Personnel management in context
the late 1980s

Personnel management in context: the late 1980s
Statistics supplement (second edition)
isbn 0 946139 40 7   £4.95
Looseleaf for ease of copying   Autumn, 1986

Tables, charts and other data to supplement and extend the book (culled from a variety of printed sources).

Personnel Management in Context
the late 1980s

Terry McIlwee

Elm Publications

This edition (second) published September, 1986
by ELM Publications, Seaton House, Kings Ripton,
Huntingdon, Cambs PE17 2NJ.

Printed and bound in Great Britain by Billings Ltd, Worcester.

 British Library Cataloguing in Publication Data

McIlwee, Terry
    Personnel management in context : the
    late 1980s.——2nd ed.
    1. Personnel management——Great Britain
    I. Title
    658.3'00941   HF5549.2.G7

    ISBN 0-946139-35-0

ACKNOWLEDGEMENT

Thanks are due to my wife Janet and my children Joanna, Ian and Kathryn for their patience and help in developing the ideas in this book and allowing parts of the house to be used as a workroom for the sifting and analysis of data.

ABOUT THE AUTHOR

Terry McIlwee MA, BTech, PGCE, FIPM, spent most of his working life as a Personnel Manager in the electronics, engineering and tyre manufacturing industries. He is now a Principal Lecturer in Applied Behavioural Sciences at Ealing College of Higher Education, where he has been Director of Personnel Management Courses in the School of Business and Management for the past eight years.

Contents

SECTION 1 — OBJECTIVES AND FUNCTIONS OF BUSINESS AND PUBLIC SERVICE ORGANISATIONS

SECTION 2 — MODERN PERSONNEL MANAGEMENT

SECTION 3 — PERSONNEL MANAGEMENT AND THE LAW

SECTION 4 — EXTERNAL INFLUENCES AND CONSTRAINTS ON THE PERSONNEL FUNCTION

List of Figures

List of Tables

INTRODUCTION

This book focuses on the organisational and environmental context of human resource management. This is done by examining the objectives and functions of business and public service organisations and the role of modern organisational management. The major functions of personnel management are discussed together with the means for measuring its contribution and evaluating its success. The book examines the main features of the external environment which influence the manner in which personnel specialists operate — especially political, social, Governmental, labour market and legislative pressures.

It covers the 'Personnel Management in Context' syllabus of the IPM Stage 1 examination and will be useful to students on BTEC Business Studies courses and other programmes of study.

A number of statements are made for which there is statistical evidence; they are supported by the tables available in a separate publication — *Personnel management in context, the 1980s: manpower statistics supplement* by Terry McIlwee, ELM Publications, 1986, Second Edition ISBN 0 9505828 9 1.

Alexander Pope: 'Essay on Criticism'

'A little learning is a dangerous thing;
Drink deep, or taste not the Pierian spring:
There shallow draughts intoxicate the brain,
And drinking largely sobers us again.'

Chapter 1
Changing Nature of Society

'Know then thyself, presume not God to scan, the proper study of mankind is man.'

Pope: Essay on Man, Epistle (ii)

Sir Derek Ezra, the retiring Chairman of the Coal Board in 'How I see the personnel function', Personnel Management, July 1982, said

'I see the role of the personnel function as creating the environment in which a contented, healthy, skilled and committed workforce can operate, with the prospect of increased rewards through increased efficiency ... Personnel experts can assist managers to motivate those who work for them, help them to be more effective in the selecting, appraising, rewarding and counselling roles.'

As this quote implies, an organisation is nothing without people; its ultimate success or failure is attributable to the efforts of those working in it. An organisation's success in meeting its desired or stated objectives accrues because of the decisions which are made at crucial times in its history by the human beings working within it. If we assume for a moment that there exists in a particular product or service market a state of perfect competition such that no new organisation is excluded from entering the market, for legal or other reasons; no organisation has an advantage by already being in the market; products or services are similar; no alteration in market price can significantly alter market penetration; all organisations have an equal ability to purchase the latest technology and raw materials are in plentiful supply; then the only factor which can make one organisation better than another is the calibre and expertise of the people working in it. For it is the labour force at all levels from top to bottom of the organisation which can assure a good quality and reliable product or service and give the organisation an edge over its competitors. This reliance on the labour force in an organisation was emphasised by Peter Drucker in *The practice of management* (Heinemann, 1955) when he argued:

'To make an enterprise out of resources it is not enough to put them together in a logical order — then to throw the switch of capital ... what is needed is a transmutation of the resources and this cannot come from an inanimate resource such as capital. It requires management. But it is also clear that the 'resources' capable of enlargement can only be human resources. All other resources stand under the law of mechanics. They can be better utilised and they can be worse utilised but they can never have an output greater than the sum of the inputs ... man alone of the resources available to man, can grow and develop.'

The Chairman of Camrex Holdings Ltd stated simply in the company's annual report of 1980:-

'It is people who make businesses.'

We are constantly being informed by the mass media, Government ministers and international organisations that Britain's productivity in steel manufacture, automobile manufacture and other crucial industries is lower than that of many of its rivals and that this inevitably has an adverse influence on our competitiveness and success in international markets. Whilst historically, technological innovation has done most to increase productivity and to produce economies of scale, the human being must be accepted as a critically important part of the operation of an enterprise and not merely as a factor of production incidental to the technical process of getting things done. If we accept this, then the skills of selecting and managing people, utilising and training them in the most appropriate way, both for the objectives of the organisation and for the motivation of the individuals themselves, becomes the key to future prosperity.

The management of the human resource of an organisation has become a more difficult art in the 20th Century than previously. In the past in the UK the individual's status in occupational life was dependent virtually entirely upon his class at birth and work tended to be concentrated in small organisations — for example in small family-owned agricultural units, small scale 'cottage' industries and 'service' in wealthy homes — other job opportunities for the bulk of the population were few and far between. Labour was available in abundance and these small organisations had little need to employ the sophisticated techniques which are practised in modern large scale organisations. In small organisations human relations problems could be (and still often can be) handled on an informal basis between the employer and the individual employee, as elaborate organisation structures with a divorce between the managerial role and ownership seldom existed. Employment arrangements could be very simple and there was no need for sophisticated selection techniques as jobs were relatively straightforward and those employed were largely unquestioning of their roles; the new employee learned the task by 'sitting by Nellie or Ned' and watching what was done; accident prevention programmes and safety audits were non-existent; and there was little legislation to protect individuals from the capriciousness of the employer.

From the start of the Industrial Revolution, the development of technology and the move towards mass production, with increasing specialisation of role, changed this picture and large numbers of individual employees were brought together into large units. Over 90% of the labour force now have the status of 'employees', from the Managing Director down to the lowest graded member of the organisation. Today's manager is now appointed because of his skill, knowledge and ability and not because ownership and control of the financial aspects of the organisation entitles him to a role in management. Now the vast majority of organisations, from the boardroom downwards, are operated by hired professional managers with individuals being employed by Limited Liability Companies where share ownership is largely separated from day-to-day management.

Increasing size of organisations has brought with it a number of

2

problems for human resource management. Decision making is often remote from the place of work and individuals are feeling an increasing sense of isolation from control. Increased bureaucratisation, which large enterprise breeds, has brought a high degree of specialisation; rigid hierarchical structures with prescribed areas of command and responsibility; impersonality into the relationship between the organisation and its members; recruitment of individuals into the hierarchy on the basis of ability and technical knowledge; and a system of control which is based on laid-down rules which are designed to regulate the whole organisational structure and process with the aim of maximum organisational efficiency. The individual member of the organisation is thus faced with limits on his discretion and is likely only to have control over a limited spectrum of work with the potential result of reduction in the satisfaction which can be achieved from task accomplishment. The increasing division of work into smaller and smaller tasks and areas of control, because of organisational and technological necessity, thus potentially creates problems of motivation (for example, the learning time of some of the tasks on a motor-car assembly line is an extensive 1½ minutes!) yet research into human needs and expectations has proved it to be a complicated set of relationships and some people are happy to operate at work within small limits of individual control.

The interdependency of departments in large scale organisations and interdependency between organisations themselves, which has been influenced by developments in technology, has placed small groups in a position to disrupt whole areas of industry. This, added to the increase generally in trade union membership density in UK enterprises, has raised the issue of trade union strength to one of concern both within organisations and in society itself and requires adept handling by managements of the industrial relationships in an attempt to minimise the effects of conflict. Trade unionists have increasingly come to challenge the exercise of managerial authority: managerial decisions on hiring, promotion, transfer, redundancy, discipline, wages and salaries, methods of wage payment and fringe benefits have become the subject of collective discussion and collective agreements. Managers have thus been forced to consider the impact of decisions to a far greater extent than ever before and the need for a total organisational consideration of the impact of decisions has been said to reduce the ability of an individual manager to control, without consultation, his own area of the organisation.

Since the 1944 Education Act educational opportunity has been seen, theoretically at least, as open to all and as a basis for the identification of talent and the development of ability. It has an influence on subsequent occupational placement across the spectrum of the different tasks and specialisms in work today. More general basic education has tended to raise the aspirations of those leaving the educational system so they now have different attitudes to work and authority than those of a generation ago. This has been partly generated by changes in the methods of education especially and education itself is now participative with learning by practical experimentation being considered in some cases to be more efective than learning by rote.

A further significant influence on managerial behaviour since the 1960s has been the development of legislation on employment which has radically increased the rights of individuals at the workplace.

All these pressures have made modern management less able to rely on the traditional idea that the exercise of managerial authority is sufficient to ensure that employees will conform to the norms and standards of the organisation and the predominant management styles now are based more on the idea of working *with* people rather than directing them.

Since modern organisations aim to use and coordinate the disparate activities of large numbers of people, personnel or human resource management is the basic management activity which permeates all levels of the organisation. This was emphasised by the Institute of Personnel Management's own definition of the personnel function in 1963 when it said:

'Personnel management is the responsibility of all those who manage people as well as being a description of the work of those who are employed as specialists. It is that part of management which is concerned with people at work and with relationships within an enterprise. It applies not only to industry and commerce but all fields of employment. Personnel management aims to achieve efficiency and justice, neither of which can be pursued successfully without the other. It seeks to bring together and develop into an effective organisation the men and women who make up an enterprise enabling each to make his own best contribution to its success both as an individual and as a member of the working group. It seeks to provide fair terms and conditions of employment and satisfying work for those employed.'

Yet the activity of personnel management occurs in the context of the organisation in which individuals work and of the society in which individuals spend their lesiure hours, which in turn influences the value systems of those same people who work in organisations.

Personnel management will have an important role in the latter part of the 20th Century if organisations wish to adapt successfully to their changing environments. We can no longer expect sustained growth in all sectors of industry as the economic environment is unpredictable. Some industries will no longer be competitive and viable and people will have to leave organisations in those sectors and transfer to the sectors which are successful, and 'High Tech' industry is not notably labour intensive. Most estimates suggest that high levels of unemployment will be the norm, while we retain the current concept of work from 16-60/65 and our current expectations about hours of work. If changes are made over the next decade to these basic philosophies, the human resource manager must be at the forefront in determining the likely operational effects of different patterns of work. Companies are increasing their use of part-time work, temporary and fixed contract work, subcontracting and as technology becomes more expensive and therefore requires more intensive use (to ensure a reasonable return on capital), shift and rota working will increase. In addition, self employment and mixed self and part time employment are growing significantly. It is likely too that an increasing number of people will not go out to work but will network from their own homes. All changes which will have major human resource implications.

The decline in employment in manufacturing industry is not speedily being offset by a sustained increase in service and public sector employment especially if we consider current Government policy on costs and manning levels in the public sector. Technology too is having implications on the nature of work and the skill mix required in the labour market. Computer aided design and manufacture, computer controlled manufacturing processes, automated handling, automated inspection, flexible manufacturing systems and computer integrated manufacture are just a few of the new developments.

Identification of manpower needs must be at the forefront in organisational planning, for without such planning help cannot be realistically generated from the educational and training systems to give people the required balance of skills, knowledge and experience.

We are also likely to see a questioning of the efficiency and effectiveness of very large organisations and their ability to adapt to changes in societal demand for goods and services. There could be a tendency to decentralise the decision making process and create smaller profit centres which are more likely to be able to adapt to change. Manufacturing policies too are changing. Organisations in virtually all manufacturing industries are developing new systems for the efficient production of a larger range of items, in smaller quantities, with quicker through-put times, lower stock levels, more rapid delivery to customers and greater quality consistency.

The increasing involvement of multi-national companies in the UK economy presents us with problems and issues which require consideration and adaptation. Where ultimate decision making comes from overseas, seemingly not considering the likely effects of decisions on the particular locations or regions in which the subsidiaries operate, the Personnel Manager or Director has an important role in communicating information both to the employees affected and to the overseas board. Work patterns and philosophies may be very different in these companies and require additional skills of recruitment, selection, utilisation, training and managing employee involvement from the human resource department and from management in general.

With the abolition of the Shop Acts and the licensing laws, Sunday opening and twenty four hour trading is only just over the horizon. Such influences are likely to have a major effect on the retail and distributive trades and require major adjustments in work patterns in such sectors of the economy.

Our Treaty obligations within the EEC mean that most of our trade and commercial practices are now determined significantly by the European Community and personnel staff will have to continue to monitor the progress of Regulations and Directives to assess their impact on work practices, procedures and costs.

Management of these changes is and will continue to be a difficult task. It will require organisations to constantly monitor and modify their utilisation of human resources and especially to train them and have them educated to meet not just current but also future needs. Whilst it is not realistic to claim that more education of itself will lead to economic growth it is true that growth does and will require educated people to sustain it. The countries which have done best economically in the last twenty years, e.g. the USA, West Germany, Japan and Sweden have all a high proportion of the educated having appropriate skills in science, technology, business and commerce. What is more important perhaps is that those with such qualifications are awarded high status and are valued by their societies.

The starting point for all personnel policies are corporate policies; personnel policies must stem from these and be an integral part of their implementation. This was emphasised by a Ministry of Labour publication in 1958 'Positive Employment Policies':

'From the management's point of view an employment policy is an integral part of the whole managerial and production policy of the firm. It has as its objective the creation of a cooperative, responsible and efficient working force. Regard must be paid to existing agreements and established practices in the industry, and the essential role of the trade union. It must be understood and applied at all levels of management. From the employees' angle the policy must provide not only fair conditions of employment but satisfaction on the job, opportunities for advancement and reasonable security.'

Policies must, therefore, be relevant to the nature and objectives of the business and constantly monitored for their relevance, not only now, but also for the future.

The Director and Ex-Chairman of Marks and Spencers, Lord Sieff, in Personnel Management December 1984 said:

'Good human relations cannot be legislated for ...

Good human relations develop only if top management believes in and is committed to their implementation and has a genuine respect for the individual. This is not something to be tackled from time to time but demands continuous action.

Human relations in industry should cover the problems of the individual at work, his or her health, wellbeing and progress, the working environment and profit sharing — providing there is a profit. Full and frank two way communications and respect for the contribution people can make, given encouragement — these are the foundations of an effective policy and a major contribution to a successful organisation.'

However we must be more positive than those people that Sir Michael Edwardes commented on at the 1984 Institute of Personnel Management Conference at Harrogate:

'I cannot honestly say that those in industry who advise line managers specifically on people matters contribute as positively as they should and I have observed an amount of clear cut negativeness from that quarter...'

We cannot afford to be conservative in our solutions to the challenges which we face as we make the decisions regarding the policies that will take us into the 21st Century.

Chapter 2
Organisations and Work

Our main concern is with people at work and their relationships within an organisation. We establish organisations to provide a product or a service for which a need has been identified by society.

1. PRIVATE SECTOR FORMS OF ORGANISATION IN THE UK

There are a number of different legal forms of organisation in the private sector of industry and commerce:-

(A) Non-commercial organisations

Individuals may join together into organisations which are of a sporting or social type with rules and regulations drawn up in the form of a constitution and self-imposed, e.g. an archery or tennis club. They will probably acquire land and property and employ labour. The members are likely to appoint officers of the club who will operate as trustees in that they have the authority to acquire and dispose of the club's property within the articles and rules laid down, for the benefit of the members, but are not allowed to make profits for themselves. They are designated in law as unincorporated associations. Trade unions are a further example of this form of organisation.

(B) Sole traders

The simplest form of business in the UK, a sole trader is the owner and only controller and in law is held entirely responsible for the success or otherwise of the activity. He is responsible personally for any debts which the business has and any property or assets he has may be used to pay off these debts. This tends to curtail the scope of the operation and the growth in size of the business. Examples of sole traders include newsagents, jobbing builders, small car hire firms, photographers, etc., where the amount of capital and the number of employees required is small.

(C) Private partnership

A partnership is merely a collection of people who wish to operate the business together and agree to share the profits and the losses. Partners in many senses are in the same position as sole traders. The advantage is that it can allow for a combination of skills and expertise and often a

8

greater availability of capital — the fact that each partner assumes an unlimited liability for the debts of the whole undertaking is an advantage when borrowing capital. Partnerships exist longer than the sole trader type of enterprise because the firm is not dependent upon the life of any one individual, although the death or retirement of a key partner is liable to bring the partnership to an end. Most solicitors, accountants, doctors and dentists operate this form of business relationship.

(D) Private limited company

The limited liability company was an extension of the partnership principle but was brought about largely because of the inability of most partnerships to obtain sufficient capital to expand. Such a company comes into existence when a number of people, who may even be unknown to each other, join together to invest their money in a common enterprise. The company is for legal purposes a separate entity, distinct from the individuals who set it up. In the event of the failure of the company, the liability of each investor for the debts of the company is limited to the amount of his original investment. Each shareholder in a limited liability company receives a share of the profits each year — a dividend — depending on the amount of money invested. Whereas the shareholders own the company, it is the company that carries on the business and the company alone that can enter into contracts and be asked to pay the business debts. The Companies Acts underpin the basic legal regulation of such enterprises. To form such a company certain documents have to be completed and lodged with the Companies Registration Office in Cardiff. These are:-

(a) The Memorandum of Association, which states the company's name, its objectives and details of how the shares are organised.

(b) The Articles of Association, setting out the internal rules of the company, as to the way it is to be run; it sets out the powers of directors.

(c) A declaration that the legal requirements of the Companies Acts concerning the formation of a registered company, have been complied with.

(d) A statement of the nominal share capital of the company and the way in which the shares are divided up.

Private limited liability companies are restricted in whom they may sell shares to; they must first offer them to one of the existing shareholders of whom there can be no more than fifty.

In 1982 there were 802,493 private companies listed by the Registrar of Companies according to the Department of Trade and Industry.

(E) Public limited liability company (PLC)

There are several main differences between public and private limited liability companies:-

(a) the shares of a public company are quoted on the Stock Exchange and are available — normally via brokers — to the general public, whereas there are restrictions on transferring shares in a private company;

(b) the number of shareholders in a public company is unlimited, but there must be a minimum of seven shareholders.

(c) there must be more than one director in a public company;

(d) before public companies are formed they must issue a prospectus setting out details of their financial records and their directors;

(e) investors' capital is more liquid because shares are bought and sold easily on the Stock Exchange;

(f) it is especially suitable, where returns may take a long time to appear, e.g. developments in balloon transportation, where a number of people can be encouraged to invest small amounts with prospect of no immediate returns;

(g) they are able to use the services of experts with keen business ability, but no capital. Thus the functions of the capitalist and the entrepreneur can be separated.

There are some disadvantages to public limited liability companies. The only link between the undertaking and the worker is a cash one in that the worker gets a wage and has little contact with those who actually own the assets of the company. In addition shareholders are in practice able to exercise little control over the actual operation of the company and over many policy matters. A further problem tends to arise, especially in these days of institutional shareholding, for the ease with which shares are transferred makes the company liable to speculative dealings on the Stock Exchange which have little to do with actual investment in a specific product or organisation.

Table 2:1 Percentage distribution of share holdings in PLCs 1963 — 81

Source — *The Observer* Nov 1983

Shareholding	1963	1969	1975	1981
Individuals	54.0	47.4	37.5	28.2
Charities	2.1	2.1	2.3	2.2
Banks	1.3	1.7	0.7	0.3
Insurance Companies	10.0	12.2	15.9	20.5
Pension Funds	6.4	9.0	16.8	26.7
Unit Trusts	1.3	2.9	4.1	3.6
Investment Trusts	11.3	10.5	10.5	6.8
Companies	5.1	5.4	3.0	5.1
Public Sectors	1.5	2.6	3.6	3.0
Overseas	7.0	6.6	5.6	3.6
	100.0	100.0	100.0	100.0

In 1982 there were 5,324 PLCs registered in Britain.

TABLE 2:2 — THE 30 LARGEST COMPANIES IN BRITAIN BY TURNOVER
Source — *The Times 1000 1985—1986*

COMPANY	Main activity	TURNOVER (£m)	employees
British Petroleum Co.	Oil industry	44,059	130,100
'Shell' Transport & Trading	Oil industry	29,522	N/A
B.A.T. Industries	Tobacco, retailing, paper, packaging, etc.	14,426	212,822
Imperial Chemical Industries	Petrochemicals, pharmaceuticals, etc.	9,909	115,600
Shell UK	Oil industry	9,608	16,731
British National Oil Corpn.	Petroleum suppliers	9,562	123
Electricity Council	Electricity suppliers	9,562	139,740
Esso UK	Oil Industry	7,565	6,619
British Telecom	Telecommunication services	6,876	244,592
British Gas Corporation	Gas suppliers, etc.	6,392	97,208
Rio Tinto-Zinc Corporation	Mining & industrial — metals & fuel	5,948	74,004
Unilever PLC	Food products, detergents, etc.	5,859	140,000
S & W Berisford	Merchanting & commod. trading, etc.	5,703	9,182
Grand Metropolitan	Hotel props, milk prds, brewers, etc.	5,075	125,074
General Electric Co.	Electrical engineers	4,800	170,865
Philbro-Salomon	Commodity brokers, etc.	4,763	532
National Coal Board	Coalmining	4,660	243,300
Imperial Group	Tobacco, food, drink & packaging	4,593	92,599
Ford Motor Co.	Motor vehicle manufacturers	3,752	58,700
Dalgety	International merchants	3,701	20,860
BTR	Construction, energy & electrical etc.	3,486	60,300
BL	Motor vehicle manufacturers etc.	3,402	80,478
British Steel Corporation	Iron & steel mfrs, etc.	3,358	78,700
Ultramar	Petroleum exploration & development	3,260	4,016
Marks & Spencer	General store proprietors	3,213	60,252
Allied Lyons	Brewers, vintners, hoteliers, etc.	3,174	71,448
J Sainsbury	Retail distribution of food	2,998	62,258
Post Office	Mail & parcel services, etc.	2,843	201,885
Gallaher	Tobacco, optics, pumps & valves disbn.	2,839	29,559
British Railways Board	Passenger railway services, etc.	2,832	207,097

(F) Cooperatives

These may take three main forms in this country:-

(a) EMPLOYEES' COOPERATIVES: workmen own and manage an organisation to derive profits as well as wages. The worker is freed from the position of a hired employee who sells his labour.

(b) RETAIL OR DISTRIBUTIVE COOPERATIVES: this generally takes the form of cooperative stores in which a number of retail shops combine to buy foods collectively at wholesale prices, sell at retail prices and divide some of the surplus among the members in proportion to their purchases. The remainder of the surplus is often devoted to social and benevolent purposes.

(c) WHOLESALE COOPERATION is the formation of cooperative wholesale societies to provide retail stores with goods on the same principles as the stores provide goods for their members. The 'members' of the wholesale societies are the individual retail stores who share the surpluses in the same way as the stores' members share their profits.

2. PUBLIC SECTOR FORMS OF ORGANISATION IN THE UK

(A) Central Government

The Civil Service

Civil servants are employees of the Crown whose salaries are paid through monies voted from Parliament. They work for the Government departments, either centrally or in the regions. Or they may work in some other independent body set up by Government, e.g. ACAS, Certification Office, Equal Opportunities Commission, Commission for Racial Equality, Manpower Services Commission. The major departments in 1984 were:

Agriculture, Fisheries & Food	Lord Advocate's Department
Defence	Lord Chancellor's Department
Duchy of Lancaster	Northern Ireland Office
Education & Science	Paymaster-General's Office
Employment	Privy Council Office
Energy	Scottish Office
Environment	Trade & Industry
Foreign & Commonwealth Affairs	Transport
Health & Social Security	Treasury
Home Office	Welsh Office
Law Officers' Department	

Each Government department is headed by a minister, some of whom are members of the Cabinet, Department of Employment, Education and Science, Home Office, etc. The departmental minister works closely with the most senior civil servant in his department, the permanent secretary (or permanent-under-secretary if the minister is a Cabinet minister) who is responsible to the minister for administrating and directing the work of the department and its finances. A civil servant, in carrying out his duties, must be politically neutral. Yet because they are permanent members of the administration, it is true to say that senior civil servants have an important role not only in implementing policy but also in formulating it.

(B) Local Government

Not all matters can be handled by Central Government because of the sheer weight of issues. In addition different parts of Britain have different needs: thus only by a form of Local Government is it possible for priorities to be established to reflect the needs of the local community. The structure of Local Government in England and Wales in 1985 was as follows:

Figure 2:1 Structure of Local Government in England and Wales (1985)

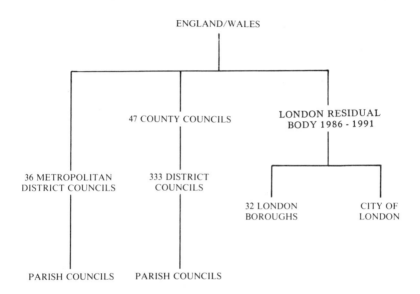

Local authorities have a wide range of services, some of which, e.g. education and the fire service, they are obliged by law to provide, whereas others, such as parks and recreational facilities, are at local discretion. We could split the services into three broad categories:

i) those offering protection to the community, such as the fire service, police service, consumer protection, environmental health (including refuse collection and disposal and street cleaning); and

ii) those concerned with the welfare of the community, such as education, social services, housing, transport, roads and local planning; and

iii) those providing communal facilities, such as parks, recreational facilities, libraries, museums.

Each different tier in the Local Government system has responsibilities for services, some of which are common (e.g. some roads are the responsibility of the County Councils or Metropolitan Councils and other roads are the responsibility of the districts or boroughs), and some of them are specific to a tier (e.g. the police and the fire service are the responsibility of the County Councils or the Metropolitan Councils, whereas housing tends to be the main responsibility of the districts or boroughs). The distribution of functions between the various councils can vary based on local catchment and local need.

Local Government authorities have powers to raise funds through rates and loans and are also allocated Central Government block grants, which enable them to finance their activities.

Generally the powers of Local Government are limited by Acts of Parliament and the Government can also influence their activities via the allocation of the block grant and by the granting or withholding of permission to borrow funds. Some Local Government services are also influenced by Central Government departments, e.g. education by the Department of Education & Science, and the fire services and police by the Home Office.

(C) National Health Service

The National Health Service was established by the National Health Service Act of 1946. Until 1974 local authorities were responsible for provision of personal health services including ambulances, health care, some nursing and midwifery, family planning, vaccination and immunisation, and hospitals were administered through Regional Hospital Boards, with dental services and the family practitioner service being administered through local executive councils. From April 1974 these services were amalgamated in a major reorganisation of the Health Service when 14 Regional Health Authorities replaced the Regional Health Boards, and (due to a further reorganisation in 1982 cutting out a tier of Area Health Authorities) these are now supported by 201 District Health Authorities. The structure from 1985 therefore is shown on page 15, Figure 2:2. This structure derives from the Griffiths Report, published in 1983. The NHS Management Board, with members from business, the health service and the civil service, plans the implementation of policies approved by the NHS Supervisory Board and manages the health service within the budget agreed by the Supervisory Board and Parliament.

The functions of the Regional Health Authorities are to draw up plans for the allocation of resources amongst the District Health Authorities who are responsible for planning, organising and administering the district's needs. The Community Health Councils act as a channel of communication between the health authorities, the consumers and the public and are consulted by the District Health Authorities on their plans.

14

Figure 2:2 Structure of the National Health Service (1985)

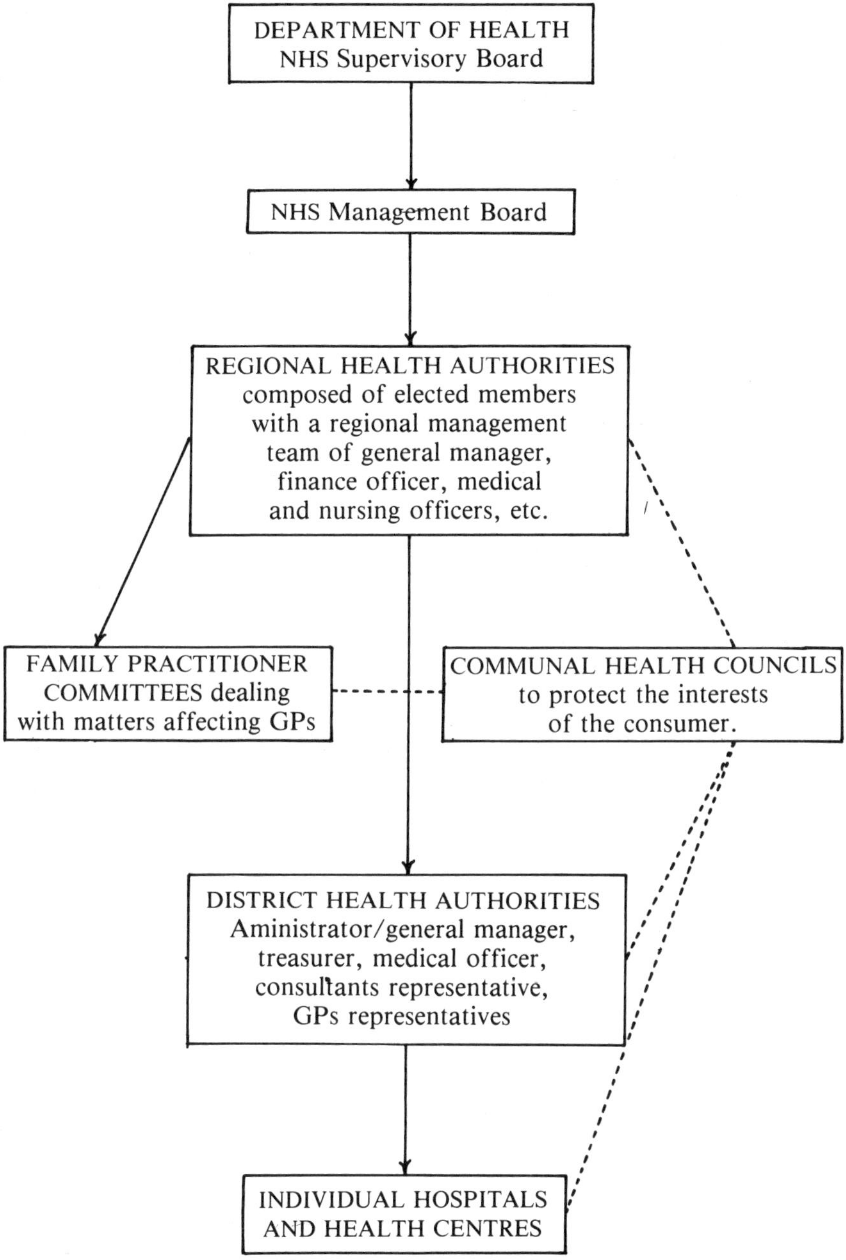

```
            ┌─────────────────────────────┐
            │  DEPARTMENT OF HEALTH        │
            │  NHS Supervisory Board       │
            └─────────────────────────────┘
                          │
                          ▼
               ┌──────────────────────┐
               │  NHS Management Board │
               └──────────────────────┘
                          │
                          ▼
            ┌─────────────────────────────┐
            │  REGIONAL HEALTH AUTHORITIES │
            │  composed of elected members │
            │  with a regional management  │
            │  team of general manager,    │
            │  finance officer, medical    │
            │  and nursing officers, etc.  │
            └─────────────────────────────┘
```

┌──────────────────────────┐   ┌──────────────────────────────┐
│ FAMILY PRACTITIONER   │   │ COMMUNAL HEALTH COUNCILS   │
│ COMMITTEES dealing   │   │ to protect the interests   │
│ with matters affecting GPs│   │ of the consumer.   │
└──────────────────────────┘   └──────────────────────────────┘

```
            ┌─────────────────────────────┐
            │  DISTRICT HEALTH AUTHORITIES │
            │  Aministrator/general manager,│
            │  treasurer, medical officer, │
            │  consultants representative, │
            │  GPs representatives          │
            └─────────────────────────────┘
                          │
                          ▼
            ┌─────────────────────────────┐
            │  INDIVIDUAL HOSPITALS        │
            │  AND HEALTH CENTRES          │
            └─────────────────────────────┘
```

15

(D) Water authorities

These are generally divided into water, river and sewage divisions.

(E) Police authorities

These are based on the county unit, although where counties are small or have a small population they may cover more than one county.

(F) Public corporations

In their early days companies engaged in supplying some form of public utility, e.g. gas and electricity, were encouraged by Government to compete with each other, for it was considered that such a policy would give the general public the best possible service at lowest cost. Gradually it was recognised that duplication of activity was inefficient and it was decided that for political, social and economic reasons certain activities were best controlled by the State. Acts of Parliament were passed to make such bodies as the National Coal Board, the Central Electricity Generating Board, British Rail, British Gas, British Airways and British Steel public corporations totally or partly owned by the State. These corporations are not Government departments. They enjoy a degree of self control with targets established by the Government and their responsibility is via a Minister to Parliament and to the general public. Each Minister has considerable financial control over the corporation and can regulate their borrowing, reorganisation and development and pricing and can demand levels of profitability. Although the Minister lays down general policy, the day-to-day operation of the corporation is left to the Board of Management which is appointed by the Minister, selection for which is based on the individual's previous experience and ability. Each Board has to present, via the Minister, an annual report to Parliament so permitting day-to-day matters to be raised and discussed. This is especially necessary as most of the State corporations are monopolies and care has to be taken to protect the interests of the consumers from inefficiency.

Table 2:3 Main public corporations — years of formation
(excluding Nationalised Industries)

Source: *Economic Trends* December, 1985

British Broadcasting Corporation (set up by Royal Charter)	1927
Scottish Spinal Housing Association	1937
New Town Development Corporations	1946
Bank of England	1946
National Dock Labour Board	1947
Commonwealth Development Corporation	1948
National Film Finance Corporation	1948

Covent Garden Market Authority	1961
Housing Corporation	1964
Highlands and Islands Development Board	1965
Northern Ireland Transport Holding Company	1968
Passenger Transport Executives	1969
Northern Ireland Housing Executive	1971
Independent Broadcasting Authority	1972
Civil Aviation Authority	1972
National Water Council	1974
Northern Ireland Electricity Service	1974
Regional Water Authorities in England	1974
Royal Ordnance Factories	1974
Trust Ports	1974
Royal Mint	1975
Scottish Development Agency	1975
Land Authority for Wales	1976
Northern Ireland Development Agency	1976
Welsh Development Agency	1976
Development Board for Rural Wales	1977
Pilotage Commission	1979
Crown Agents & Crown Agents Holding & Realisation Board	1980
Her Majesty's Stationery Office	1980
British Technology Group	1981
Urban Development Corporations	1981
Water Authorities Association	1983
Audit Commission	1983
London Regional Transport	1984

Table 2:4 The ten largest nationalised industries by employment (1983)

Corporation	Employment at end of March 1983
British Telecom (Privatised 1984)	245,694
British Railways Board	220,370
National Coal Board	212,843
Post Office	205,829
Electricity Council	141,385
British Gas Corporation	101,225
British Steel Corporation	81,100
British Shipbuilders	66,600
National Bus Company	51,951
British Airways	37,517
Total	1,364,511

Source: *Various*

3. DEVELOPMENT OF ORGANISATIONS

To operate organisations we need to employ people. At first a small organisation may require little specialisation and the people concerned with it get on with whatever task is most urgent, but gradually organisations recognise a need to add other individuals with particular expertise to the labour force.

When an organisation starts it probably has an 'ideas' person who has identified the societal need. He rarely has cash to spare and usually finds someone who will finance him. Dependent upon the 'product' of the organisation, whether it be to make motor cars, print cards, bake bread or sell holidays, some technology may be required and our ideas person may not have much in the way of technical knowledge, so he attempts to find someone who can provide that necessary skill. To begin operating the organisation suitable premises must be found and then he may want some appropriately-trained workers.

Thus, as an organisation grows necessary expertise is acquired — marketing experts, salesmen, development engineers, social workers, nurses, doctors or whoever is required to fulfil objectives. We hire people for their strengths and we combine them with other people who individually have complementary strengths. We can view organisations as entities which attempt to maximise their use of each individual's strengths whilst, at the same time, minimising their weaknesses by employing others to cover these skill deficiencies. Gradually a hierarchy will develop as we establish control within the organisation by means of an authority network to coordinate the division of labour we are creating. As organisations grow, the complexity of control becomes greater and organisations differ from each other in their methods of coping with these complexities. It is possible to define the common elements of organisations and for this a good statement is given by Schein in *Organisational Psychology* 3rd edn Prentice Hall, 1980 who defined an organisation as:

'the planned coordination of the activities of a number of people for the achievement of some common explicit purpose or goal, through division of labour and function and through a hierarchy of authority and responsibility.'

This definition examines the essential elements of organisation:

1. Organisations have *purposes* and these purposes have to be made clear to all workers so that they can work collectively.

2. To carry out the purposes of the organisation *division of labour* is required to use the expertise of each individual to the full.

3. *Authority* is required to ensure that individuals work consistently towards the organisation's objectives.

4. Organisations employ those 'activities' of people which help in attaining objectives and, although individuals can belong to a number of different organisations, only some activities are relevant to each organisation.

Thus each organisation produces a different working environment. One of the essentials of human resource management is the recognition that this environment influences the behaviour of the individuals working in it. We have to understand the particular influences which exist in our own organisation and how they affect the behaviour of the individuals working there.

Organisations are composed of people with different sets of values, beliefs and skills; they have structures with different characteristics, depending upon the type of product produced, the technology used and the tasks performed. This creates different kinds of relationships between people and their work. The processes and structures are concerned with authority, communication, goal setting and the decision making necessary to fulfil the task of the organisation whilst, at the same time, considering the objectives of the human resources.

4. OBJECTIVES OF ORGANISATIONS

Modern organisation theory recognises that to define the objectives of an organisation at any one moment is not simple. Any organisation may have multiple goals, for the immediate priorities of organisations change due to pressure from the environment in which they operate. These goals may overlap in their effect. For example, if we examine a business organisation, at one time the priority may be an increase in profits. This could be achieved by an increase in price, but the organisational ability to benefit from such an increase will depend on the nature of competition in the market. A different strategy could be an increase in efficiency, which in turn will be influenced by the commitment of the employees or the ability to purchase or introduce technological change. A parallel emphasis, however, could be on gaining a larger share of a particular market. This may only be obtained by freezing and even lowering prices, which could actually reduce profitability in the short term. In a different period, the objective could be compliance with new health and safety legislation, again necessitating a reduction in profits as cash is used to fulfil this objective. Perhaps, at another time, the use of resources may be necessary to develop new products, as consumer research shows a fall in demand for the current range.

(a) Objectives of private sector organisations

A list of a business organisation's objectives could include the following:

— do research
— make a profit
— diversify
— develop new products
— control other organisations
— maximise sales
— provide an enhanced range of products
— move into new national or regional markets

19

- provide a healthy and safe working environment
- offer education and training
- minimise unnecessary expenditure
- have the best terms and conditions of employment
- promote the personal growth of individuals within the organisation
- create jobs
- serve the community
- survive
- grow

all of which may operate together or individually from time to time.
The following examples illustrate stated company objectives:

The Unigate company objectives were stated as follows in their 1981 Company Report:-

> 'It is our intention to continue to upgrade our manufacturing and distributive facilities and services to customers, despite the temptation to delay vital investment until the economic climate appears more favourable ... We place the highest possible priority on the elimination of waste and of inefficiency in order to derive maximum benefit from our assets.'

BP Ltd in their 1980 Annual Report said :

> "Group policy recognises that BPs primary responsibility to society is to increase wealth by conducting its business successfully and efficiently with group profitability being the principal measure of this success. As well as the distinct economic benefits that successful BP companies provide through employment, in paying taxes and by purchases from suppliers, it is group policy to make a wider contribution to the community through sponsorships and donations, educational support and other educational activities. The emphasis is particularly in localities where there are many group employees and in fields related to group 'activities'."

Reckitt and Colman, in the 1982 Chairman's statement, argued;

> 'As a company we have to compete internationally and it is important that our UK costs should enable us to be competitive, both at home and in export markets. We accept this challenge and recognise that we must always strive to improve productivity in order to trade successfully in these recessionary times ... '

J Harvey-Jones, Chairman of ICI at the AGM 1983 and quoted in the Guardian, said:

> 'Our first and overriding aim is an increase in profits. It is only through success in that key factor that we can properly meet the justifiable expectations of you, our shareholders, our employees, and our customers.'

The complexity of objectives and the interdependency between them is illustrated in the following statement by Eliot Jaques on the objectives of the Glacier Metal Company, which was given in *The Changing Culture of a Factory* Tavistock, 1951:-

> 'The purpose of the Company and those working in it shall be the continuity and expansion of the working community the coordination of which will enable its members to serve society, to serve their dependents, to serve each other and to achieve a sense of creative satisfaction.

This purpose will best be accomplished by:

1) seeking the maximum technical ability;
2) seeking the utmost organisational efficiency;
3) seeking to establish an increasing democratic government of the company community, which will reward fair responsibilities, rights and opportunities for all its members, consumers and shareholders;
4) seeking at all times to earn such revenue that the company will be able:

   — to provide such reasonable dividends for its shareholders as to represent a fair return on their capital investment for the speculative risk incurred;
   — to undertake research and development in order to enable the company to attain a high position in the competitive market;
   — to provide those who work in the company with working conditions which will promote their physical and mental wellbeing;
   — to improve its equipment to enable those who work in the company to do so with the greatest possible effectiveness;
   — to raise wages and salaries in order to enable those who work in the company to live full and happy lives;
   — to improve the company's service to its customers by reducing the price or improving the quality of its products;
   — to make reserves to safeguard the company and those who work in it.'

Objectives of public sector organisations

Organisations in the public sector have a variety of different objectives. We look to the State and the public bodies to:

— educate children, young people and adults
— build and maintain roads and streets
— dispose of refuse
— provide adequate sewerage facilities
— supply water
— supply transportation including railways, bus services and an airline
— establish a stable money supply and control the banking system
— establish weights and measures
— predict the weather
— keep the society safe by providing armed services and the police
— control traffic
— reduce crime
— operate postal and telephone services
— inspect restaurants and licensed premises
— represent our interests abroad
— conserve the environment and reforest land
— help to encourage research by the provision of funds
— provide basic social services and prevent people starving
— provide hospital and health care services
— provide rehabilitation services for the handicapped and disabled
— maintain parks and other recreation areas and amenities
— create jobs or provide conpensation for the unemployed
— guarantee free speech

— guarantee the individual's freedom to worship

These are only a few of the aims of public sector bodies operated directly by the State, Local Government bodies, the Health Service and the public utilities and corporations. For example, the primary objective of the Health Service is defined in the National Health Service Act, 1946, Section 1(1) as:

> to secure improvement in the physical and mental health of the people ... and the prevention, diagnosis and treatment of illness.

The specific objectives of the hospital services are stated in the Act, Section 3(1):

> to provide ... accommodation and services of the following description:-
>
> (a)   hospital accommodation;
> (b)   medical, nursing and other services required at or for the purpose of hospitals;
> (c)   the service of specialists...

In addition the Act states the duty of teaching hospitals in Part II Section 12(3)(a):

> 'to provide for the university with which the hospital is associated such facilities as appear to the Minister to be required for clinical teaching and research.'

However, it is left to the statutory hospital authorities to define specific objectives so that the hospital service remains effective. These tasks can include:

(a)   the provision of beds, meals and other services for patients;

(b)   the provision of general nursing services for patients;

(c)   the provision of specific nursing facilities for patients, as prescribed by doctors;

(d)   the provision of medical diagnosis, prescriptions and appropriate treatment by doctors;

(e)   the provision of other services for patients, including medical social services, occupational therapy, chiropody and physiotherapy;

(f)   in teaching hospitals, the provision of training facilities for medical students;

(g)   in training hospitals, the provision of training facilities for nurses;

(h)   the provision of research facilities for doctors and scientific and other technical staff;

(i)   in psychiatric hospitals or psychiatric wings of general hospitals, the provision of facilities for detaining patients under compulsory orders of the Mental Health Act, 1959;

(j)   the provision of medical laboratory services to General Practitioners;

(k)   to continually assess and review the services offered by the hospital in response to the needs of the patients it is likely to serve and consequentially to provide the relevant building and technical facilities and the required medical, nursing and other services.

The Royal Commission on the National Health Service, reporting in 1979, argued that the National Health Service should have the following objectives:

— encourage and assist individuals to remain healthy;
— provide equality of entitlement to health services;
— provide a broad range of services to a high standard;
— provide equality of access to those services;
— provide a free service at the time of use;
— satisfy the reasonable expectations of its users;
— remain a national service, responsive to local needs.

The objectives of any organisation are a function of the environment in which it operates and are the result of a combination of internal and external factors. Organisations are essentially open systems which influence their environment and are influenced in turn by it; they exist in a highly interdependent relationship of exchange with their environment and other organisations. They utilise a wide variety of inputs of people, materials, machines and capital and their ability to operate depends on the availability of these inputs and their ability to adapt to the changing demands of their customers. Thus a tyre manufacturer will be affected by the customer's demand for a long-lasting tyre but also by the availability of the raw materials he uses and the efficiency with which he can manufacture the product.

The particular objectives at a given moment are a feature of the internal and external forces on the organisation at that point in time. This is illustrated in Figure 2:3 on page 24

The State may itself provide products or services which it feels producers in the private sector might not. In the UK these products include vehicles, fuel, transport facilities, communication services, education, health and defence.

In the public sector the objectives of the public corporations have changed due to Government pressure. Whereas in the past the Government was prepared to subsidise their operations, increasingly in recent years they are required to become self financing. For example, British Airways' financial objective, as stated in their Annual Report and Accounts for 1978/79, was:

'to generate a cash flow that will pay interest on loans and currently payable tax, pay an appropriate dividend on Public Dividend Capital and fund all capital expenditure on the replacement of assets and a proportion of capital expenditure on assets needed for expansion.'

As we can see, from the example of the public corporations, in all sectors the objectives of public sector organisations are heavily influenced by

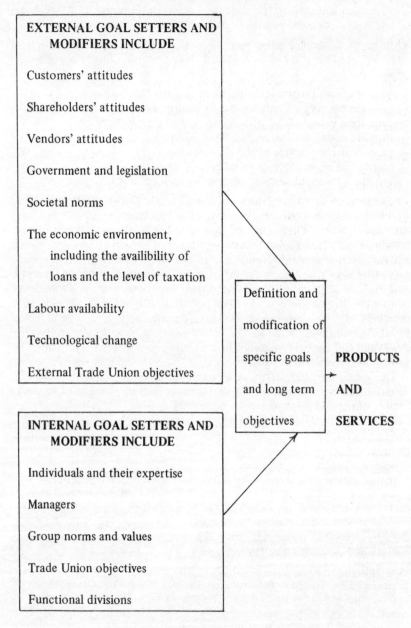

EXTERNAL GOAL SETTERS AND MODIFIERS INCLUDE

Customers' attitudes

Shareholders' attitudes

Vendors' attitudes

Government and legislation

Societal norms

The economic environment,
    including the availibility of
    loans and the level of taxation

Labour availability

Technological change

External Trade Union objectives

INTERNAL GOAL SETTERS AND MODIFIERS INCLUDE

Individuals and their expertise

Managers

Group norms and values

Trade Union objectives

Functional divisions

Definition and modification of specific goals and long term objectives

PRODUCTS AND SERVICES

Figure 2:3 Internal & external forces on the organisation

political policy. The actual operation and spending of a local authority will be influenced by the 'members' who sit on the various committees which agree budgets and policy, and by the money made available from Central Government.

5. NEED FOR CLEARLY DEFINED OBJECTIVES

Without clearly defined objectives the activities of an organisation will become confused and erratic, the resources required hard to control and keep in balance. It is also likely that the management of one process may interfere or conflict with the management of another.

An organisational objective can be viewed as a field of possible action, defined by constraints, which are both internal and external to the organisation. The quality of labour available constrains the objective of producing a product of superior quality, or the minimisation of breakdown in equipment; the availability of finance may reduce the ability to purchase new technology; Government influence may prevent an organisation producing military equipment being able to sell its products directly to a particular country; developments in medical science may improve a hospital's ability to cure the sick; and cuts in Government spending may reduce the availability of jobs in the public sector. The imagination and capability of a particular organisation's management may result in the perception of business opportunities which other organisations fail to see.

Sir Adrian Cadbury in How I see the Personnel Function, *Personnel Management* April 1982, emphasised the importance of renewing objectives and that personnel should be part of the planning team:

'In planning ahead we are continually trying to determine the direction of change in consumer tastes, in costs, in regulations and in patterns of distribution. If we read the signs of change correctly, they will provide the opportunities for growth we need; if we fail to do so, the business will decline. It is the task of a small team in the company to look ahead and discern what threats and opportunities different futures might hold in store. Personnel is represented on that team and so is right in the centre of our strategic planning...

In the next 20 years we will be more dependent than ever, not just on forecasting our future markets aright, but on guessing how the behaviour of individuals as customers and as employees will change and what constraints on society and the pressure groups within it will exercise on our business. On these interpretations of the future we will build our plans and agree our aims. From there we have to develop patterns of organisation which will enable those aims to be carried out, this means devising structures which encourage change, allow for individuality, and operating autonomy and yet fit within a policy framework.'

Any individual working within an organisation is selecting courses of action within a set of constraints determined by the objectives which are set by the executives. Thus each department sets sub-goals for the members of that department, which reflect the higher overall goals of the organisation. There is thus a hierarchical structure of ends or goals, ranging from broad general ones at the top of the organisation to more specific ones at lower levels. We might represent these as follows:

Figure 2:4 Hierarchy of organisational objectives

Overall objectives

↓

Divisional objectives

↓

Departmental objectives

↓

Sectional objectives

↓

Individual objectives

Thus for example, we would probably find that the specific goal of profit is unlikely to be found among the goals of a foreman at Metal Box, British Airways or British Gas, but we do find foremen very interested in reducing costs, which for them is a logical objective within the constraints set by the overall objective of profit.

We can, therefore, argue that the objectives of the organisation are paramount in determining the nature of work within it. They will also determine the capital and monetary resources required. If we wished to establish an organisation with the aim of producing cheap family motor cars, the finances required would be much greater than if we wished to produce and sell bread in a small village. The objectives also influence the types of technological equipment we need. The technology required for the mass production car market is much more advanced than that required to produce custom-built cars from bought-in components. The type of equipment required will, in turn, influence the qualifications or skills of the people we require; the nature of the training we will need to give; the systems of reward; and the size of the labour force. Objectives will influence the channels of communication and the kinds of information we develop to control and monitor the success or otherwise of our activities. There is a direct relationship between objectives and the structure which is consequently adopted for the organisation. This in turn, influences its systems of control and the provision of information for management decision making. It is necessary, for the efficient operation of organisations in society, that the employees are made aware of the general objectives so they can relate their efforts to the resultant success.

There is no general magic blueprint, for each organisation has different needs and influences, although there are common elements like legislation and the economic and social environment. Each organisation comprises individuals whose skills and expertise differ. The strengths of

26

each individual need to be considered when deciding how to spread responsibilities to ensure fulfilment of organisational objectives. For instance, the Chief Accountant may be a fine financial and budgetary administrator, but have no concept of the needs of marketing or production. It is important to develop a team of people who are sensibly organised and skilfully led so that together they will succeed in developing and managing a successful organisation.

The organisation structure may change, dependent upon the key objectives of the moment. For example, project teams may need to be created to cope with specific challenge but may be disbanded when that challenge has successfully been met. Individuals need to change as new roles and functions arise and as they themselves develop through training and maturation. Growth in size always demands organisational changes, both to be able to respond to outside factors and because growth requires that the structure and methods of management which people adopt must adapt to cope with the increasing volume of information and the greater complexity of business problems.

6. AUTHORITY AND CONFORMITY

When tasks are delegated some responsibility is of necessity also delegated and the Manager recognises two important features:

— Firstly that the individual taking over part of the responsibility from another member of the organisation will not and cannot do the job in the same way as it was done in the past.

— Secondly that information will be required to enable the manager with overall responsibility to monitor the efficiency with which the delegated task is being accomplished and to ensure that the task holder is contributing efficiently towards the organisation's overall objectives.

These twin problems of how much and what authority and responsibility to delegate to whom, and of how to obtain sufficient information to control what is happening in delegated functions, are key issues, especially for large organisations.

The problem is compounded when we consider organisations which operate on more than one site. For example, control is more difficult for a large Building Society where autonomy may be given to each Branch Manager to make key decisions on loans and to decide who is hired and fired. How can we ensure fairness and equity in decision making, whilst at the same time allowing a large degree of local autonomy?

Any individual, when joining an organisation in a new role, needs to be made aware of certain facts about it. Some of these may be expressed in the job specification; some may be included in the terms of reference of budget responsibilities; some can only be communicated by word of mouth; and others will depend on the progress expertise and derived experience of the individual postholder. We can all probably recognise elements in our own jobs which have developed because of our individual abilities and which are often not captured within any existing formal job specification.

Among the things an individual holding a particular job needs to know are:

(a) a knowledge of which people are directly responsible to him;

(b) knowledge of the tasks he is expected to perform and the responsibilities he has;

(c) what results he is expected to achieve and the time span within which they are to be achieved;

(d) what are the parameters of his authority on such matters as wages and salaries; prices; disciplinary action; responsibility for engaging staff; obtaining and purchasing supplies etc;

(e) what figures must be prepared on the performance of his function, in what form and how often should these figures be presented;

(f) what information he is entitled to from the activities of the other functions within the organisation; how often should he be furnished with it; and from whom does he obtain it.

The more precisely an individual can be told what job he has to do, the objectives he has to achieve and the constraints on his actions and methods of reaching those objectives, the more likely he is to be able to contribute effectively to the operation of the organisation and the attainment of its objectives. Therefore, the individual responsible for making decisions and performing his task, within the overall objectives of the organisation, should know what norms and values the organisation has and what specialist assistance he can obtain. This is important because the amount of specialist assistance varies, with greater specialisation tending to occur in large organisations.

Organisations use a number of methods to ensure that each individual uses his expertise to work towards the objectives. It has been argued by Schein (in *Organisational Psychology* 3rd edn Prentice Hall, 1980) that when an individual joins an organisation he enters into a *psychological contract*. Thus the organisation and the individual himself have expectations about the required behaviour of the other, not only on the amount of work which is wanted but also on the whole pattern of rights, privileges and obligations which are attached to employment within the specific organisation.

To ensure that individuals perform to the required standards, organisations develop a series of rules and regulations which control the behaviour of the individual while at work. The amount of discretion allowed to each individual often depends on the nature of the work which he is performing. For example, someone working on a continuous process assembly line is likely to find that their ability to determine when they go for a cup of tea or to fulfil natural bodily functions is dependent, either upon specific break times, or upon the ability of the supervisor to provide a substitute while they are absent from the line. They are also likely to find that if they do not arrive at work on time or if they are late back from a break they may be subject to a sanction of loss of wages or some other form of disciplinary action which is specified in some formal rule or procedure. The organisation thus imposes authority on the individual employee. Employees in turn, however, expect that the organisation will be reasonable in the exercise of that authority and, for example, not unnecessarily withhold permission for them to leave the production line.

Individuals accept, when they join, the authority relationship which is granted to their superiors and the rules and regulations on hours and the amount of work expected for payment. The psychological contract for individuals is implemented through an expectation that they can, either through individual or collective action, influence the organisation's treatment of them and be treated in an acceptable manner. What is considered acceptable treatment inevitably changes as the norms and values of society change. Nowadays, many of the minimum standards are laid down by statute law.

Individuals in joining a particular organisation thus accept a reduction of their freedom of action. As discussed earlier, the actual duties and responsibilities may be transmitted to the individual by means of job specifications, etc. which attempt to establish the expected roles, duties and behaviour expected. Organisations also use a number of other devices to ensure individual conformity, e.g. works rules, collective agreements etc.

7. SOCIALISATION OF INDIVIDUALS

Within the recruitment and selection process the organisation is attempting to select those with the required skills, knowledge, experience and attitudes to fit the need, and will reject those who are not considered suitable. Organisations attempt to portray the desired traits and expected behaviour through the induction process, which is designed to explain the aims and objectives of the specific organisation, the rules and regulations which apply to the individual and the benefits which will accrue because of his employment. Superiors, subordinates and colleagues in the department in which the job is located further act as transmitters of group norms and values within the organisation. These norms will not only include formal standards expected by the organisation but also the informal ones to which the individual must conform to become accepted as a member of the work group or team.

Socialisation continues through initial skills training which establishes the patterns of acceptable output and the work methods which are to be adopted. With time, the individual's behaviour continues to be moulded by the workplace environment. He finds that his ability to obtain merit-related wages increases, to be granted his holidays when he wants them, to be considered for promotion, to be encouraged and developed for

29

wider responsibilities or transfers, depends primarily on the acceptability to his superiors of his overall pattern of behaviour and his willingness to conform to the standards and rules.

The socialisation process attempts to ensure that the individual is clear about the objectives of his work and enters into what the organisation considers appropriate activities, minimising his attempt to attain inappropriate personal objectives which may perhaps interfere with those at work.

8. MEASUREMENT OF ORGANISATIONAL SUCCESS

Analysis of success in carrying out work or tasks will be inadequate if individuals have no idea of the objectives of the organisation or they do not know how successful or unsuccessful it is in reaching them. As we have implied, the basic reason for having an organisation in the first place is that there are objectives which cannot be attained by the efforts of individuals alone or resources are required beyond the skills, knowledge, experience and finance possessed by individuals or capable of being used by individuals in isolation.

To examine whether an organisation is moving in the right direction and fulfilling its objectives we must consider its performance in the light of the available resources and environmental constraints which influence it. We could for instance, measure the success of a hospital in terms of the number of patients who regain their health; yet this is not a suitable measure for those units or hospitals which care for the terminally ill or for the small cottage hospital which is faced with a 'flu' epidemic in an area where the general population are in the main elderly.

Consider also profitability of a business enterprise as a measure. We would inevitably expect a higher level of profits from a well-established organisation than perhaps from one which is only just entering into a particular market and is not yet known. Profitability is also something which is influenced both by internal efficiency and by the general economic environment which prevails. In a period of depressed economic activity we would expect profits to be lower than in a boom. The level of profits demanded can also vary from organisation to organisation. For instance, we may demand high profitability in the oil industry to be able to fund future investment, whereas we may only demand break-even profitability from London Regional Transport. Profits may also be easier in industries where demand for the product is little affected by increases in price, because the product concerned is essential to the consumer, e.g. water. Where the product is not essential, but a luxury item, e.g. video recorders, prices may have to be low because of other manufacturers' competition.

Our objective may be to increase our share of a particular market and we may need to undercut the prices of our competitors. Yet, if we consider this objective in isolation, without considering profitability, we may find that this leads to our firm going out of business. A well known example of this was the electronic calculator market.

A further objective which could be measured is that of level of sales; yet high sales are not merely a result of an organisation's efficiency and success. For example, high sales of umbrellas could result from unusually high rainfall. We may use the wrong measures to analyse success. For example, firms which use returns of discount vouchers on items bought in shops may find, when these vouchers are counted and measured against items actually supplied, that there is a discrepancy, because some stores are less honest than others in being strict about the named items for discount.

It may at times be difficult to measure success because of the interdependency of factors which impinge on ability to attain objectives; yet organisations will need to constantly monitor their progress to ensure that the structure, labour force, products manufactured, quality of those products etc. are adequate to cope with the opportunities in the market place. Certainly personnel departments are becoming increasingly involved in analysing the success of current organisational structures.

9. ORGANISATION STRUCTURES

An organisation differs from an uncoordinated interrelationship of people because it has a structure which is specifically derived for it to be able to reach its objectives. The prime concern of organisations is getting work done, but work is done by people. One of the major problems for an organisation is to create a structure which aids communication and the attainment of work objectives. Structure comprises a series of hierarchical relationships which establish the accountability and responsibility of individuals in the organisation and are designed for the organisation to achieve its objectives. It thus groups jobs in a particular pattern and the people filling those jobs are expected to carry out a collection of specific activities to cope with a variable workload. There is no best or 'right' structure in a particular situation, but there are certain arrangements of jobs which are likely to be more effective than others for organisational success whilst providing individuals with an acceptable degree of attainment of their own aims and aspirations. Structures also need to be flexible as organisations are continuously and inevitably changing in line with market or product conditions and the general attitudes of society on the morality or immorality of business operations. Patently a business cannot remain static or it will not survive; it needs to adapt and respond to its opportunities and to minimise the effects of external threats. We cannot talk of organisation structure as if it is a static thing; it is dynamic. Organisation charts imply rigidity and this is enhanced when we consider that often job descriptions may be removed and dusted off from time-to-time and used when a vacancy occurs, without being examined to see if they are currently or futuristically viable. Such actions overlook human influence.

Inevitably jobs grow and shrink because of the nature of the person in post as well as due to reactive changes in the organisation. Think of your own job and those around you and see if they have changed recently, either because you or others have matured or grown more experienced and examine these jobs against the current job descriptions.

Many books on organisation seem to start from the premise of freezing the organisation at a moment in time and dissecting it, rather like a cadaver on a mortician's slab, to see what has gone wrong and terminated its existence.

We cannot do this as easily with organisations, for the very investigation process itself often changes the nature of the organisation and because organisations are dynamic living entities which are always undergoing subtle changes over time. Certainly we may be able to see how well the organisation was coping or is coping today by examining particular incidents, but these occur in the context of slow, and in some cases, hardly-perceivable change.

J Child in *Organisation: a Guide to Problems and Practice,* Harper & Row 1984, argues that the following are essential elements for consideration in designing and reviewing organisation structure:

—   to allocate jobs to individuals giving them some personal control over the methods of working and the utilisation of resources.
—   to clearly formalise the hierarchies within the organisation and the breadth of spans of control.
—   individuals should be united together into divisions which fit and contribute loyally to organisation objectives.
—   authority should be delegated where appropriate and procedures developed so that the parameters of decision making could be monitored for success or failure.
—   communication systems should be designed to be efficient and effective in co-ordinating effort and encouraging involvement in the decision making processes.
—   the organisation should design systems which motivate individuals to give of their best and which rewards them appropriately for doing so, perhaps by linking where appropriate appraisal of performance with reward.

With these factors in mind let us examine some of the most common forms of organisation structure.

(A)   Functional structures

The classical structure which is commonly used in organisations of all types is the one which is formed around the primary tasks which require to be done. An example could be given as in:

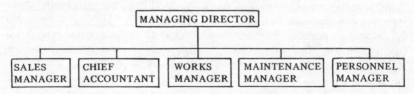

Figure 2:5 Classical form of organisation structure

32

In this structure work activities are organised into separate departments. Such a structure often tends to be centralised for the purposes of decision making. This structure is very common in small companies or in large companies with a small product range. It tends to be found in situations where the environment is changing slowly and there is little need for the organisaton to react quickly to market opportunities.

This form of structure has lasted for a long time and has the advantage that the Managing Director is in close touch with all the operations and can thus coordinate the whole enterprise. Lines of command are relatively simple to understand and control and people are grouped together on the basis of their technical or specialist expertise, which provides clearer opportunities for promotion and career development. One of the strengths of this form of structure is that people with certain skills or disciplines tend to be managed by those with similar skills or disciplines; thus attention to specialist career planning and training tends to be good.

There are disadvantages with this type of structure:

(i)   Internal conflict and competition can occur as sectional interests develop, for example, over budgets or available resources; perceived departmental needs may conflict with the needs of the organisation as a whole and loyalty may be given to the departmental or specialist function.

(ii)   This structure is difficult to adapt in situations of growth and diversification, either of product of geographical location, as the total responsibility falls on the Chief Executive for ensuring overall profitability and it is difficult to split up this responsibility without creating greater potential internal conflict. Thus, for example, projects which require the involvement of all functions, like new product development, tend to provide stresses for the organisation as no one function has overall responsibility for the task.

(iii)   Due to the inherent specialisation within this form of structure it is more difficult to develop successors for top management who have the necessary across-the-board organisational skills and expertise.

(B)   Divisional structures

As organisations develop and outgrow the functional type of structure or where that type of structure is not as apposite, as in, for example, local authorities or the Health Service, the trend is towards divisionalisation. This is a popular form in organisations with a wide range of products or services where fairly identifiable splits can be made between profit or cost centres. There are two main ways of creating divisions depending on the type, emphasis and size of the organisation concerned:

(i)   One frequent form is *divisionalisation by product or market* where fairly clear product or market differentiation is possible. For example, in local authorities, the Chief Executive has responsible to him Chief Officers who run the various services, within the budgets allocated centrally, e.g., as in Figure 2:6.

In the National Health Service the key groups of employees — doctors, nurses, paramedical and ancillary staff — are organised around the service provided, e.g., prenatal and natal, psychiatric, dentistry, general surgical, orthopaedic and so on.

This form of organisation is also found in many large private organisations, e.g. ICI has separate product divisions for Paints, Alkalis, Dyestuffs, Pharmaceuticals, etc.

(ii) *Geographical divisions* may be formed where differentiation between types of customers is considered important or where distances or communications costs favour this type of structure. It is usually adopted where essential decision making is better handled locally. Examples of this form of organisation occur in the brewing industry and amongst pharmaceutical companies, e.g., as in Figure 2:7.

Within such a structures it is usual to find a group of senior functional managers or directors located at headquarters to provide centralised direction and guidance for regional managers in the performance of their line function and to provide help to functional managers in each region on aspects which need to be handled on a company-wide basis. Yet each region or product division acts in an autonomous way in producing and marketing the products developed, within the overall control of the head office functional specialists.

Divisionalisation is the most common form to be found in large organisations in both the public and the private sectors of industry. The advantages of a divisionalised structure can be listed as follows:

(i) More products or services can be encompassed within the organisation by creating new divisions;

(ii) Where technological change is faster in one product sector of the market than another, differential adoption can take place, the appropriate expertise can be developed and specialised equipment purchased in each major unit without creating major problems for other units;

(iii) With both product and regional divisionalisation, profit responsibility can be delegated down the chain of command allowing the main activities of the organisation to be separately evaluated and major decisions can be taken nearer to the interface with the appropriate market;

(iv) It is easier to acquire and dispose of major activities within the organisation;

(v) A team is developed with loyalties to product or knowledge of an area;

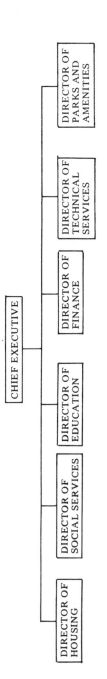

Figue 2:6 Divisionalised organisation structure

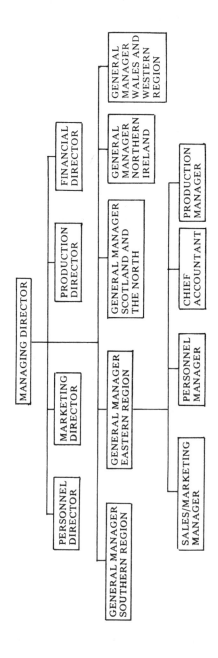

Figure 2:7 Geographically divisionalised organisation structure

35

(vi)   More scope is provided to develop divisional managers, who have overall control over sections of the organisation, for succession to top management posts.

Yet disadvantages also accrue to such structures:

(i)   Where product divisions are created, there is a danger that each General Manager could promote each product group in a way which creates problems for other product divisions or the organisation as a whole, e.g. retail — and wholesale — tyre sales departments at the fringe of the two markets could find themselves competing with each other on discount policy. Some form of centralised control may be necessary without reducing the motivation of such General Managers to produce satisfactory results themselves.

(ii)   Conflict between divisions may occur, e.g. as above, where they compete against each other in the same markets, or where transfer prices have to be negotiated for internal trading between them, perhaps where the product of one division, whilst having a market of its own, is also an important bought-in-part of another division.

(iii) There may be conflict between short term divisional objectives and long term company objectives.

(iv)   With divisional profit structures the effects of recession may hit some regional or product divisions harder than others and may lead to stress between divisions.

(v)   A further problem is that specialist functional experts may be spread through the organisations and feel isolated from each other.

(C)   Mixed structures

With increasing complexity and size of organisations, many companies are attempting to develop structures which incorporate elements of both the functional and divisional to reduce conflict and optimise the use of resources:

(i)   Project structure

A structure which may be found in the high technology industries, such as aeronautics and electronics, which are given powers to demand and control resources and are created and superimposed on the existing functional and divisional structure of the organisation. People with the relevant skills, knowledge and experience are brought together, perhaps for product development or some other multidivisional or multifunctional purpose. They work together for the life of the particular project and are usually disbanded once the team is no longer necessary, the extant structure reasserting its control.

The main advantages of such a structure are :

(a) It utilises the mix of skills within the company and in so doing helps to develop management teams for the future benefit of themselves and the organisation;

(b) By getting managers to work together on a common project it aids in helping them to understand more of each others' skills and reduces the mystique which can surround specialist functions;

(c) If all groups within the organisation realise that a common approach has been developed, there is greater likelihood of cooperation when the outcome of the project has been determined.

There are also potential problems with such an approach:

(d) There may be conflict between the line units which continue to operate during the life of the project and the project teams as to responsibilities and accountability, creating control problems. For example, those who are not members may resent the involvement of such a team in those areas which they perceive as their long-term responsibility.

(e) There is also the danger that the best managers will become overloaded with work and will neglect either their permanent jobs or their projects as a result.

(ii) Matrix structure

A matrix structure usually combines a functional form with a project-based structure. It differs from a project structure in so far as project teams (as described previously) are disbanded at the end of the project, whereas a matrix structure tends to be operated on a permanent basis. A project manager will coordinate and be responsible for the work carried out by the project team and he will deal with the client. This, for instance, is often seen in civil engineering contracts. He is still responsible to his own departmental manager, but will be functionally involved with other departmental managers, depending upon the complexity of the specific project. These managers will provide his with specialists responsible to him for the specific project, but reponsible for departmental matters to their own managers. Matrix structures combine vertical and horizontal lines of communication and authority. Thus, a division of an engineering organisation, which has four projects being undertaken simultaneously, may have a matrix organisation as in Figure 2:8.

Project managers, whilst having responsibility for funding and budgets, planning, scheduling and quality control of the project, usually have more responsibility than formal authority for the staff, hence they often get results by persuasion and informal appeals for cooperation.

Advantages claimed for the matrix structure include:

1. It enables the organisation to improve the quality of decision making over particular projects because decisions are made by the project leader who is in direct contact with the client.

Figure 2:8 Matrix organisation structure

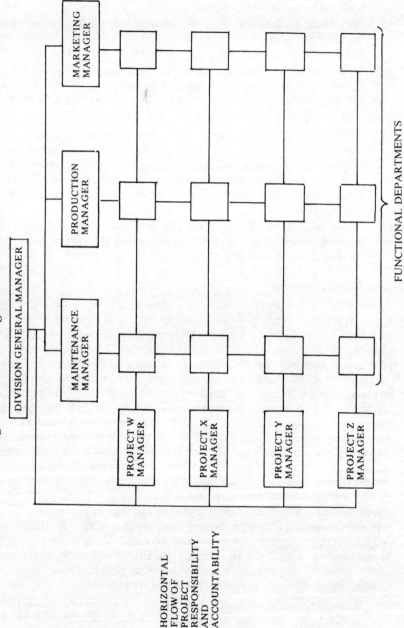

FUNCTIONAL DEPARTMENTS

38

2. It encourages functional managers to understand the contribution they are making directly to each project, because the focus of effort becomes the project, and not departmental functional needs.

3. Interested departments are involved from the inception of the project and thus in the decision making process from the first phases.

As in the other types of organisation structure mentioned, disadvantages do accrue. These include:

1. Decision making may take longer as the consultation process often takes time.

2. It may be felt that there is a dilution of functional specialist responsibilities within the organisation and, consequently, managers of functional departments may feel their authority as 'experts' threatened.

3. Potential conflicts may arise over the allocation of resources and division of authority between functional groups and project groups.

4. There is also potential danger that individual members of project teams may feel their loyalties divided between their project manager and colleagues and their own functional manager and specialist colleagues.

10. CENTRALISATION AND DECENTRALISATION

The trend towards increased specialisation of function leads to a diffusion of accountability and authority to attain organisational objectives. An organisation's structure requires the allocation of authority to those responsible for undertaking specific activities; and consideration of how much power and authority should be allocated to the various activities and key roles. In every organisation which has multiple levels of management in the hierarchy and multiple specialism, there is delegation. The question is not whether it occurs, but how much it actually takes place. With centralised structure, the major decisions on all significant aspects of the organisation's work are made at the top. A decentralised structure, on the other hand, places the authority and decision making process as close as possible to the level at which the work is done. Only very small organisations can maintain a centralised structure where effective authority can be retained at the top by one individual or by a small group of senior executives.

Whether a particular organisation is managed on a centralised or decentralised basis depends on a number of factors:

(i) The absolute size of the firm or organisation is a key factor. It is very difficult to coordinate all day-to-day decision making in a large multiproduct organisation, in a local authority or a large general hospital. The number of units or different specialisms and the total number of employees controlled are significant factors. Efficiency and the ability to respond quickly is improved by making subordinate units semi-autonomous with long term planning being coordinated from the top.

(ii)   The nature and history of the organisation can also be a significant influence. If there is only one product and the organisation is located on only one site, then centralised control is likely. If, on the other hand, the organisation is a multiproduct conglomerate, operating on a number of different sites nationally or internationally and it has grown through mergers and takeovers, it is much more likely to have a decentralised structure. In such a diverse organisation, the speed and efficiency decision making and the flexibility of the organisation in responding to customer requirements are enhanced through a decentralised authority network.

(iii) A further consideration is the philosophy and personality of top management. Thus, for example, Henry Ford used to make all the major decisions in the Ford Motor Company and this centralised control is also familiar in many other owner-managed organisations. If the Chief Executive is autocratic in his control and also owns a substantial proportion of the enterprise's assets, a centralised form of control will tend to prevail.

(iv)   In practice some management functions are more easily decentralised than others. In large multiplant organisations such functions as financial planning, research and development and some aspects of personnel can be usefully centralised — albeit there are people who carry out some aspects of day-to-day control at each site — whereas cost accounting, purchasing, production, quality control and some marketing and sales functions are probably decentralised.

The main *advantages* of decentralisation can be listed as follows:

1.   It permits speed in decision making by enabling line managers, who are closer to the work in hand, to take local decisions without waiting for decisions from the highest authority.

2.   It enables local management to be flexible in their approach to decisions, in the light of local market opportunities or needs, and thus to be more adaptable in situations of change.

3.   It prevents top management being overloaded with minutiae, by freeing them from operational matters, and enabling them to concentrate on the essential strategic decisions which are necessary for an organisation's long term survival and competitiveness.

4.   It encourages subordinates at each level in the structure to exercise greater initiative and ingenuity and can contribute to staff motivation by enabling middle and junior managers to take and be respon-

sible for local decisions. This ensures the development of capable managers groomed for more senior coordinating posts.

5. Problems of coordination, communication and bureaucracy are reduced, thus cutting down on local management frustration.

6. It focuses attention on cost control and profitability locally, which enhances management awareness of cost effectiveness and success in reaching revenue targets, thus minimising the ability to blame others where difficulties are encountered.

For all the advantages which decentralisation of decision making can bring, there are *disadvantages* which must be considered and the repercussions of which must be controlled if the organisation is to reach its long term objectives. These have been identified as:

1. It requires an appropriate and adequate control system if major errors of judgement are to be avoided by local management. Decentralisation can only succeed with competent, well-trained managers who are able to judge when centralised advice is required.

2. It requires coordination from senior management to ensure that individual parts are not working so that their objectives conflict with those of the organisation as a whole.

3. The decisions made by individual units may lead to inconsistency in the treatment of employees and of customers or clients.

4. There is a danger that loyalty may be encouraged to individual units and unit managers rather than to the enterprise.

5. Local units may fail to utilise the expert services which are available centrally: there is the danger of duplication of effort by local units who may try to solve problems from scratch, which have already been adequately solved in another unit.

To reduce some of these disadvantages it is essential that decentralisation should be adequately planned and not happen by default. The managers who operate with local autonomy must be well trained and made aware of the overall aims and objectives of the total organisation on a regular basis. Logical decisions must be made on which types of decision will be decentralised and what the limits of discretion are. The more competent and effective the key employees are in their individual unit, the more likely it is that problems will occur with decentralisation and the more difficult it will be to control the organisation. The main difficulties likely to occur are influenced by the differing views of the extent of autonomy of each unit; the interactions between key central and key subsidiary staff; and the different styles of management and different cultures that may develop between the main organisation and the individual operational units, especially where there is geographical separation between the units and head office.

The degrees of autonomy allowed to specific units can vary from organisation to organisation, depending on the nature of the market served. This relationship can vary along a continuum from the individual unit having complete freedom of action, controlled only by levels of investment and a laid down profit objective, to that where the subsidiary unit is completely controlled by the parent organisation, having little freedom of action except over day-to-day operations. The most important element is not where the freedom of discretion lies along the continuum but that the parties mutually understand the amount of licence which is allowed.

11. LINE VS STAFF MANAGEMENT

In small organisations all employees tend to be line personnel, but as organisations grow it becomes necessary to employ specialists who give technical advice and provide support services for line personnel. The terms line and staff are usually explained in two senses: firstly in the sense of functions which contribute towards the organisation's overall objectives, and secondly as authority relationships.

Line positions and the individuals employed in them contribute directly to the provision of the goods and services which are demanded by the customer or client. Generally the organisation could not operate, even in the short term, without the functions which comprise the line. In a manufacturing organisation manufacturing and sales functions are line functions; in a department store both buying and selling are line functions; and in a hospital so are both nursing and medical. They are seen as primary functions and they act to ensure that objectives are met. Line authority is central to the chain of command and members of line functions have direct authority over others.

Staff functions can be split into two categories, specialised staff and service staff:

Specialised staff functions provide planning, advice and control: engineering, research and development, legal, finance, audit and personnel departments fall into this category. Such departments are usually composed of people with technical and professional expertise. In addition to providing advice and control functions for all line departments, they are also involved at senior levels in policy formulation. They have direct authority over others in respect of their specialist functions only. Thus there tends, for example, to be a hierarchy within the personnel department of superior-subordinate relations, and there are line responsibilities within specialised staff functions. Because line authority is not totally dependent on line functions, it can be better understood as a central feature of the total chain of command within the overall organisation structure.

Service functions aid the organisation in the predominantly physical sense and some give technical counsel and perform control functions. Examples of service staff are purchasing, maintenance, inspection, quality control and typing pools.

It is most sensible to consider the concepts of line and staff in terms of authority relationships rather than in terms of functions and their direct contribution to products or services. This is because most organisations have complex relationships between functions which are often dependent on each other to a greater extent than direct classification into traditional staff or line compartments would imply. Some areas of the staff function may merely provide services, e.g. recruitment, market research, legal advice and guidance,whereas others may establish key standards of performance for other sections of the organisation, e.g. setting and monitoring key quality standards for the customer or installing and controlling industrial relations procedures to maintain common standards of treatment of employees. It can be argued that staff managers have functional authority in relation to agreed aspects of their own particular expertise. Thus, the personnel manager of a company is not only responsible and accountable for the conduct of personnel matters, but may also have authority to ensure that line managers adhere to the organisation's procedures and policies in their treatment of staff individuals and groups within their departments. This overall authority for personnel matters inevitably reduces the power of line managers to exercise their own discretion but, given the external pressures of legislation and Codes of Practice in the 1980s, it is only by having expert advice that organisations can fulfil the responsibilities demanded of them by society.

The amount of actual power to enforce his authority which a functional staff manager has varies from organisation to organisation, dependent on the particular traditions which have evolved.

Certainly the relationship between line and staff personnel has the potential for disagreement and conflict:

1. A potential cause of such conflict is the dual authority that can exist when members of staff or advisory departments attempt to give instructions to line management. For example, a safety officer who is a member of a personnel department may order a foreman to shut down a defective piece of equipment because there is a potential danger for the operator. The foreman's line manager may have instructed the foreman to keep the machine running because he considers the dangers minimal to the experienced operator in charge of the machine. Unless the safety officer has earned the respect of the foreman and line manager, conflict can result if higher levels of the executive hierarchy are asked to adjudicate.

2. The task of many staff units is to initiate improvements and change in an organisation's operation, policies and procedures. Line personnel often have a different orientation; their job is to produce a product or provide a service within an appropriate time-span and, to do this, they may prefer stability to changes for which they cannot immediately see a return.

3. A specialised staff function usually consists of staff who are expert in a limited field and who have often undergone professional or specific technical training. A line manager, on the other hand, tends to be a generalist who has obtained his position because of hard work within the organisation. There are likely to be conflicts because of different perceptions of the value of practical experience compared with further education and training.

4. Different staff specialists may be called upon to help solve the same problem in a line department and may offer different solutions. For example, if a specific department's accident record is poor, the plant engineer may advise improvements in the fencing and guarding of equipment, whereas the personnel and training officer may recommend improvements in, or intensification of, safety training for the operators and departmental supervisors. The line manager must then reconcile the differences and determine an appropriate solution.

5. Staff departments also serve as an instrument of top management to control the performance of operating managers and others. This monitoring of performance against objectives and standards, for example, — How are payroll costs rising? What levels of overtime are being worked? How high is labour turnover or absenteeism? — can cause problems between line and staff functions unless cooperation occurs and constructive diagnosis and recommendations are made jointly.

Line and staff managers should work together in solving problems and in attaining objectives; the degree of staff advice to line managers and the degree of functional authority within the structure varying from organisation to organisation.

12. ORGANISATION STRUCTURES IN THE 1980s

The past 10-20 years have seen a remarkable degree of change within organisations. Apart from the influence of technological innovations, such factors as mergers and takeovers have led to new structures developing. Organisations have combined with others horizontally, vertically and laterally.

Horizontal combination or integration occurs when firms making the same kinds of products merge to become more competitive in the market-place. One example was the combination of the separate motor car manufacturers to form British Leyland. The aims of such combinations are to reduce price cutting and competition; to encourage economies of scale by increasing efficiency; and to buy raw materials and sell a broader range of products.

Vertical combination or integration occurs when organisations acquire the different stages and processes of production perhaps back to raw materials or essential components or forward to the point of sale to the customer. The aims of this form of combination are to reduce costs, by cutting out the middleman or wholesaler; to obtain the sources of raw materials; to reduce the likelihood of failures in supply due to other purchasing competition; and to obtain the economies of linked processes and unified control.

Lateral combination or integration occurs when firms producing allied or complementary products, or products for different markets, join together. The aims of this form of amalgamation are to be able to reduce the effects of loss of markets for one particular product and to increase profits.

Such combinations rarely take only one form and many large companies have practised all three. Such amalgamations can cross national boundaries and lead to the increased development of international multiproduct organisations, which practise division of operation across national boundaries to increase efficiency; to reduce their reliance on one individual economy; and to increase their penetration of difficult markets. Well documented examples are Ford, Alfa Laval, ICI and the major oil and chemical-producing companies.

These combinations have forced organisations to change their structures to take advantage of the benefits. Traditional centralised functional or divisional structures will not be effective in such organisations and a mixture of forms is often to be found. These past trends will still be discernible in the 1980s as organisations attempt to survive in a depressed economic environment, by shedding their unprofitable units and consolidating their operations.

This is likely to cause a trend towards intermediate matrix-type structures as groups or teams form or reform to do different tasks or work processes change with technological innovations. Organisations will face pressures to change and to be flexible; to adapt to such changes, on the one hand, whilst retaining stability and coherence of objectives on the other. The structures will have to be developed against the background of the human need for stability, career development and participation in organisational decision making. Adequate communication systems will need to be created so that people do not lose sight of the overall long term goals of the organisation and are able to operate in ways which can be seen to be contributing fully to those objectives.

Obviously not all organisations will have to develop new structures; the traditional functional or divisional systems are still suitable for many, especially those where market changes take place slowly.

The trend towards decentralisation of operations is likely to continue to increase the consciousness and entrepreneurial ability of the decision makers in units which can respond to the needs of the client. This will increase the speed with which organisations can respond to technical innovation, which will occur at different rates from sector to sector and process to process.

At present it would appear that organisations will either have to grow or stagnate. Growth, however, is unlikely to be in terms of expansion but rather in terms of increased efficiency; better use of resources; better quality of output; and greater awareness of client needs. This will require more effective management, both in terms of efficiency in decision making and awareness of human needs and fears. Information flow will increase with developments in computer technology — it is thus likely that organisations will have to become more participative and democratic in their decision making.

It must thus be recognised that if an organisation is to survive, its structures, policies, operations and style of management must be developed by deliberate design and must be examined continually, consciously and critically. Techniques of organisation development will, therefore, be required as part of the personnel management role.

Examine your own organisation against the background of this chapter. What objectives does it currently have in the short term and long term? How and why have these objectives changed? What structure does it operate? How centralised or decentralised is it? What degree of autonomy is allowed to each division or branch? What staff/line conflicts exist? What significant changes will it face in the future? What do you believe will be the resultant employment and employee relations issues?

Chapter 3
The Major Functions of Enterprise : Marketing

Personnel management occurs within the context of organisation, alongside other functions and contributes with those other functions to the attainment of organisational objectives. Before we examine the nature of personnel management itself, it is worth examining two of the major functions of business — marketing and production. In this chapter we shall examine marketing and, in the next, production.

1. WHAT IS MARKETING!

Marketing is a major function of the management of an enterprise which is more concerned with what is happening outside the particular organisation than inside. Marketing as an activity has been described in a number of different ways. Here are some examples:

1. The British Institute of Management (BIM) defines marketing as:

    'The creative management function which promotes trade and employment by assessing consumer needs and initiating research and development to meet them. It coordinates the resources of production and distribution of goods and services, determines and directs the nature and scale of the total effort required to sell profitably the maximum production to the ultimate user.'

2. Peter Drucker in *The Practice of Management* (1954) has said:

    'Marketing is...looking at the business through the customer's eyes.'

3. The Institute of Marketing, (1966) stated that marketing was:

    'The management function which organises and directs all those business activities involved in assessing and converting customer purchasing power into effective demand for a specific product or service and moving the product or service to the final consumer so as to achieve the profit target or other objectives of the company.'

The origins of marketing can be traced back to the period following the Industrial Revolution when, for the first time, there were indications that the means of production were capable of meeting and even surpassing the actual stated demand for goods. Before techniques of mass production were developed, there was generally a shortage of manufactured goods and this demand and supply lag meant that most products and services were assured of an immediate sale. Productive processes were given a great stimulus by the two World Wars and, despite an increasing population (because of medical developments and enhanced survival prospects) by the early 1960s, in developed industrial countries, the supply of manufactured goods had outstripped demand. Companies found that competition had increased; they could no longer sell all that they made. The position had changed from one in which the manufacturers had to a great extent determined the quantity and the type of goods supplied, to one in which the consumer had a choice — especially affecting the consumer goods industry — the cash to be able to purchase goods and was able to discriminate in his purchases.

For businesses to sustain their share of the market and to grow it was necessary to conduct research into the needs of the consumer and to develop products of a price and a quality that was acceptable. This has been recognised for years. Adam Smith wrote in his *Wealth of Nations* 1775:

'Consumption is the sole end of production'.

In this lies what has been termed *the marketing concept* : the appreciation that far from being the last link in the business chain, it is the customer who initiates the whole business cycle. This does not mean that the customer is always right, but that customer need should be the starting point for the organisation's corporate strategy. Wealth is only created when goods are sold, not when they are made and goods are sold when there is an identifiable consumer need which can be satisfied by the organisation. It is the first concern of marketing to identify those needs and, having defined them, to devise methods of meeting them at a profit.

One important differentiation needs to be made. In marketing there is an identifiable difference between people's *needs,* which can be defined as the physical and psychological drives which stem from being human, e.g. the need for food, clothing, shelter, etc. and to differentiate these from people's *wants* which are the specific fancies which are directed towards satisfying those needs. Thus, the need for food can be directed by a confectionery firm into a specific fancy for jelly babies or liquorice allsorts rather than another organisation's food products. Marketing often concentrates on creating and changing people's wants to satisfy their human needs.

The specific elements in the marketing function can be represented as in Figure 3:1

Figure 3:1 – Elements in the marketing function

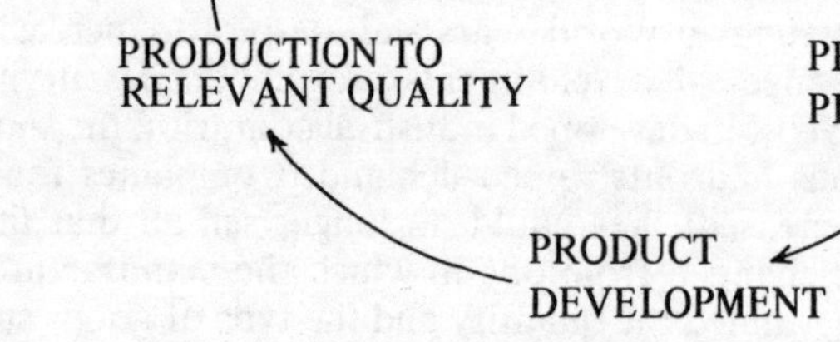

2. COMPANY ORIENTATION

Organisations can take a variety of orientations towards their customers and potential customers in the consumer market. The four most commonly identified are:

1. Production orientation

The organisation concentrates its attention on efficiency of production and distribution and maintaining low costs to encourage customers to purchase their products. Mass production car manufacturers tend to adopt this approach.

2. Product orientation

The organisation competes on the basis of the quality of its products. Examples are found in the high quality 'hi-fi' market.

3. Sales orientation

The organisation's philosophy is dominated by the idea that customers will need to be persuaded to buy the product by positive selling. Hence, the focus of attention is on sales skills and techniques. Some companies in the insurance and double-glazing industries adopt this type of approach.

4. Market orientation

This focus is on the needs of the customers and the company will make every attempt possible to ascertain their real wants. It then responds to customer demand. This is quite common in the kitchen design industry.

3. IDENTIFICATION OF THE MARKET

The first task of marketing, however, is to identify what the market is. It is not just Shepherds Bush or the UK or the World; used in the context of modern marketing, the work 'market' is taken to mean people or groups of people having in common the need or desire for a particular commodity or service. Two broad categories of market can be identified:

1. *Industrial markets,* which may represent a relatively small number of customers who require technical advice and support after the sale has taken place and who may require products tailored to individual requirements. Some industrial and commercial markets do purchase large quantities of similar products.

2. *Consumer markets,* where lower costs of producing and selling may be influential in tempting people to buy.

Marketing managers have a special interest in classifying potential consumers, whether of the industrial or private kind, to discover differences in taste, spending habits and attitudes, which may be used as the basis for designing relevant marketing programmes.

The term *market segmentation* is based on the idea that most, if not all, markets are composed of different types of customers with distinct product preferences. Segmentation identifies that consumers are different in some way; they may buy the product at different times, or for different reasons, or perhaps the product can be put to a different use in a segment which is not general for the rest of the market. The most frequent methods of segmenting a market are based on demographic, geographical and buyer-behaviour variables, which may overlap. Figure 3:2 illustrates these variables.

Figure 3 : 2
Variables affecting
market segmentation

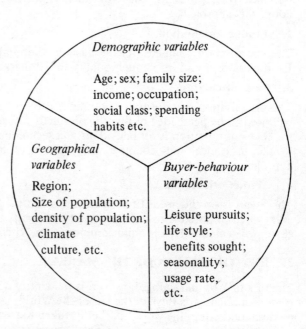

Demographic variables

Age; sex; family size;
income; occupation;
social class; spending
habits etc.

Geographical
variables

Region;
Size of population;
density of population;
climate
culture, etc.

Buyer-behaviour
variables

Leisure pursuits;
life style;
benefits sought;
seasonality;
usage rate,
etc.

1. Demographic variables. A convenient way of classifying the population is according to social class on such characteristics as occupation, education and income. This has a correlation with spending habits and life style. The common classification of classes and approximate percentages of the population in such categories is given in **Table 3:1**. The categorisation has a weakness as it tends to be based on the occupation of the head of the family.

    Magazines, newspapers and journals are examples of products which can be directed towards carefully segmented markets and this is of interest to advertisers who will choose the medium which is orientated towards the consumer groups they are trying to reach. What characteristics do you think consumers have who read the following?

The Observer	The Sunday Times	The Sun
Playboy	The Economist	Woman's Realm
The People	Financial Times	Woman and Home
New Society	Daily Telegraph	Cosmopolitan

TABLE 3:1 SOCIAL CLASSES — BROAD CLASSIFICATION

Code	Broad Category	Occupation of Head Household	Approx. Percentage of of Population 1983
A	Upper middle class	Professional and senior managerial	16%
B	Middle class	Intermediate managerial administrative or professional staff	
C_1	Lower middle class	Junior managerial, supervisory, senior clerical	22%
C_2	Skilled working class	Skilled manual	33%
D	Working class	Semi-skilled and unskilled manual	29%
E	Subsistence levels	Persons living on pensions and social security or in casual work	

2. Age is a further basis of segmentation because of the different attitudes and preferences between age groups and because of the different domestic circumstances which ageing brings, e.g. clothes can be aimed at different age groups.

3. Geographical segmentation, which covers aspects such as regions and their density of population, has significance for suppliers of such goods as pork pies, which are more popular in the Midlands and North, and clothes, which are required to deal with certain variations in climatic conditions. Attempts to maximise sales without segmenting the market would probably lead to wasted effort. Large retail stores are only likely to establish shops in areas with high population density, to gain maximum returns.

4. Buyer-behaviour variables. Such items as the frequency of use of particular products or seasonality may have major repercussions in some industries. For example, small off-licences are likely to keep a small stock of liqueurs throughout the year but are likely to increase their stocks around Christmas and Easter when families are more likely to indulge. Some industries may also be affected by weather patterns, e.g. certain brands of beer are more likely to be

purchased in good weather or hotels may have to improve their attractions for year-round guests. Other examples of products with a seasonal demand include bedding plants and Christmas cards. Seasonality factors are of considerable importance in relation to production schedules, distribution and storage arrangements.

Thus the nature of a particular market is likely to have profound effects on the techniques employed in identifying the needs of each sector.

4. THE MARKETING MIX

An important element in every marketing strategy is (termed in the 1940s by Professor Neil Borden of Harvard University) the *Marketing Mix.* It identified twelve key influences on marketing programmes. Borden's model has since been refined and the variables have now been reduced to four, product, promotion, price and distribution. Once the decision has been made to penetrate a particular market, the influence of these variables operating together on success is crucial. The Marketing Mix can be represented in Figure 3:4. These various elements are outlined later in the chapter.

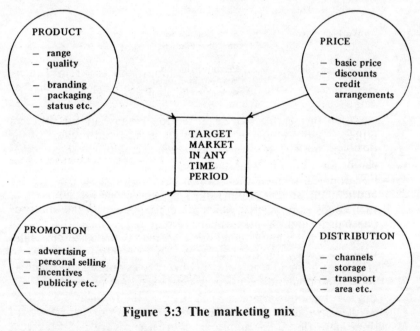

Figure 3:3 The marketing mix

5. MARKET RESEARCH

Market research attempts to acquire and analyse information to make marketing decisions. Thus information is gathered which tries to answer

the following questions:
1. What products are being sold?
2. In what quantities?
3. Where?
4. How?
5. When?
6. At what price?
7. What is the total potential size of the market?
8. Is it an industrial or consumer market or a mixture of both?
9. Is the market growing, saturated or declining?
10. What are the characteristics of competitors' products?
11. How successful are advertising strategies?
12. Do customers require an after sales service?
    — and so on.

Thus it is concerned with assessing the demands for new products and the acceptability of existing products. In both instances, it will study the organisation's position and that of its competitors. The data which forms the raw material of market research falls into two broad categories, primary and secondary:

1. *Primary data* — is gathered directly from the customers and those handling the commodity, e.g. wholesalers and retailers. This data is most frequently collected by means of surveys, which may either be based on questionnaires or on interviews. Often surveys are undertaken by specialist research organisations who use trained interviewers asking structured questions to ensure comparability of data. Questionnaires have the advantage that they obtain wide coverage at a relatively low cost, but this is offset by the usually low rate of response. Interviews have the advantage that they are more flexible than questionnaires and the target population can be effectively controlled, but they have the main disadvantage that they are costly and time consuming.

2. *Secondary data.* There are two main sources of secondary data — firstly, external information from Government statistics, trade reports, and press and private marketing research agencies; secondly, internal data can be obtained from sales information including field sales reports and letters from consumers.

6. PRODUCT PLANNING AND PRODUCT DEVELOPMENT

This translates customer needs, as identified by market research, into acceptable products or services which can be sold to the consumer to meet that need. People, as we have already mentioned, do not necessarily purchase products for their intrinsic value, but because they believe their needs will be satisfied by the product. For example, people buy motor cars for what they provide in terms of convenience and comfort as a means of transport, but also possibly for psychological reasons of status or self-expression.

Product planning is concerned with any or all of the following:

1. Completely new products
2. Changes in existing products
3. Extensions to an existing range of products
4. Introducing an established product from another market.

Market research will establish the nature and extent of the potential market and will also evaluate the extent and quality of competitive activity. If the findings are favourable for a new product, the preliminary product specification will be passed to the Research and Development department for production of a prototype for testing. At the same time, preliminary costings will be calculated so that estimates can be made of the profit margins. Tentative advertising and sales plans will be prepared and, depending upon the results of product testing (perhaps with potential consumers) and evaluation of the results, a decision will be taken as to whether to launch the product or not. Production capacity and equipment will be necessary for production of the appropriate quality and numbers.

Product quality may be designed into the item, so that benefits of reliability, long product life and value for money can be used in advertising and selling. In some products quality may not be important, e.g. certain types of disposable goods, like plastic spoons for picnics, do not need to be durable or aesthetically pleasing so long as they are hygienic and functional.

7. DISTRIBUTION

The objectives of distribution are to ensure that the right goods, in the right quantities, are in the right place. The producer must choose the most suitable *channel or channels of distribution* — a channel is a combination of organisation, transportation and storage. The most common channels can be depicted as in Figure 3:4.

The first channel is more often found in industrial than in consumer markets. Manufacturers of goods such as machine tools, turbines, computers and other large and expensive items tend to move them directly to the consumer without involving any middleman. Channel 2 is often found in mail-order business operations and large cash-and-carry warehouses which are increasingly developing their coverage. Channel 3 represents the situation where manufacturers sell direct to large national, retail chains who buy in bulk from manufacturers and distribute directly to their own retail outlets, e.g. Woolworth's, Marks & Spencer, British Home Stores and Sainsbury's. Channel 4 represents the typical chain for mass-marketed consumer goods where products are sold over a wide geographical area, perhaps both nationally and internationally, wholesalers buy in bulk from the manufacturers, store the goods and sell them in smaller quantities to individual retailers.

Three major influences affect the physical storage and distribution of goods from the manufacturer to the customer:

Channel

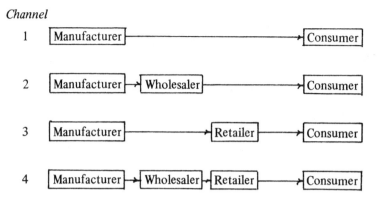

Figure 3:4 Common distribution channels

1. Market considerations

Some examples are:

(a) The channels of distribution chosen to satisfy the industrial sector of the market will usually differ from those chosen for the consumer sector.

(b) Where seasonal demand cannot be met by seasonal production, storage facilities may be required for the goods which are accumulating as a result of continuous production — these stocks can be known as *buffer stocks*.

(c) Variation in purchasing habits between different parts of the country will have an effect on distribution methods and costs.

2. Product considerations

The composition, size, weight or technical complexity of the product can all affect distribution. For example:

(a) Perishable products will require special transport and storage facilities.

(b) The actual size and weight of the product can also impose limitations and some products may need to be shipped partially-assembled for final reassembly at the point of sale.

(c) Complex products may require installation by qualified technicians and perhaps after-sales service, including the distribution of spare parts.

55

3. Economic considerations

In Europe distribution accounts for between 35% and 50% of the retail price of the product. Capital is tied up in finished goods and so a manufacturer will tend to choose a channel of distribution which does not necessitate his holding an inventory and thus releases, and perhaps even reduces, the working capital he requires for his business.

8. SALES PROMOTION

Every product needs to be brought to the attention of the customer in the market-place and its benefits identified. One important method used to sell benefits is termed *branding,* which can be thought of as the naming of a product to give it appeal and recognition. Famous brand names include Coke, Biro, Mars, Wilkinson Sword and Hoover, all of which are synonymous with particular products. Thus, for instance, most domestic vacuum cleaners are referred to as Hoovers, whether they are made by Hoover or not. Branding is used a lot in selling beers, cigarettes, detergent, and perfumes. Some of the large retail stores successfully sell products manufactured by other well-known suppliers under their own brand name, e.g. Sainsbury's, Woolworth's, Marks & Spencer and Bejam.

Sales promotion is merchandising the product in such a manner that it attracts prospective customers and induces them to buy. This may take a variety of forms with different emphasis, according to whether thay are used for consumer or industrial markets. The principal methods are:

1. Advertising
2. Personal selling
3. Incentives
4. Packaging
5. Sponsorship and publicity

1. Advertising

This communicates information about the product or service by means of the written word, the spoken word and visual material. There are five principal media of advertising:

(a) Newspapers, magazines, journals, trade publications, etc.
(b) Television
(c) Direct mailing
(d) Commercial radio
(e) Hoardings, transport advertisements, trade and country fairs etc.

In the UK something like 70% of advertising is via the press and about 30% on commercial television. There are various options open to an organisation in deciding how much to spend on advertising. It can be based on a relationship of advertising expenditure to sales expenditure, on what competitors are spending and on special budgets to increase awareness of particular products. Examine the impact of advertising by listing some products of which you are aware and try to analyse why the advertising is a success.

2. Personal selling

Personal selling is an important adjunct to advertising. Personal selling is especially important in the industrial market. The basic sales process contains six elements or stages:

(a)   Arousing interest in the product;

(b)   creating a preference for the organisation's product rather than that of another organisation;

(c)   establishing contact with the customer;

(d)   encouraging interest in a sale;

(e)   completing the sale;

(f)   keeping the business.

In consumer markets the first three stages are often handled by advertising, but in industrial markets it is more usual for representatives or salesmen to handle them. Companies allocate the following tasks to sales representatives:

(i)   Communicating regular information to customers on the products and their uses and advantages;

(ii)   obtaining new customers;

(iii)   gathering information on customer satisfaction;

(iv)   dealing with technical queries and ensuring delivery at the right time.

This requires knowledge of   —   the range of products
                               —   the customers and likely customers
                               —   other organisations' products
                               —   techniques of selling.

Sales forces may be organised on a number of different bases or combinations of different structures. These include organisation on:

—   a geographical or territorial basis

—   a product or range of product basis, where specialist knowledge is important

—   a customer basis, e.g. consumer or industrial markets.

The success of a salesman or representative can be evaluated in a number of different ways. These include:

—   net sales achieved for product or customer

—   number of calls made in a given period and value of sales per call

— number of new customers
— costs of selling as a proportion of sales achieved.

3. Incentives

The offering of incentives to promote the organisation's product or service and to encourage customers to buy, is most common for consumer products. The hope is that various incentives will draw attention to a new product or improved product; encourage sales of slow moving items; and stimulate higher customer usage of particular items, which perhaps they have not used before. Incentives are also offered to trade purchasers to develop goodwill and encourage wholesalers or retailers to 'push' various items and to increase the amount they buy. Incentives may take a number of different forms and include:

— free samples
— bulk purchase bargains
— temporary price reductions
— special discounts for the trade
— provision of display material
— stamp trading and gift catalogues
— competitions
— free demonstrations
— reductions on holidays etc.

4. Packaging

This has two functions; firstly, it provides protection for the product, and secondly, it creates a brand image. Certainly packaging becomes important at particular times of the year, for example, Christmas when many cigarette companies produce more large 200 boxes with wrappers which reflect the season and Easter when the confectionery firms produce Easter eggs. Odd shapes or large packets with small objects inside produce problems of storage and distribution and this needs to be considered at the design stage.

5. Sponsorships and publicity

Some publicity, in the form of press-releases on new products or articles in trade or specialist journals, has the advantage that it often costs nothing. Other, more expensive forms include sponsorships of football, cricket, tennis tournaments and other sporting events. Organisations who sell products which have medical lobbies attempting to reduce consumption by individuals, often enter into this form of publicity.

9. PRICING

Price is important because it produces the revenue which is required for the organisation to remain in business. The main objectives of pricing policy are twofold —

1. To achieve a target return on investment
2. To maintain or improve a company's share of the market

Pricing policy can be subject to short term or long term considerations and price is particularly important when introducing new products or breaking into new markets. When a new product is introduced which has substantial development costs, the price may tend to be rather high yet, as the product attracts buyers and these initial costs are covered, prices may be reduced. One danger is to ensure that initial prices are not too high to deter customers. An example of a product which had a high initial price, but which dropped very rapidly as customers saw its advantages, was the biro.

Some products need to be sold at a higher price to retain credibility on quality. An example was Babycham which, when introduced at a very low price, was not purchased but, when prices were increased to cover costs, sold more.

It may be necessary to sell a product at a low price to ensure market penetration: a bargain price may attract considerable sales and, at the same time discourage further competitors from entering the market. The cheap-fares policy attempted by Laker Airways was an example. The price was so low, however, that it failed to generate sufficient revenue to cover investment costs on new capital equipment.

Certainly we cannot underestimate the effect that competitors can have on pricing policy. For example, in the sale of petrol, prices change as each company attempts to increase their share of the market by reducing prices. Some companies, like Conoco, even operate a policy which insists that they undercut their competitors. Much depends on the sensitivity of the market to such price changes.

Demand patterns in the market may be categorised along a continuum from elastic to inelastic. Demand can be said to be *elastic* when demand can be increased or decreased by levels of price which may be affected, not only by internal pricing policy but also by economic, political and social considerations. For example, the market for motor cars tends to be elastic because the demand can be affected by such factors as hire purchase restrictions or Value Added Tax. Demand, on the other hand, tends to be *inelastic* when it is not subject to variation, as with the market for bread or salt.

Pricing policies can be based on a number of different methods as the following examples illustrate:

1. *Cost plus pricing* : This is pricing which is based on covering total costs and adding a margin of profit for each item sold. This method requires a very accurate knowledge of the structure of costs and the ability to distinguish how various categories of costs are likely to behave at different levels of output and over different time-spans.

2. *Contribution pricing* : This attempts to balance market demand and costs of production by developing tables which reveal the level of sales required to enable a company to break-even. Sales above this level make a contribution to profit. It is an important method of pricing for large items with heavy development costs, for example, aeroplanes. A graph can be derived as in Figure 3:5 — Break-even pricing.

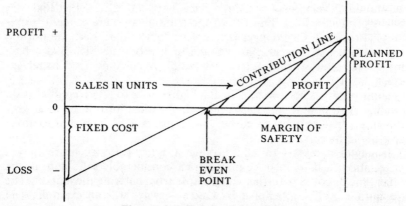

Figure 3:5 Break even pricing

3. *Competitive pricing* : Prices are largely determined by competitors already established in the particular market. Newcomers have to judge their ability to penetrate the market by offering lower prices. Care must be taken because they may find that customers have accepted a price structure which yields relatively high profits to existing organisations and to react to this by offering a new product at a substantially lower price may court disaster from two sources:

(a) the customers — who may not believe initially that it is as good as existing products, *or*

(b) the competitors — who may have the resources to undercut the organisation and force it out in a price war.

Where a range of products is offered, companies may use the 'loss-leader' concept, which means that one product in the range is reduced in price to below-cost levels with the objective of attracting attention to the range as a whole, and to establish the organisation's name in the market.

In pricing policies, companies need to keep a regular check on costs. Labour costs, for example, have changed from year to year in the post-war era; so have material costs for oil-based products, raw materials like copper and aluminium; and energy costs have increased substantially over relatively short periods during the 1970s and 1980s. Some cost increases may be offset by productivity changes, but the most crucial costs are those which can fluctuate upwards suddenly and which cannot easily be absorbed in the short term by productivity increases. Such changes pose problems for organisational marketing strategies.

10. ORGANISATION OF THE MARKETING DEPARTMENT

The organisation of a marketing department depends on the way that the company views marketing and on its size. In small companies marketing may merely be seen as an extension of the selling function; in larger organisations marketing may be seen to have a much deeper and more general role and may give predominance to marketing executives over those in sales and separate out the functional specialisms within the marketing department. Figure 3:6 illustrates a possible structure.

In very large organisations where a divisionalised structure has developed because of geographical or product specialisms, the marketing function may be split into a headquarters function and regional or product functions with authority being delegated by top management, allowing a degree of autonomy to each subdivision. In organisations offering a range of products, a matrix type of structure may be developed with responsibility allocated to particular products or ranges of products, or even based on types of customer.

What sort of structure does your organisation have and what specialisms exist within the marketing function? How are the products marketed?

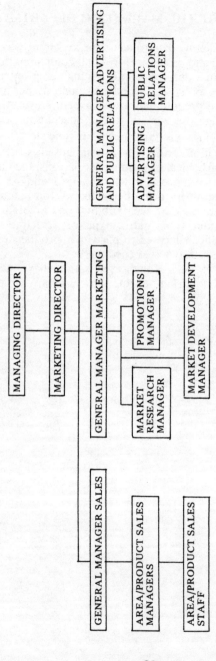

Figure 3:6 Example of a specialised marketing department

Chapter 4

The Major Functions of Enterprise : Production

The production function has the objective of transforming the organisation's raw materials into finished products to make available the goods and services demanded by the customer. Modern production systems and processes are complex and can be costly to install and operate. People, materials and machines have to be integrated to develop a system which is efficient in both cost and human terms.

TYPES OF PRODUCTION SYSTEM

It is possible to distinguish four types of production system, normally determined by the scale of operations employed in the organisation. These are unit or job production, batch production, mass production and process production.

1. Unit or job production

A single product, often to customer's specific requirements, each product is a 'one-off job' which may never be repeated in that exact form, for example, the production of a turbine for a ship, a particular system of electrics, a particular market survey for an unusual product, or a civil engineering project. In job production in the first place the job is put out for tender and, in the case of specialised manufacture such as shipbuilding and some types of civil engineering work, only one or two specialist firms will be asked to submit proposals for the work. Thus, on large projects, it is always necessary for a great deal of designing and planning to be done in order for a tender to be submitted and one of the main problems is to decide how much time and money is to be spent in preparing the data for a contract which could be awarded to a competitor. The prime features of unit or job production are:

(a) a relatively high-price product;

(b) the use of highly-skilled labour;

(c) relatively low capital costs of the production system — equipment often has more than one purpose;

(d) the organisation requires a fairly high degree of flexibility of structure and amongst staff, as the sequencing of operations is not standardised;

(e) centralisation of management, although employees are expected to show a high degree of discretion in their work;

(f) unpredictability of demand for stores;

(g)   a comparatively large technical organisation

These conditions make production difficult to plan, control, sequence and accurately time. It is sometimes difficult to obtain manpower with the appropriate versatility of skills, as there is fluctuating demand for labour during the cycle of the work.

2. Batch production

This type of production system is designed to produce a batch of standardised units, sometimes in small, sometimes in large, numbers, without continuous production. Unlike jobbing production, operations and sequences of work tend to be standardised. Examples of batch production items are aero-engines, components for the machine tool industry, and certain forms of electronic equipment.

Batch production is often used for goods for stock as well as to meet specific orders. One of the major problems is to ensure that too many units are not produced, especially where items are expensive and difficult to store, but that sufficient units are made to meet particular, urgent demand. The prime features of batch production are:

(a)   A relatively standardised set of operations, carried out intermittently, as production runs tend to be short, therefore there is a lack of balance in the workload of different departments;

(b)   equipment is generally grouped in batches of the same type;

(c)   although operatives tend to be less skilful than in job production, because there is less demand for adaptability, a relatively high degree of skill is still demanded;

(d)   emphasis is required on production planning and processing;

(e)   comparatively large product design department;

(f)   large production stores areas.

3. Mass production

Production is continuous and all units of production are so highly specialised that each is employed continuously upon the same operation. The range of products made on each line of equipment is restricted and, consequently, output is very high. One operation follows on from another and leads to the next in a continuous flow. Mass production systems are heavily dependent on high market demand to maximise the utilisation of equipment and minimise costs. A highly developed marketing organisation is needed to make continuous production possible. Examples of mass production manufacture include the production of biscuits, soap powder, motor cars and washing machines.

Since mass production is production on a large scale, its prime features are in direct contrast to job production:

(a)   Production of a relatively low priced product;

(b)   product specifications are standardised;

(c)   high capital costs of production systems;

(d)   highly standardised methods, costs and materials, thus little flexibility of equipment;

(e)   long production runs for individual products;

(f)   a high proportion of semi-skilled and unskilled labour;

(g)   less centralisation of management and greater emphasis upon specialised services to management;

(h)   a tight system of production control;

(i)   strict control of flow of raw materials into the organisation.

Its greatest drawback, although it theoretically is an efficient way of producing large quantities of goods, is that it requires human beings to adapt themselves to the production process and this can bring reaction to the tedium and monotony of tasks.

4. Process production

This is the continuous output of a product for weeks and months at a time. There tends to be a high degree of automation. Like mass production, process production requires an effective marketing organisation so that its expensive equipment can be employed without interruption. It also requires a steady supply of raw materials to avoid complete plant shutdown, owing to unforeseen shortages. Just as batch production can be seen as an extension of job production, so process production can be viewed as an extension of mass production, since the process production systems include oil refining, steel making, paper making, brewing and food manufactures.

Its prime features are:

(a)   Production of a relatively low priced product;

(b)   high capital costs of production systems;

(c)   highly sophisticated mechanisms and procedures of control;

(d)   lower labour force than mass production, but a high level of technological skill as well as semi-skilled and unskilled employees;

(e)   little flexibility of equipment;

(f)   high levels of planning of essential raw materials.

SCOPE OF THE PRODUCTION FUNCTION

The production function encompasses all activities directly concerned with the manufacture of goods and services. A typical production division within a company may be subdivided into Production Administration, Production Management, Production Design and Production Ancillaries. There is no ideal production structure and the organisation of any one will be largely a question of administrative convenience and company practice. The arrangements in any two organisations are unlikely to be identical and the titles of tasks in the function will probably vary from one organisation to another.

1. Production administration

Production administration is the process of planning and regulating the activities of that part of an enterprise which is responsible for the production of goods. It usually incorporates such activities as production engineering, production planning and production control.

(a) Production engineering

Production engineering determines and specifies work processes. The functions of a production engineer are:

— to investigate alternative methods of production and keep the organisation up to date on new methods;
— to design the processes of work including the layout of tools and equipment and the modification of tools and equipment, where necessary, within appropriate safety standards;
— to measure the rate of work flow by analysing the time span of each task, using work study and work measurement techniques.

Work study was developed in American industry during the 1920s by F W Taylor and others. It has been defined as:

'A generic term for those techniques, particularly method study and work measurement, which are used in the examination of human work in all its contexts, which lead systematically to the investigation of all the factors which affect the efficiency and economy of the situation being reviewed in order to effect improvement.' (British Standard BS 3138)

These techniques of work and method study are thus aimed at eliminating inefficient work methods and improving work methods to increase production, reduce costs, and increase the productivity of people and machines. They require the observation of working practices to ask — What is done? When is it done? How is it done? Who is doing it? Where is it done? and, How long does it take? Work study and method study are used to aid solutions to a variety of potential problems, including layout of work, handling of materials and efficiency of storage of materials, equipment design to increase efficiency and productivity.

Standard task times can be derived, which can be used as the basis of a wages system.

(b) Production planning

Production planning translates customer demand into short term and long term production schedules and programmes. This usually includes the maintenance of material and stock records, progress chasing and machine loading. Production schedules are usually detailed, specifying the timetable for precise operations and jobs and setting out the sequence of priorities. The major aim is to ensure that work is completed on time and within the laid-down cost budgets. Production planners have to work closely with marketing departments to ensure that customer needs are being met as to types of product, time of availability and quality, or where there are production difficulties, to keep the customer informed of progress. They will also have to work closely with purchasing departments to ensure raw materials are available on time.

To be successful production planning must be:

(i)   Geared to a suitable production policy; which is aimed at producing what is required, when it is required, at minimum cost.

(ii)   Realistic and based on facts; which requires that production schedules, machine loading schedules and labour schedules do not conflict with sales forecasts and are not based on sales delivery dates which are excessively optimistic.

(iii) Explained and a series of attainable targets set; so that the workforce have some idea of the objectives required.

(iv) Flexible; so that inevitable delays can be offset.

(v)   Not merely for the short term; but based on medium and long term considerations to obtain a balance of work between departments.

(vi) Subject to controls which enable adjustments to be made, when the plan runs into problems.

The order book shows the pattern of demand for the company's products in the coming months. Orders are often characterised by market (home or export), type of customer etc. as different standards may be incorporated into production plans.

If the order book shows a *decrease in demand,* production planners will have to make provision to compensate. Action taken could take several forms:

(i)   maintaining existing production schedules and letting stocks accumulate;

(ii)   discontinuing overtime;

(iii) introducing short time working;

(iv) creating redundancy.

Where there is a sharp *increase. in demand,* production planners will examine the following possibilities:

(i)   cutting stocks of finished products to a minimum;

(ii)   introducing rationing by permitting customers only a proportion of their orders;

(iii) introducing overtime;

(iv) sub-contracting work to other manufacturers;

(v)   looking at the need for long term expansion or re-equipment.

Production planners will need to liaise with the personnel function, as many of these strategies have manpower implications.

(c) Production control

Production control ensures the progressing of orders through the production process and monitors results and efficiency. It is an inevitable consequence of the production planning activity. Any plan must incorporate controls to ensure that targets are achieved. In particular, there must be provision for managers to be informed of and to investigate, unexpected variances from the plan. In a large organisation a wide range of factors will be analysed and controls instigated:

(i) Progress control — the control of production programmes and schedules to ensure that each department is maintaining its planned output at the right time;

(ii) Cost control — control of budgets, including such aspects as material costs and labour costs and ensuring that significant variances do not arise;

(iii) Machine utilisation control — ensures that planned maintenance takes place where appropriate;

(iv) Stock control — the control of stocks of both raw materials and finished products to ensure that supplies are available as required and that raw materials are present in sufficient quantities.

2. Production management

Production management ensures (in liaison with the personnel function) that the labour force involved in the actual production process is adequately trained, organised and supervised to achieve the required targets. These managers are responsible for the manufacturing and assembly processes and have to ensure that the work is carried out in accordance with the schedules prescribed and that employees are treated in a fair and equitable manner.

3. Production design

This area of production is concerned with the designing of products which consumers demand and which the organisation can produce. It will also be concerned, together with the production engineering function, with analysing equipment suitability for producing the new products developed. In those organisations operating with unit or batch production methods, the designer is likely to work closely with clients to meet their requirements. In some organisations the production design function is separated from the other production activities and given the umbrella title of *Research and Development* (R & D). This is likely to be a department in which expert scientific staff are organised to make the products of the future. One of the problems which R & D departments are likely to ignore is the production of an item at a reasonable cost. The production engineer may have to modify the prototype into a product which can be feasibly and cheaply made without major restructuring or re-equipment of the organisation.

Two problems can occur with the use of a continuous research and development department:

(i)   The results of research are not capable of accurate prediction. A firm might spend large sums on research, only to find no opportunity for its commercial application. For example, work on a new product may be negated and result in a financial loss because a rival firm reached the development stage first.

(ii) Costs may be considerable, not least in attracting suitably experienced and qualified staff.

4. Production ancillaries

A number of other departments may come under the production function. These may include purchasing departments, inspection and quality control and maintenance engineering.

(a) Purchasing

It is important that the necessary raw materials are available so that the production process is not impaired through shortages. The costs of bought-in materials and parts often represent a significant part of the total costs of production. The purchasing department has to liaise with the various sub-units of production and has to maintain links with a variety of external suppliers. A purchasing department can be said to have the following responsibilities:

(i)   It should appraise the efficiency and reliability of suppliers and ensure that supplies obtained are of the appropriate standard and in appropriate quantities.

(ii) It will need to be aware of the current range of suppliers for each item and the reliability of their distribution methods.

(iii) It should purchase the relevant raw material and other inputs, representing the best value to the business in both the short and the longer term. For example, the cheapest supplier may not necessarily be able to provide appropriate quantities or be the most reliable in the long term.

(iv) It will have to ensure the maintenance of adequate stock levels, whilst, at the same time, being aware of the costs of storage and likely future trends in costs which might warrant larger purchases than normal.

(v)   It will need to maintain good relations with all departments and with present and potential suppliers.

Depending upon the nature of the organisation's products, specialist purchasing officers may need to be employed who have technical knowledge of products and purchases.

(b) Quality control and inspection departments

The responsibility of checking the quality of the work on the shop floor is usually that of an inspection department whose staff ensure that standards are maintained. There are two main methods of doing this:

(i)   All stages of the process can be inspected on a regular basis, against the appropriate laid down standards or

(ii) Inspection can be done by sampling batches of the product.

The standards of inspection required will depend on the degree of sophistication of the product.

Quality control tends to have a wider function. It involves itself with production engineering in building quality into the production system itself and in constantly reviewing the system to try to improve the process and work methods.

The aims of both activities are the same:

(i)   To ensure that products are satisfactory to the customer in terms of quality and reliability and that the products are those which were actually demanded;

(ii) To ensure that the products are safe when sold;

(iii) To reduce the costs of wastage of raw materials and partially finished products and to ensure that the workforce are encouraged to take pride in the product.

(c) Maintenance engineering

The prime responsibility of the maintenance engineering department is to ensure that production is not held up because of lack of serviceability of plant or equipment and that, if unexpected breakdowns occur, the equipment is repaired and returned to service as quickly as possible.

To achieve this the maintenance staff and production personnel must cooperate. Sometimes maintenance departments are organised so that each production area has a resident engineer, who is under the control of the relevant production manager, whereas, in other cases, the production manager has to call when appropriate for service from a separated department.

Maintenance can take a number of different forms, these can include:

(i)   Preventative maintenance, which regularly maintains equipment to prevent or reduce the likelihood of it failing. This can involve a planned programme of maintenance so that servicing and overhaul schedules are prepared and operated, with least disruption;

(ii) Breakdown maintenance, which only deals with equipment when it physically fails. Such a policy can be very costly when compared with regular, planned maintenance.

One of the roles of the maintenance department will be to ensure that key spares are ordered and available so that delays can be reduced. This requires an analysis of machine failures so that common problems and problem parts can be identified.

The ability of a maintenance department to fulfil its role will depend on the nature of the productive process. Where process or mass production occurs, it will probably necessitate running maintenance being carried out while the plant continues in operation; shutdown of equipment, especially in a process organisation, may incur large losses.

Examine your own organisation, if it is a manufacturing concern, and see which of these activities operate and how they are organised or structured.

Chapter 5
The Function of Management

The function of management has existed as long as organisations to accomplish work have existed; no one person alone can administer an organisation of any size. We read in the Book of Exodus, verses 13—26, the following:

> 'on the following day, Moses took his seat to administer justice for the people, and from morning till evening they stood around him. Observing what labours he took on himself for the peoples' sake, the father-in-law of Moses said to him, "Why do you take all this on yourself for the people? Why sit here alone with people standing around you from morning till evening?" Moses answered his father-in-law "Because the people come to me to bring their enquiries to God. When they have a dispute they come to me, and I settle the differences between the one and the other and instruct them in God's statutes and his decisions." "It is not right" the father-in-law of Moses said to him "to take this on yourself. You will tire yourself out, you and the people with you. The work is too heavy for you. You cannot do it alone"..."choose from the people at large some capable and God-fearing men, trustworthy and incorruptible, and appoint them as leaders of the people: leaders of thousands, hundreds, fifties, tens. Let these be at the service of the people to administer justice at all times. They can refer all difficult questions to you, but the smaller questions they will decide for themselves, so making things easier for you and sharing the burden with you"...Moses took his father-in-law's advice and did as he said. Moses chose capable men from the ranks of the Israelites and set them over the people: leaders of thousands, hundreds, fifties, tens. They were at the service of the people to administer justice at all times. They referred hard questions to Moses, and decided smaller questions by themselves.'

There is no general definition of 'management', although the classic definition was given by Henry Fayol in 1916 when he said that:

> 'To manage is to forecast and plan, to organise, to command, to coordinate and to control.'

and these concepts have permeated all definitions of management since.

Peter Drucker has argued that management is:

> 'The organ of society specifically charged with making resources productive.'

E F L Brech, in 1957, stated:

> 'management is a social process...the process consists of...planning, control, coordination and motivation.'

A manager is:

> 'Someone who directs the work of others and who does his work by getting other people to do theirs.'
> (Peter Drucker)

> 'Someone who decides what should be done and then gets other people to do it.'
> (Rosemary Stewart)

> 'A member who has subordinate to him authorised roles into which he can appoint members and determine their work; he is accountable for his subordinates' work in these roles.'
> (Wilfred Brown)

'Managers are those who use formal authority to organise, direct, or control responsible subordinates...in order that all service contributions be coordinated in the attainment of an enterprise purpose.'   (Tannenbaum)

These statements are expanded in the Glacier Metal Co. Ltd's policy document which provides a specification of the work of a manager in controlling others, quoted by Wilfred Brown in *Exploration in Management* (1960).

'Assignment and Assessment of Work

E.3. A manager shall be accountable for the work assigned to him including the work which he assigns to members under his command. In assigning work, a manager shall determine the extent to which he requires his subordinates to make reference to him before making their own decisions.

E.4. A manager shall appoint, train and maintain at his immediate command a team of subordinates who are competent to carry out the work he requires of them and who conform to the generally acceptable standards of conduct. He shall assign and display an order of seniority among a sufficient number of his subordinates to ensure that his work is done in his absence.

E.4.1. He shall set standards of executive performance and attainment for his immediate subordinates and shall make these standards clear to them.

E.4.2. He shall assign work to his immediate subordinates consistent with the standards he has set.

E.4.3. He shall judge the executive performance of each of his subordinates in relation to the standards he has set, and their conduct in relation to the standards accepted by the company.

(a)   He shall ensure that each subordinate is rewarded at a level appropriate to the work of his executive role.

(b)   In the event of a subordinate performing below the standards he has set or contrary to the generally accepted standards of conduct he shall acquaint him of this fact and, in the event of continued inadequacy, he shall decide whether to retain him in his command...

E.4.4. A manager shall limit his immediate command to a number of people he can effectively control, and amongst whom he can maintain cooperation...'

1. TRADITIONAL FUNCTIONS OF MANAGEMENT

There is apparently broad agreement amongst writers on management that the management function is comprised of the following activities: planning, organisation, control, coordination, motivation, communication and the development of the human resource within the organisation. Let us examine briefly each of these activities in turn.

(1) PLANNING is that management activity which involves formulating the future strategy and policy of the organisation. Planning is concerned with the formulation and establishment of measurable objectives and is a decision making process. Once plans are implemented, results have to be monitored to provide feedback on performance.

(2) ORGANISATION — Here the manager's task is to determine what activities are necessary to achieve objectives and to develop an appropriate organisational structure so the work is distributed

logically and relevant responsibilities assigned.

(3)   CONTROL — Controlling activities are essentially concerned with measuring progress and correcting deviations from objectives. The basic functions within control are establishing standards of performance, measuring actual performance against standards and taking correcting actions, where appropriate.

(4)   COORDINATION — Coordination requires working with other groups and ensuring that subordinates work together in order to reach the desired results. The strengths of individual members of the department are exploited and weaknesses minimised.

(5)   MOTIVATION — In setting plans and in executing them managers have to gain the commitment of their subordinates. They must encourage staff to work towards objectives.

(6)   COMMUNICATION — Communication is vital to organisational success; managers must ensure that their subordinates are given sufficient data about the objectives of the organisation and the progress which is being made on each task to operate effectively. It is also important that they be made aware of their own strengths and weaknesses and how well they are performing.

(7)   DEVELOPMENT OF HUMAN RESOURCES — Peter Drucker and Wilfred Brown argue that training and developing his subordinates is one of the key elements of the manager's role. He is the one in the best position to develop strengths and help the individual to overcome problems and learn from experience.

Whilst it is easy to identify these traditional functions of management, it is very difficult in large scale modern organisations to classify easily the work done by managers as different responsibilities belong to different jobs, depending upon their position and level within the hierarchy. Some of the specific duties and responsibilities are stated in job descriptions. The only danger in using them to analyse managerial jobs, however, is that job descriptions may be limited in that they often describe not what actually happens but what ought to happen or what people think is occurring.

2.   FACTORS INFLUENCING MANAGERS

We can broadly identify the factors which are influencing the manager at any one moment as falling into three categories:

(a)   the *manager* himself, due to his experience, education, values and position in the hierarchy;

(b)   the *subordinates* who work for him, who are in turn influenced by the nature of their work, the skills they possess and the people with whom they work;

(c)   the *environment* of the organisation itself and the society in which it operates.

These features overlap with each other, varying over time, and can be pictured as in Figure 5:1 Factors influencing the manager.

Figure 5:1 Factors influencing the manager

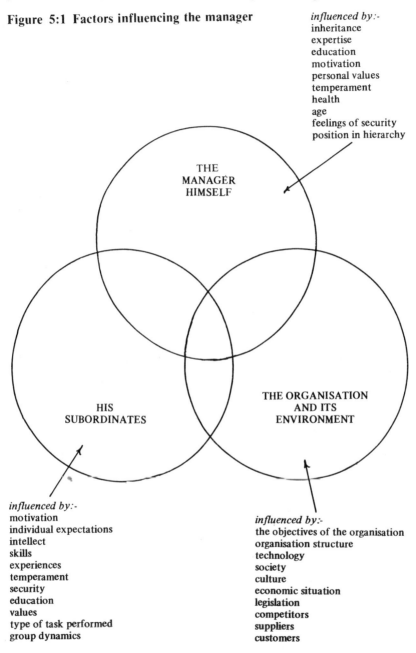

influenced by:-
inheritance
expertise
education
motivation
personal values
temperament
health
age
feelings of security
position in hierarchy

THE
MANAGER
HIMSELF

HIS
SUBORDINATES

THE ORGANISATION
AND ITS
ENVIRONMENT

influenced by:-
motivation
individual expectations
intellect
skills
experiences
temperament
security
education
values
type of task performed
group dynamics

influenced by:-
the objectives of the organisation
organisation structure
technology
society
culture
economic situation
legislation
competitors
suppliers
customers

The manager can be perceived as a PEST controller — that is he controls *people, economic factors of production, the structure of the organisation* and *technologies.*

3. WHAT MANAGERS ACTUALLY DO!

Attempts have been made to analyse the content of managerial jobs and how time is actually spent. Some of the questions which have been asked have included:

1. How specialised is the particular job?
2. To what extent does the job involve working with other people both inside and outside the organisation?
3. What work pattern does the task tend to impose?
4. What kinds of decisions does the job involve?
5. How much time is spent on different aspects of a manager's work?
6. What kinds of variety are provided by the job?

The three main approaches used by researchers have been:

(a) *Self reporting,* where managers are interviewed and estimate themselves how they spend their time between different activities.
(b) Managers are asked to keep *diaries* where they keep a record of what they actually do and record the data in specific time periods.
(c) *Observers* actually watch managers over an extended period of time.

One example of the problems which managers have in reporting what they actually do was quoted by Leonard Sayles in *Managerial Behaviour* (1964) where he gave the following account of a member of middle management who said:

'I have a terrible time trying to explain what I do at work when I get home. My wife thinks of a manager in terms of someone who has authority over those people who work for him and who in turn gets his job done for him. You know she thinks of those nice neat organisation charts...she also expects that when I get promoted I'll have more people working for me...Now all of this is unrealistic. Actually I have 18 people reporting directly to me. These are the only ones I can give orders to. But I have to rely directly on the services of 75-80 other people in this company, if my project is to get done. They in turn are affected by perhaps several hundred others and I must sometimes see some of them, too, when my work is being held up.

So I am always seeing these people, trying to get their cooperation, trying to deal with delays, work out compromises on specifications, etc. Again when I explain this to my wife, she thinks that all I do all day is argue and fight with people.'

This communication aspect of the manager's task has been further identified in the UK by Rosemary Stewart, in *Managers and their jobs* (1967), who supervised a major piece of research which included detailed studies from diaries kept by a sample of 160 managers employed by over 100 companies. These were found to spend an average of 60% of their working time in conversation of one sort or another. The average time spent with their own subordinates was 26% of these contacts in their working week, which averaged 42 hours, with 8% being spent with their own superior and 12% with fellow managers. In addition to communications activities, they spent on average 36% of their time on paperwork.

Yet these averages do not represent all managers' tasks, for in the book Rosemary Stewart identified five different types of manager — the the *emissaries,* the *discussers,* the *writers,* the *trouble-shooters* and the *committee men.*

(i) The Emissaries — sales managers and general managers who spent a significant amount of time away from the company on visits to other companies, conferences and exhibitions, and hence spent a lot of time travelling and entertaining or being entertained.

(ii) The Discussers — these managers spent most of their time with other people and colleagues solving the day-to-day problems of business.

(iii) The Writers — who spent most of their time by themselves and who were less concerned with the day-to-day problems of business. Most of their contact was with only one other person, who tended to be a specialist adviser like themselves. Often they were involved in engineering or research and development activities.

(iv) The Trouble-shooters — spent most of their time coping with crises concerned with industrial relations, man management, supplier shortfalls and work-in-progress. Most works and factory line managers fell into this category.

(v) The Committee Men — spent most of their time in group discussions of both a formal and an informal type. Again many works and factory line managers fell into this category, as well as those in the designing and marketing function.

Many of the management jobs studied were shown to have a highly-fragmented work pattern with managers having to shift their attention every few minutes from one person to another. Very little of their working day was uninterrupted and there was little opportunity to give sustained attention to one problem or issue. This often meant that sustained attention was needed for problems away from the place of work.

Rosemary Stewart, in a later work *Contrasts in Management* (1976), suggested that managers' jobs differ in how far they demonstrate a recurrent work pattern, where the manager does work of a similar kind every day or every week, although in most there was a monthly or annual pattern imposed by reports and budgets which were required for company control purposes. This research studied 450 managerial jobs in industry and commerce, 16 of which were examined in depth. It identified the fact that jobs could be differentiated by the following characteristics:

— the duration of the activities undertaken;

- the time span of problems handled or decisions made regarding those problems;
- the periodicity and recurrence of work;
- the amount of expected, compared with unexpected, work;
- the incidence of urgent work and crises;
- the extent to which work had to be completed in a time period laid down by an external agency to the manager himself;
- the origin of work activities, whether these were determined by the need to respond to others whether they be employees, customers, superiors or other managers on the same level or whether work was self-generated.

In examining the jobs studied a matrix was derived as in Figure 5:2

Figure 5 : 2 –

Type of work pattern : characteristics and sample membership

Source: *Personnel Management,* June 1976. Patterns of work and dictates of time, R Stewart.

TYPE OF WORK PATTERN	1. Systems Maintenance	2. Systems Administration	3. Project	4. Mixed
Characteristics	Recurrent Fragmented Trouble-shooting	Recurrent Time-deadlines a. expected b. unexpected	Non-recurrent Sustained attention Self-generating Long-term	No dominant characteristics
Sample Membership	Works manager Production manager Production Supt.	a. Financial accountant b. Staff manager	Research manager Product sales manager Group product manager (some overlap with 1.) 2a/3 Management accountant Commercial manager	General manager Area sales manager Head of admin. Production engineer

Definitions: The description of each type means that these characteristics are a marked feature of that type, not that they never occur in other types.

Recurrent: does work of a similar kind every day or every week;

Fragmented: switches attention from one person or problem every few minutes;

Trouble-shooting   has to cope with sudden problems;

78

Time deadlines:	work to be done by a particular time which is not self-imposed;
Unexpected:	the timing and precise nature of work which cannot be predicted;
Self-generating:	work or systems originating with the individual, rather than in response to other people;
Long-term:	One year plus.

1. Systems Maintenance — a major task in some jobs is to handle exceptions, e.g. to keep operations within target completion times. Thus, the manager has to deal with problems that prevent completion on time. In addition, such managers need constantly to check that the system itself is retaining its efficiency. Most operational jobs fall into this type of work pattern.

2. Systems Administration — is concerned primarily with the processing of information and the administration of the system. Such jobs are generally found in junior and middle management posts in formally-structured organisations.

3. Project work — is characterised by involvement in tasks very often of a unique type which have a long term time horizon. There is less imposition of structure from the organisation and there is a greater need for work to be self generated.

4. Mixed work patterns — are less capable of rigid classification and include elements of the first three types. They are concerned with system design in reaction to environmental pressures rather than with operational problems.

An alternative approach to studying managerial jobs, that of structured observation, was adopted by Mintsberg in *The Changing Nature of Managerial Work,* Harper & Row 1973. His studies emphasise interpersonal relations, the amount of time spent on obtaining or disseminating information, and the rather erratic nature of the managerial activity. Mintzberg showed through his studies of all levels of management, chief executives, administrative managers, sales managers, supervisors, etc. that major roles:

1. The interpersonal role — to ensure the task is accomplished:
   - the figurehead role — where the manager is the representative of the unit or specialism he manages, with people from both inside and outside the organisation;
   - the understanding role — where the manager interacts with his subordinates to motivate and encourage them to fulfil the task;
   - the liaison role — where the manager liaises with people

inside and outside his specialism to obtain supplies, meet customer specifications, obtain data, etc.

2. The informational role of obtaining and giving information, which is probably the most important managerial function. This role sees the manager as:

— a monitor, who gathers and stores information from all sources in the organisation;

— a disseminator, who in his turn distributes information to others within his department which he has synthesised and which otherwise would probably not be available to them;

— a spokesman, who fulfils the same role of disseminator to those outside his own area of control.

3. The decision making role — where the manager synthesises and translates the information he has obtained from all sources to make his decisions. Within this role he is:

— an entrepreneur, who uses his expertise to make changes within his area of control, or within the organisation generally;

— a disturbance handler, who is responsible for taking corrective action when the organisation faces unexpected situations which could not be planned for;

— a resource allocator, who decides how to use any of the resources available to him at any moment;

— a negotiator, who deals with those individuals and groups whose help, cooperation or consent is necessary for the oganisation to fulfil its goals.

These three major role groupings and ten major subsets encompass the managerial function, but the degree to which these are found in an individual manager's role will vary from task to task and from organisation to organisation. Mintzberg, however, concluded that there were eight major types of managerial jobs;

i) The contact man, who is a figurehead and liaises with outside organisations;

ii) The political manager, who spends much of his time external to the organisation trying to reconcile the conflicting forces that influence it;

iii) The entrepreneur, who seeks future opportunities and implements change within the organisation;

iv) The insider, who tries to build up and further internal activities by 'fire fighting';

v) The real time manager, who attempts to construct and maintain a stable system through time;

vi) The team manager, whose primary concern is to create a team which will work together effectively;

vii) The expert manager, who fulfils a specialist role advising other managers and who is consulted because of his expertise;

viii) The new manager, who has not found his feet yet and who lacks the interpersonal contacts and information channels of the other seven categories.

4. DIFFERENT LEVELS OF MANAGEMENT

From these studies we can see that it is difficult to talk generally about the manager's role, because management is not a unitary activity but is a feature of the organisation in which it takes place and changes according to the time and the environmental influences.

H I Ansoff in *Corporate Strategy* (1968) sees management as having three principal decision areas — strategic, operating and administrative. These can be differentiated as follows:

1. Strategic decisions: These are concerned with the examination of the external influences and opportunities which influence the organisation's objectives and the products and services it sells or provides. Such decisions set the principal goals and objectives of the organisation and determine the product mix and the markets in which it will operate. They will also tend to be non-routine and non-repetitive decisions which are frequently complex, especially in terms of the number of variables which have to be considered before final choices are made betweeen the alternatives available.

2. Administrative decisions: These are concerned with the structuring of the organisation's resources in such a way as to be able to reap the benefits of the opportunities available to it. Essentially they are concerned with structuring the authority and responsibility relationships; work flow; information needs and flow; location of the organisation; determining sources of raw materials and bought-in-parts; obtaining and developing the relevant labour force; and the acquisition of the technology required to produce the goods and services. Such decisions arise from, and are subject to, the sometimes conflicting demands of strategic decisions and operational problems.

3. Operating decisions: These can be the short term decisions which attempt to maximise organisational efficiency on a day-to-day and a week-to-week basis. They settle issues, such as the scheduling of operations, manning levels of machines and departments, keeping a watch on performance and initiating appropriate action to enhance performance, by applying appropriate sanctions. They cover other key areas such as pricing, budgeting, stock inventory levels. Fewer variables are involved in the decision making process as they are reactive to situational pressures and the decisions

themselves tend to be routine and repetitive. They generally aim to produce results in the short term.

The degree to which an individual manager becomes involved in these levels of decision making depends on his position in the hierarchy. Perhaps only managers at the highest level will have responsibility for deciding the future course of the organisation, but managers at all levels have the responsibility to ensure the success of the organisation in both the long term and the short term and to use resources effectively.

Dr John Adair has emphasised that there are three major areas of concern for managers at whatever level in an organisation; the task to be accomplished, the group who are performing the task and the individuals who comprise the group. Managers need to concern themselves with all three areas as neglect of any one area can result in adverse effects on the performance of work groups in achieving their objectives.

The key features of this *functional* model of leadership can be illustrated as in Figure 5:3.

Figure 5 : 3 – Functional model of leadership

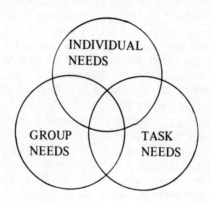

Achieving the task

Purpose	—	am I clear what the task is?
Responsibilities	—	am I clear about these?
Objectives	—	have I agreed these with the group?
Programme	—	have I worked out how to achieve the objectives efficiently?
Working conditions	—	are these right for the job?
Resources	—	are these adequate?
Targets	—	has each member had these defined and agreed them?
Authority	—	is the line of authority clear?

Training	—	are there any gaps in the group's abilities?
Priorities	—	have plans taken these into acount and the timing required?
Progress	—	do I check regularly and evaluate?
Example	—	do I set standards by my behaviour?

Developing the individual

Targets	—	are these agreed and quantified, where possible?
Induction	—	does the individual understand the organisation and his position in it?
Responsibilities	—	is the individual aware of, and does he agree with, his job description?
Authority	—	is this adequate for the task in hand?
Training	—	has provision been made, where necessary?
Recognition	—	do I emphasise success and give praise where earned?
Growth	—	has the individual a chance to develop?
Performance	—	do I perform regular reviews?
Grievances	—	are these dealt with quickly
Attention	—	is enough given?

Maintaining the team

Objectives	—	does the group understand them?
Standards	—	does the group know what to expect?
Personality	—	are the right people working together?
Team spirit	—	is the job structured to encourage this?
Discipline	—	is it reasonable? Is it impartial and consistent?
Grievances	—	is the procedure sound? Are they dealt with quickly?
Consultation	—	do I welcome and encourage ideas?
Briefing	—	is this regular?
Support	—	do I represent the feelings of the group?

Adair's concept is basically a contingency theory of leadership. It stresses that the manager's behaviour in relation to task, group and individual needs has to be related to the prevailing situation and task and, therefore, has to be adaptive. It recognises that management is a function of the situation. Management's task is to enable the organisation's purposes to be defined and fulfilled by adapting to change and by main-

83

taining a balance between the various and frequently conflicting internal pressures.

This feature is summed up by Professor Handy in *Understanding organisations* (2nd edn 1981) where he suggests that the key variables a manager has to cope with are:

(i)   People
(ii) The nature of the work and organisation structures
(iii) The prevailing systems and procedures which have been developed
(iv) The organisation's specific goals
(v)   The technology which is being used or is to be introduced
(vi) The values and beliefs or the culture of the specific organisation.

In addition to the undoubted human relations skills which all managers need to possess, the knowledge and experience needed will vary dependent on the nature of the industry, the particular organisation in which they operate and the position which they hold within it. How much the knowledge and skills are organisationally biased and how much the environment needs to concern them depends on their job. Generally those managers making operational decisions are most concerned with the short term. Administrative decisions are concerned with three factors; the service which the organisation is receiving from its suppliers, the success it is having in meeting customer needs, and the changes which are being made in company strategy and their likelihood of affecting existing structures and procedures. Strategic decision making is far less concerned with the situation pertaining within the organisation, as that is the main responsibility of the other two levels of decision makers, but is extremely concerned with environmental pressures and their influence on the future. Some of these aspects can be illustrated as in Figure 5:4.

Each level has to be given the skills, knowledge and experience to cope with the predominant pressures. Thus the modern manager must be trained to cope with the technology of his particular industry and given administrative and personal communication skills. The higher up the organisation he progresses, the more knowledge he requires of the economic and social and political environment in which he operates.

As we have already inferred, when looking at the structure of organisations in Chapter 2, modern management now consists of a number of different functional specialisms. Each individual has defined for him the tasks and responsibilities that relate to his job and his position in the organisation.

5. ORGANISATIONS OF MANAGERS

Most managers today are employees and there are few who own the organisation in which they work. Yet management has a different sort of task from other employees. Part of their job is to plan, coordinate and control the work of others and they have a responsibility to ensure that

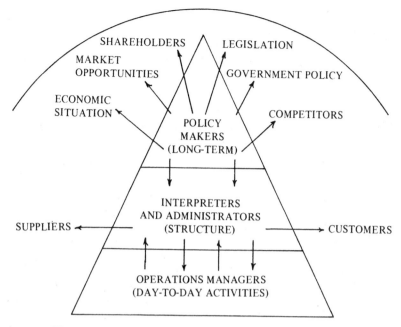

Figure 5 : 4 – Factors influencing strategic decision making

targets are met. They are granted authority and responsibility and use this for the benefit of the organisation. To their subordinates they are seen as the 'boss' and can be viewed as the employer — the hirer and firer. Within the structure of society, managers are given a status and class which significantly differentiates them from a shop floor worker or a clerk. Managers are also more likely to find their psychological needs are satisfied at work. Our society has seen a great proliferation of the task of management in large organisations. According to the 1981 census there were some 2½ million managers in the UK — over 10% of the total labour force.

(A) MANAGERS AS PROFESSIONALS

This increase in management numbers, coupled with increasing specialisation, has brought into organisations people who have loyalties outside, especially to professional bodies, e.g. accountants, lawyers, engineers.

Alvin Gouldner in *Patterns of industrial bureaucracy* (1954), which studied an American factory, identified two types of company executive; the expert who had a wider loyalty than merely to the organisation and the company man who identified primarily with the organisation. According to Gouldner, 'experts' or cosmopolitans as he calls them, are less likely to identify themselves as company men because their previous formal training provides employment opportunities in a wide range of different organisations. The cosmopolitan often looks for recognition of his specialist abilities to the members of his profession. To summarise:

Cosmopolitans tend to have:

(a)   a low degree of organisational loyalty;
(b)   a high commitment to their own specialised skills;
(c)   an identification with a peer group which exists outside the organisation.

Company men or 'locals' on the other hand are assessed on their loyalty and service to the organisation in which they work and are less mobile than those who are professionally trained.

Locals, therefore, tend to have:

(a)   a high degree of organisational loyalty;
(b)   low commitment to specialised skills, except those pertaining to knowledge of the organisation in which they work;
(c)   an identification with a peer group situated inside the organisation.

Professions can be viewed as occupations in non-manual activity areas. The key to professionalism is competence. The professions each possess and foster a body of knowledge which enables them to establish high standards of practice to protect the client from incompetence. The important knowledge base is handed down via a rigorous training and education system and entry to the profession is regulated by the professional body by its membership policies. Explicit control of members is exercised over conduct and the profession itself recognises achievement by entry to higher grades of membership. It thus creates a power base which means that the professional organisation increasingly attempts to control rewards and expectations and constrains the performance and authority of the individual. Professional bodies thus seek to gain exclusive rights over particular areas of knowledge and socialise professionals in such a way as to diagnose problems in terms of the objectivity which education has sought to inculcate. We can summarise the characteristics of a profession as follows:

1.   Professions are founded upon the existence of a systematic theory, i.e. a body of knowledge.

2.   Professions establish a degree of professional authority based on the body of knowledge.

3.   Professions have an established code of ethics or statements of appropriate behaviour by which the professional's behaviour and expertise is judged.

4.   Professions often have a language of their own which is understandable to the professional and attain their professional knowledge in recognised, established training centres.

5. Professionals typically remain as members of the occupational group in which they have invested time and money and move from organisation to organisation as 'experts' in their particular field.

Carr-Saunders in an early work on *The Professions*, differentiated four major types of professions within society which are still valid today:

1. *The old-established professions* — founded upon the study of a particular area of learning which is used in the practice of the skills developed from that learning. Examples include religion, the law, medicine and education.

2. *New professions* — again founded on a body of knowledge which has developed, often because of new technologies and work environments. Examples include chemists, engineers and other natural scientists.

3. *Semi-professions* — which replace theoretical study of a field of learning by acquisition of a precise technical skill. Examples include nursing, pharmacy, social work and optometry.

4. *Would-be professions* — where members aspire to professional status. Examples include personnel, sales, business consultants, managers and estate agents.

We can also identify a fifth group which was not mentioned by him —

5. *Marginal professions* — which are comprised of those who perform technical assignments which are associated with professional roles. Examples are medical and laboratory technicians, draughtsmen.

One of the most significant changes in our society has been the employment of professionals and semi-professionals in business, commerce, central and local Government. Most modern organisations tend to be based on what Weber has conceptualised as the idea of a bureaucracy, a system which is characterised by a rigid hierarchical structure where work activity becomes subject to rules which are laid down by the superiors within the hierarchy. This sort of structure can lead to conflict for the professional employed in a large organisation. Four areas of conflict can be identified:

(i)   the professional's resistance to bureaucratic rules;
(ii)   the professional's rejection of bureaucratic standards;
(iii) the professional's resistance to bureaucratic supervision;
(iv)   the professional's conditional loyalty to the bureaucracy.

Professionals who participate in the two systems — the professional and the bureaucratic organisation — can find that their dual membership places important restrictions on attempts to deploy and control them in a rational manner with respect to the attainment of the organisational goals. Professions and bureaucracy are founded on fundamentally different principles of organisation; professions tend to be structured on a colleague basis with status being conceded to those with a greater knowledge of the particular specialisms. Thus, for example, the heart surgeon in a hospital will defer to the anaesthetist on matters of anaesthetics, whether he has higher bureaucratic status or not. Organisations, on the other hand, are controlled by rules and regulations and status is conferred by appointments to levels in the hierarchy.

If an organisation is to operate as a rational structure, it must to some extent be insulated from the surrounding environment, although we must remember that organisations can be classed as open-systems. Specifically the organisation will demand the power to select employees and promote them and control their contributions to implement and attain its goals. Yet organisations are often unable to fully control the criteria by which professional personnel are to be recruited; co-professionals are likely to demand some voice in the selection process, especially where the person to be recruited will work with existing professional staff who require complementary skills. Organisations may also have difficulty in controlling the efforts of professionals once recruited, in so far as they retain an identification with the profession and attempt to adhere to its norms and standards. In addition, the salaries which an organisation may have to pay to obtain people of the right calibre, may be influenced by the degree to which the profession limits entry.

A professional, therefore, comes with acquired skills which equip him to perform an entire task and he has internalised norms which control the application of those skills. He expects to direct those activities and be free from constraining regulations and interference. He demands autonomy and, at the same time, expects to assume responsibility for his decisions and actions. Bureaucrats, or 'locals' in Gouldner's terms, are less likely to come in contact with a set of standards other than those espoused by the organisation in which they are employed.

The following quotation, from *Fortune* magazine in 1965, serves to illustrate the problems which occur in integrating the professional manager into an organisational context. It was written by an industry-employed scientist:

'Research Directors sometimes fail to realise that the scientific standing of a scientist is determined primarily by the opinion of his colleagues in his speciality throughout the world. Actions that enhance his standing may bear little or no relation to actions that enhance his corporate standing. To achieve recognition from his professional colleagues he must communicate his research in the open literature, but publication in technical journals may be of little interest to the company or even damaging to it. To achieve company recognition, his research must lead to a marketable product or technique, but such research may not help his scientific reputation one whit. It is an error to think that all a creative scientist requires for happiness is to create. His creation exists scientifically if he can communicate it to his peers for evaluation. He not only needs to communicate his research, he wants it, and therefore wants himself to be thought of highly (by members of his profession) ...'

Simon Coke in an article 'Putting Professionalism in It's Place', *Personnel Management* February 1983, also notes the emphasis of the professions on encouraging professional allegience and following professional methods:

'In the case of UK chartered accountants there is a long three to five year apprenticeship spent in auditing firms whose ethos and objectives are quite different from those of commerce and industry at large. A quick look through accounting examination papers suggests an emphasis on the highly technical and detailed aspects of the auditing function. No one can doubt the thoroughness of training given young accountants ... but these are formative years in their development. The particular emphasis paid on attention to detail, the need to check and check again, the cautious, considering approach are all ideal of course, for the business of auditing, but — I venture to suggest — not for the ideal company accountant. It militates against the creative instinct in top management decision making, kills any suggestion of justifiable risk taking, stifles the entrepreneurial spirit.'

A further problem for the professional is that organisations are demanding greater integration between specialist activities yet, as each profession widens its sphere of interest while at the same time trying to deepen and develop its specialism, this need is likely to lead to a higher degree of interprofessional conflict and hence problems in coping with interdisciplinary change.

(B) MANAGERIAL UNIONISM

An additional source of external influence on those in management positions is the increasing development of managerial trade unionism. We can identify four major determinants of managerial unionism:

1. There is little doubt that pay figures predominantly in managers' decisions to join trade unions. Particularly at junior and middle managerial levels, they are concerned to maintain or increase their standard of living and frequently to retain or restore their differentials over those that work for them.

2. Other managers are influenced by insecurity in job retention. The great expansion in managerial jobs has resulted in the paradox that, whilst there are more such jobs, the increasing consolidation of organisations when business is poor or depressed and the increasing numbers of mergers, takeovers and closures have led to organisations being increasingly prepared to make managerial jobs redundant. Often mergers take place to acquire productive capacity and managers are superfluous.

3. More management jobs also mean that the average manager is more likely to find himself stuck part-way down a bureaucratic pyramid with very little power to influence objectives and organisational behaviour.

4. Whilst promotion may be available in the early part of his career, the top posts in all types of organisations are limited and many a competent manager finds himself without promotion opportunities. His needs and problems can be easier resolved in a small organisation; in a large one he will tend to become entangled in bureaucratic procedures. Hence frustrations increase and managers become more willing to combine with others to represent their

point of view.

These points were emphasised in the Commission of Industrial Relations Report on *White Collar Trade Unionism* (CIR study No.3) where is said:

'the need and wish for a collective voice can apply among managerial staff in particular when the organisation is large and where there are collective issues ... Increasing bureaucratisation and employment concentration are also affecting managers. The result is that in some circumstances quite senior managers are now finding it increasingly difficult to air their grievances, especially where terms and conditions of employment, having become standardised, leave little room for individual negotiation. Moreover redundancies are no longer uncommon in managerial areas and many managers therefore see collective organisation primarily as an insurance policy in the event of redundancy or some other mishap outside their control.'

In examining the expansion of managerial unionism there is a distinction between general practice in the public and private sectors of the economy. In the public sector, since the Whitley Committee Report in 1918, trade unionism amongst staff at all levels has been accepted as a natural and normal development. This has been enhanced by the nature, size and structure of public service: in Central Government, Local Government, the health service and nationalised industries terms and conditions of employment have been developed in a rational way such that there is general uniformity of employment conditions, based on grade structures from the lowest to the highest levels. This has tended naturally to encourage collective representation. Unions like COHSE (The Confederation of Health Service Employees), NALGO (National and Local Government Officers' Association), NUPE (National Union of Public Employees), CPSA (Civil and Public Services Association), NUT (National Union of Teachers), RCN (Royal College of Nursing) and AUT (Association of University Teachers) have a long history of negotiation.

In the private sector the norms and practices are generally different. Some employers still practice overt opposition and many managers will not join a union against the known wishes of their superiors, either because they feel it is disloyal to do so, or from fear of the potential consequences to their career and their relationship with the organisation. Despite legal protection against dismissal for union activity, the manager may feel it will affect his chances of promotion. Evidence suggests that supervisors and middle level managers are more likely to join trade unions than more senior levels of manager.

(C)   OTHER MANAGERIAL ORGANISATIONS

i)   The British Institute of Management (BIM)

The BIM was established in 1947, and is an independent and nonpolitical organisation which is concerned with the development of the principles, practices and techniques of management and the encouragement of management education, training and development. The central policy and decision making authority of the BIM is its Council, which is comprised of nationally elected members and representatives of its local branches. The Council establishes and keeps under review the Institute's policies and objectives.

The BIM represents the views of management to Government and non-Government organisations. Its other activities include the provision of conferences and seminars on matters of interest to managers; in company training provision; the provision of an advisory service to the individuals and organisations who are members. It also publishes a range of books, management check lists, information sheets, information summaries, information notes and occasional papers on matters of interest and surveys of practices amongst organisations. Topics included are labour turnover, performance appraisal, management development and training, and employee relations. It publishes the monthly magazine, *Management Today*.

ii) The Institute of Directors (IOD)

The IOD was founded in 1903 and was incorporated by Royal Charter in 1906 and is the representative body for a considerable number of business leaders in the UK and abroad. It represents directors on the boards of over 90% of the country's largest organisations, including the nationalised industries. Its members are all individuals, there is no corporate organisation membership. It is dedicated to preserving free enterprise, although it claims to be a nonpolitical organisation. It's stated primary objectives are:

i)   providing an effective voice for members both inside and outside Parliament;

ii)   providing the help and encouragement the members need to improve their own competence as business leaders.

The Institute's Industrial Relations Advisory Service can be used by small companies who do not have an industrial relations department and provides guidance on legislation and several employee relations questions.

The Institute also provides a business information service which covers such matters as salary surveys, industrial relations, company law, taxation, financial planning and exporting. It has a Council as its governing body which has elected members and representatives of its branches and it publishes a monthly magazine, *The Director*.

iii) The Institute of Personnel Management (IPM)

The IPM was founded in 1913 and is an independent nonpolitical organisation which aims to develop comprehensive professional knowledge and experience in the field of personnel management. In pursuit of this objective the Institute aims:

- to provide an association through which knowledge and experience can be exchanged;
- to develop a dynamic body of knowledge in response to changing conditions and demands;
- to develop and maintain professional standards of competence and to issue codes of practice to further this;
- to encourage research in subjects of interest to the profession;
- to present a national viewpoint on personnel management and develop links with other bodies, both at home and abroad, which are concerned with personnel matters;
- to represent the views of its members to Government departments, employers' associations, trade unions organisations, and any other national or international organisations which concern themselves with manpower matters.

The Institute is governed by an elected Council drawn from the membership and its members are individuals. It collaborates with education establishments for education and training for personnel management, as well as offering a range of relevant short courses for both members and non-members.

The Institute, through its seven national committees on Education, Employee Relations, International, Membership, Organisation and Manpower Planning, Pay and Employment Conditions, and Training and Development, and its two standing committees on Public Services, and Discrimination, prepares and distributes a variety of reports and surveys on matters concerned with personnel policy and practice. It also publishes a wide range of books on management and personnel management topics and two magazines monthly, *Personnel Management* and *The IPM Digest*.

Examine the management structures, roles and responsibilities within your own organisation against the ideas represented in this chapter.

Chapter 6
Major Functions of Personnel Management

1. INTRODUCTION

The personnel function operates in different organisational contexts and its current activities are influenced by the history, the organisation culture, the ideology of senior management, the size, the geographical spread and the technology of the organisation concerned. All of these create expectations about the personnel department's role in decision making and the actual nature of its activities and major responsibilities. Thus the type of function which the organisation demands will influence what is done from day to day. Before we examine the major functions which can be identified in organisations, with varying degrees of importance and time spent on each, let us briefly examine some features of the history of the function.

2. HISTORICAL DEVELOPMENT AND GROWTH

The personnel function can be said to have begun life as a largely welfare-oriented activity. It emerged first in firms which operated a primarily paternalistic philosophy. Examples included Quaker firms like Clark's, Rowntree's and Cadbury's.

Three factors can be identified in the development of personnel management:

(a)   First the need for a human concern or welfare function developed with the Industrial Revolution and the rapid extension in the use of machine power, which resulted in work being transferred from agriculture, small factory workshops and cottage industry to the creation of large factory units reliant on large numbers of unskilled employees. Although the overall prosperity of the nation developed, it was mainly the engineers and the new middle-class entrepreneurs who benefited, whereas the working classes lost their traditional agricultural skills and became appendages to machines, prone to the diseases which developed with the overcrowding and slums of the new urban industrial areas.

In the latter part of the 19th Century family firms were being replaced by limited liability companies where ownership and management became divorced from each other. The owners and shareholders had little knowledge of the lives, thoughts and needs of the workpeople employed by their companies. Paid managers acting as the agents of ownership were in more contact with the employees, but they seldom had the familiar personal knowledge of the individual workmen which the employer had under the old family-run system and were generally more concerned with efficiency of technological processes and work output than with the people who operated the processes. The increased size of firms, the size of operations and the numbers of workmen thus made personal relations difficult.

(b)   In addition, the welfare and well-being of workpeople became a public issue when the debate occurred over Lord Althorpe's Factory Act of 1833, which set legal limits on the working hours of children and young people. Its provisions were enforced by the appointment of Factory Inspectors, who had powers of entry into the factories and textile mills.

The British Factories Regulation Act, Circa 1835

The new Factories Regulation Act applies to all cotton, wool, flax, tow, hemp or silk-mills, of which the machinery is driven by steam-engines or water-wheels. Where the machinery is moved by animal power, the act does not apply, not to bobbin-net lace factories.

No child can be employed at all before it is nine years old.

No child younger than eleven must work more than forty-eight hours in any one week, or more than nine hours in any one day.

After the 1st March, 1835, this restriction extends to children under twelve; and after the 1st March, 1836, to children under thirteen.

To render these restrictions effective, no child must remain on any pretence more than nine hours a day in any working apartment of the factory.

Persons under eighteen years of age must not work more than sixty-nine hours in a week, or twelve in a day; nor at all between half-past eight o'clock at night and half-past five o'clock in the morning.

Children under nine may be employed in silk-mills.

One hour and half must be allowed for meals to all young persons, but that time is exclusive of the nine or twelve hours' work.

Two entire holidays and eight half-holidays are to be allowed to all young persons who are under the restrictions.

Every child restricted to forty-eight hours' labour in the week must attend a school for at least two hours a day, for six days out of the seven. The mill-owner is not allowed to continue in his employment any child who does not regularly attend school as above stated; for which purpose he must be certified every week of the child's attendance by the teacher.

Source: Andrew Ure, *The Philolsophy of Manufacturers,* 2nd ed. (London: Charles Knight, 1835), pp.358-359.

Out of this Act grew the 'Ten Hour' Bill of 1847 which limited the daily working hours of women and children in textile factories to 10 hours. This principle of regulation was extended by a series of Acts to other areas of work, e.g. Lord Shaftesbury's Mines Act of 1842 by which the underground employment of women and children was forbidden.

(c)   A third influence was the development of trade unions which were concerned with the improvement of working conditions and themselves were struggling for life.

Early welfare workers were mainly women because it was the plight of women and young people which had caused most societal concern. They were primarily of the upper middle-classes and were the output of university social work courses which focused on overall social, and not industrial, issues. No-one was very clear what they should be doing to raise standards of welfare at work, apart from trying to see that legislation was implemented, providing personal counselling when it was requested and looking after amenities such as canteens, recreation facilities, restrooms and administering benevolent funds as they developed. Some managers and owners, however, found that their welfare workers, far from being innocuous easers of conscience, actually wished to contribute reforms to the employment conditions in factories. Ann Crichton in *Personnel Management in Context* (1969) said on this point:

'One cannot blame the paternal employers for their vagueness. The welfare workers were not helped to see what to do any more clearly in their courses of preparation at their universities. These courses were really intended for social workers and their theoretical studies were about social philosophy and social economics which encouraged them to be concerned about social justice and reform, hence very often they had considerable difficulty in realigning their objectives with those of the rest of management. They saw the need for an active management role in order to achieve changes and tried to press for major amendments in terms and conditions of employment, changes which were often unacceptable to management because they seemed unrealistic and visionary rather than practical and of immediate consequence.'

One of the early pioneers in the field of welfare work was Miss Eleanor Kelly who was successful in a firm of metal box manufacturers in Carlisle at the turn of the century. She persuaded management to install six washbasins in the factory for the use of 1500 men and women employees. She went on in 1913 to found the Welfare Workers Association, the embryonic professional body, now the Institute of Personnel Management (IPM). Alongside the welfare-oriented function other areas of personnel work were also developing. The sheer number of employees in the growing firm led to the control needs of owners and management being met by the appointment of people to look after wages, addresses, other personal records and initial screening for employment. So men, either appointed from the shop floor or junior clerical positions, were employed as labour officers or employment officers (the title varied from one organisation to another) and were involved in recruitment and selection. Records were also maintained of discussions and agreements with trade unions so that matters in dispute could be compared with previous agreements. In some companies, therefore, these employment officers were also used within the collective bargaining function.

A major impetus to the welfare role was given during the First World War by various Government reports, in particular the Health of Munition's Workers' Committee which urged the appointment of Welfare Supervisors in all factories where women were employed. It was actually made compulsory to have welfare workers in all factories where explosives were used.

The main emphasis was still on work carried out by female workers, hence the proliferation of the welfare function, as more and more women were employed to replace the men who were away in the armed services. Occupational psychology also developed to meet the recruitment and selection needs of employers in allocating personnel to suitable occupations. Due partly to the work of the Industrial Fatigue Board, which investigated the effects of variations in hours of work, breaks and other working conditions, more serious concern developed for the working environment. At the same time, more formal apprenticeship schemes were developed so that they became not just a matter of serving time but also an educational experience. In fact the interest which was taken in those young people was to help the personnel function retain its credibility during the difficult years of the 1930s. Apprentices became supervisors and managers themselves and retained a close relationship with the employment and welfare officers over many employee matters.

The economic depression which followed the First World War led to the closing down of many welfare departments. As a result, especially in the older industries of mining, shipbuilding and textiles, the function of personnel lost ground as only the minimum standards of working conditions laid down by legislation were retained. It was not until the end of the 1930s and the beginnings of labour shortage, exacerbated by the Second World War, that there was sufficient concern for an improved evaluation of the personnel management function. Yet even during the 1930s the function was give credibility, especially in the new industries which supplied consumer goods like cars and electrical appliances.

In 1939 the Institute of Labour Management (as the IPM was known until 1946) defined the nature of personnel management as:

'that part of the management function which is primarily concerned with the human relationships within the organisation. Its objective is the maintenance of those relationships on a basis which, by consideration of the well-being of the individual enables all those engaged in the undertaking to make their maximum personal contribution to the effective working of that undertaking.'

and went on to list the activities of personnel specialists as:

'In particular personnel management is concerned with methods of recruitment, selection, training and education and with the proper employment of personnel; terms and conditions of employment; methods and standards of remuneration, working conditions, amenities and employee services, the maintenance and effective use of facilities for joint consultation between employers and employees and between their representatives and of recognised procedures for the settlement of disputes.'

The Second World War established the personnel function as an important specialism within management, recognised as such by Government, employers, employees and their representative bodies, trade unions. Industry had a need to maximise production and so selection for appropriate jobs, and especially the training of staff, were recognised as essential features of the war effort.

The Engagement and National Arbitration Order ensured that work people in controlled occupations should have fair wages and reasonable terms and conditions of employment. The Schedule of Reserved Occupations specified essential jobs and labour officers were reserved, not having to join the forces, from the age of 25 (industrial welfare officers from the age of 35). Essential Work Orders prevented unnecessary labour turnover and people could only be sacked or move with the permission of the National Service officer. This led to the development of formal disciplinary procedures in many firms.

By the end of the Second World War, personnel management had been assured an essential place in industry and commerce and the state of full employment which prevailed for the next 30 years or so helped to maintain this importance. Organisations found themselves with a perpetual shortage of key skills and it became necessary to attract people to a firm, instead of picking and choosing from those who were looking for work. In many organisations wages were increased on an annual basis, from the early 1950s, and arbitrary dismissal was no longer a threat to the individual as there was inevitably a vacancy in another organisation desperate for the individual's skills.

As time went on the impact of full employment encouraged competition between employers for the scarce labour resources. Despite the warnings that were given by employers' organisations of the dangers of wage competition, firms and industries offered wage increases to gain and keep employees. Sir Ernest Field, Director of the Scottish Engineering Employers' Association, issued a circular in February 1952 which reflected the concern:

"All members are earnestly reminded that, in the interest of Federated firms in general and in their own ultimate interest, they should never offer inducements of any kind which may reasonably be expected to entice people away from a Federated employer ...

...Inducements take many forms —

Time rates higher than is normal for the job;

Overtime, which is not really necessary in the interests of production at the time;

Systems of alleged payment by results which bear little or no relation to effort and are in effect what are commonly referred to as 'gift schemes';

'Merit', 'Experience' or 'Ability' increments paid without any real regard to the possession of these qualities, or before there has been sufficient time properly to assess them ...

...I must also stress the proved fact that the results of enticement are of only transitory advantage to the firm and of boomerang effect: sooner or later, the labour position being what it is, the losing firms are forced into the position of having to adopt the same methods to fill their vacancies, with obvious effect on the wage structure and costs ..."

Such problems made firms realise the need for sound and logical wages, salaries and fringe benefits packages and personnel officers became increasingly responsible for the monitoring of local rates and for advising on policy.

Partly because of the labour shortage, and partly because of the increasing complexity of technology and the need to have people who were unlikely to cause damage, through inexperience, to valuable equipment, training became more systematic and assumed greater importance during the 1950s. It was given a further boost by the Industrial Training Act of 1964.

The general pattern of industrial relations activity also changed in the post-war era. Trade union influence, credibility and bargaining power had increased during the Second World War and this continued during the next thirty years. From the 1950s, as we mentioned earlier, wages were negotiated annually and were under constant review. Whereas, before the war, much negotiation had been handled centrally by employers' associations and trade unions nationally, in the post-war era, the trend has been towards plant and company level bargaining with local lay workplace representatives or shop-stewards. Such local negotiation gradually tended to involve the personnel officer maintaining the industrial relations control function. This involvement was increased due to the criticisms of the Royal Commission on Trade Unions and Employers' Associations under Lord Donovan (1968) which urged a tightening up of local industrial relations practices and procedures. Paragraphs 94 and 95 of the Donovan Report emphasised the key role of personnel policies in improving industrial relations:

'(94)...If companies have their own personnel specialists, why have they not introduced effective personnel policies to control methods of negotiation and pay structures within their firms?

(95) Many firms have no such policy, and perhaps no conception of it. They employ a personnel officer to be responsible for certain tasks: staff records, selection, training, welfare negotiation and consultation. Many of the older generation of personnel managers see themselves simply as professional negotiators. Even if a personnel manager has the ability to devise an effective personnel policy, the director responsible for personnel (if there is one), or the board as a whole, may not want to listen to him. Many firms had acquired disorderly pay structures and uncoordinated personnel practices before they appointed a personnel manager, and the burden of dealing with disputes and problems as they arise has absorbed his whole time and energy.'

In Paragraph 179, Donovan argued for a more professional approach by specialists in industrial relations:

'(179) Over recent years growth in the size of companies has emphasised the unsuitability of the existing institutions of industrial relations to large companies. Most of them have factories in various parts of the country which do not fit into the regional or district structure of many employers' associations and collective bargaining procedures. This structure therefore fails to recognise the prime responsibility of boards of directors for industrial relations throughout their companies and it thwarts attempts to design company personnel policies. Even greater obstacles are placed in the way of the growing number of companies which operate in more than one industry. Large companies maintain, or should maintain, competently staffed and adequately equipped personnel departments. Many large companies are innovators and therefore in special need of negotiating arrangements linking improvements in pay with improvements in methods of operation. Many of them are pace-makers in pay and the problems which arise from the gap between industry-wide rates and actual earnings are therefore especially acute for them. Moreover competition for higher earnings between different factories within the company can be effectively controlled only by negotiating pay structures on a company basis, making agreed allowances for any appropriate regional differences.'

The recruitment and selection process also became more important, partly because the size of organisations was such that vacancies usually needed to be filled but also because of the increasing importance of new specialisms, particularly the increase in the numbers of administrative, technical and clerical staff.

During the 1960s it became clear that there was a trend towards the employment of specialist staff within the personnel function; recruitment and selection, training and development, industrial relations, wages administration, welfare etc. Personnel management also began to spread into Central and Local Government, health, education, nationalised industry and other service sectors of society. Even relatively small concerns employed personnel specialists. Reorganisations especially influenced the development of these departments, for example, in Central Government after the Fulton Committee Report in 1968, and with the reorganisations of both Local Government and the health service in the early 1970s. Influence can also be seen in these last two sectors due to the increasing activity of trade unions like COHSE, NUPE and NALGO and the recognition of the shop-steward role.

Finally, a further major influence on the development of the personnel management function over the last 20 years has been the need for organisations to conform to the increased amount of legislation in the employment field and the concomitant need for specialist advisers. From small beginnings there are now over 24,000 members of the Institute of Personnel Management alone.

2. WHAT IS PERSONNEL MANAGEMENT?

Personnel management can be seen as that part of the management task which is concerned with the human resources of the organisation and their contribution to its effectiveness. It exists wherever one person employs another and can be said to be part of the role of everybody who is responsible for the work of others, as was outlined by the IPM's definition quoted in Chapter 1. The personnel management tasks which a supervisor performs in any factory or office throughout the economy are likely to be as follows:

— he participates in the selection of new employees;
— he very often 'inducts' the new employee into the organisational environment, explains what his duties and responsibilities will be and explains his rights and privileges;
— he outlines departmental objectives;
— he appraises performance and motivates employees;
— he counsels and helps employees with their personal problems;
— he recommends wages and salary increases, promotion and transfers;
— he enforces the rules and maintains departmental discipline, warning employees of unacceptable behaviour;
— he ensures safety standards are adhered to;
— he negotiates with shop-stewards representing work groups.

We can see that all managers have a responsibility of communicating with, and directing the activities of, individuals in the workplace. Thus, to emphasise a special function of personnel management runs the risk of undermining the personnel responsibilities of the managers. This makes personnel different from all other staff or advisory functions, whether in the public or private sectors, because the concerns of personnel specialists pervade the whole organisation: regardless of level, every manager who directs staff is in some sense a personnel manager.

Rules and problems in employing people are now so complex that many organisations feel that they need guidance in their interpretation and in designing adequate policies and procedures. They employ personnel specialists who provide an independent comprehensive expertise. In 1963 the IPM clearly stated that they did not see a conflict arising between the personnel professional's role and that of the direct management of human resources carried out by line managers:

> 'It is not the personnel manager's job to manage people but to provide the specialist knowledge or services that can assist the management team to make effective use of the human resources of the organisation' (IPM 1963).

Thus personnel specialists exist to help line or operating departments do their work more effectively.

In most organisations the personnel department has usually been established as an advisory or staff function, although there may be executive or line function over certain matters, for example, the final say in disciplinary or dismissal issues or the development of appropriate training programmes. The key role will be in establishing conformity of employment conditions and ensuring that all employees are treated in a fair and equitable manner.

Because there is an overlapping of responsibility in manpower matters, most personnel specialists experience some degree of suspicion, antagonism and resentment from the line managers that they service. This occurs for a variety of reasons. Line managers may feel personnel specialists are interfering and making their jobs more difficult by, for example, refusing to permit the sacking of an employee in a way that may be against company procedures. They may feel personnel are acting in a 'spying' role, looking for weaknesses on the part of individual managers in relation to their human relations skills. They may feel that personnel specialists are taking over duties which, historically, were those of line managers and so on. The extent to which personnel professionals gain acceptance from other managers depends very much on the quality of service which is given. As Tom Lupton said in *Industrial Behaviour and Personnel Management* (1964):

> 'The recognition of the policy making role of the personnel manager depends upon the extent to which he can demonstrate that he possesses a degree of expertise in the systematic analysis of the social consequences of economic and technological decisions which other members of top management do not possess. When his colleagues turn to him for professional advice in the same way as they would turn to an accountant, an engineer, a market research man or an expert in operational research, and he is able to give such advice, he has become the new style personnel man to whom I have been referring. I am arguing that only if he has a good working knowledge of

the theories of behavioural science and an ability to apply this knowledge to the analysis of the problems of organisation, he will generate confidence in his ability as a professional.'

In order for the organisation's objectives to be reached, however, both line and staff managers must work *together*. This was described realistically by Sir Alex Jarrett, Chairman of Reed International in *Personnel Management*, June 1982:

'It is my abiding conviction that individual managers in their own departments must carry the prime responsibility for industrial relations and the outcome of pay bargaining. No one else can carry that responsibility, though they can look to personnel for expert assistance and they may, in some cases, delegate the negotiating role itself. Further, it is no good having as I do, highly professional personnel staff, if I and my board and our senior line managers are not committed to the objectives and strategies they are pursuing.'

Personnel managers sometimes have difficulties in their relationships with trade union officials and lay officers. This difficulty often concerns perceptions of the power of the individual personnel specialist to concede in collective bargaining. Personnel specialists should be given enough authority when they fulfil a negotiating role.

The success of the personnel function can probably best be evaluated by examining the use line managers make of the specialist services available and whether employees recognise its significance as part of management.

Three main principles tend to underpin the activities of personnel professionals in organisations:

1. That all employees should be treated with justice, i.e. that no favouritism or antagonism should be shown towards individuals and that there should be consistency of treatment of all employees, at whatever level or performing whatever function.

2. That the needs of the individual member of the organisation should be recognised, particularly in relation to personal development and job satisfaction.

3. That employees should be given knowledge of what is happening within the organisation and should be consulted when changes are taking place.

3. ACTIVITIES

The essential nature of a personnel department's functions can be summarised as:

1. Constructing and formulating a company's manpower policies in line with specific corporate objectives and ensuring that the policies and practices conform with the relevant statutory provisions and the collective agreements previously entered into with any representatives of the workforce.

2. Ensuring that the policies, where appropriate, are applied throughout all sectors of the organisation in a fair and equitable manner.

3. Assisting and guiding line management in the application of policy by providing advice and specialist services on manpower matters.

4. Constantly monitoring and evaluating the manpower policies of the organisation to ensure that they relate to the prevailing values of society and practices in other organisations.

Within these overall functions the general activities which may be encompassed by personnel specialists, depending on the size of the organisation, have been identified by the IPM as:

1. *Corporate planning:* This activity aims, by integrating with other functions in the organisation, to review the company's forward objectives and plans. It is concerned with specifying objectives, considering needs which arise from those objectives and planning methods of satisfying those needs.

2. *Organisation:* Examines the efficiency of the management structure and arrangements for authority and responsibility. It is concerned with job analysis; structuring of individual and groups of jobs; defining the roles within a job; and the allocation of intermittent tasks outside the normal job structure.

3. *Manpower planning:* This activity can be divided into four subsections:

    (a) Forecasting manpower requirements and manpower supply at all levels in the organisation, especially in relation to the number of people and the knowledge and skills required.

    (b) The recruitment and selection of employees, advertising, selection interviewing and testing.

    (c) Dealing with the transfer, promotion and termination of existing employees.

    (d) Maintaining an administrative system to provide relevant information to monitor performance, e.g. labour turnover and absenteeism analysis.

4. *Manpower training and development:* Analyses and determines organisational training needs and individual development programmes; integrates training with other functional specialisms; and conducts performance appraisals.

5. *Remuneration:* Considers the total remuneration structures of the organisation, based on external relativities. This could encompass the monitoring of job evaluation, merit rating, pensions, and sickness pay schemes by local and national surveys.

6. *Employee relations:* Concerned with the relationships between employers and employees and their representatives and with overall productivity. Mainly concerned with trade union recognition and relationships, consultative machinery, and disputes procedures.

7. *Employee services:* The range of services relating to the health, safety and welfare of employees, including the prevention of

accidents, the provision of medical and nursing facilities, canteens and employee counselling.

Shaun Tyson's article in *Personnel Management* in May 1985, 'Is This The Very Model of a Modern Personnel Manager?', suggests that there are currently three common models of personnel management activity in the UK.

(i)   *The administrative support model:* personnel management is a routine activity which acts in support of line management and there is no real expectation that the function will contribute to major decision making in the businesss itself. It concentrates on the administration of recruitment and selection, wages administration, and health and safety. Probably the most typical of personnel roles and found in most small organisations, hotels and retail outlets, factories, and the subsidiary decentralised units of large conglomerates.

(ii) *The systems/reactive model:* a model which exists in more sophisticated environments and has a strong industrial relations bias. The personnel department's main activity and influence lies in the creation, and maintenance, of policies and procedures to control the work activity and the interface between the employee and the organsation. The function in such organisations thus, not only administers personnel systems and provides guidance on them to line managers, but also instigates and develops them.

(iii) *The business manager model:* here the personnel management function is integrated into business decision making, people are to be motivated to achieve the organisation's objectives and personnel policy objectives are perceived in the language of business ratios — value of sales per employee, value added per employee, employment costs as a percentage of profit, etc. Personnel policies are considered automatically in the achievement of the wider business organisation objectives and labour is manipulated to achieve these organisation ends.

4. STRUCTURE OF PERSONNEL DEPARTMENTS

The extent to which consideration of the above activities leads to sub-division in the personnel department structure varies considerably and is influenced by the size, the structure and the type of organisation which hosts the specialism. There are four main ways in which the department can be structured:

1.   A central personnel office which provides a total personnel service for the whole enterprise. This is typical of the small firm and also in the retail trade where a company may have many branches but with none big enough to develop their own specialism. A personnel officer in this latter type of structure may find himself in a peripatetic role.

2.   Central and branch personnel offices: In this structure a central

103

personnel office, which establishes overall policies and procedures, is supported by branch personnel officers with executive responsibilities for routine staff acquisition and administration and who are responsible on a day-to-day basis to the senior line manager at the branch, but refer to the central functional organisation over matters which have broader ramifications.

3. Central and divisional personnel offices: Here one or a number of central personnel offices are supported at divisional, but not at branch, level with divisional personnel offices reporting executively to divisional senior managers. They have a functional responsibility to a central personnel officer or offices for overall policy. There can be many variations of this depending on the overall organisational form and structure. In some cases, divisional personnel offices may tackle local divisional policy as well as routine staff administration. This structure is seen in large organisations in both the public and private sectors.

4. Central, divisional and branch personnel offices: In this structure the personnel function is represented at all major organisational levels with, in each case, a specialist relationship to the central personnel office and executive responsibility to local management.

These four main ways of organising the personnel function represent increasing functional decentralisation and are largely a result of organisational size. Organisations usually develop a structure over time which is most appropriate for them.

Within these overall structures three common personnel department functional structures may exist. In some structures the personnel staff may be expected to fulfil a *generalist* role where they provide a total range of personnel skills in each division or plant, perhaps with the ability to turn for advice to personnel advisors or specialists in a central or headquarters function. These central specialists have the task of defining policy, but within this policy overall responsibility for all matters at branch or local level is left with the local generalist.

Some organisations prefer to organise the function at all levels into *specialist* units, for example, training, manpower planning, recruitment and selection, welfare, industrial relations. The few generalists are either in small units or in the top-line posts of the personnel function.

Finally, other organisations find it more logical to mix the two functional structures and have generalists and specialists represented at all levels.

The current trend is for a growing number of personnel departments to be organised on specialist functional lines, especially over such matters as training and development, manpower planning and wage and salary administration. Other tasks including, for example, recruitment and selection, industrial relations and health and safety at work which require continuous consideration, discussion and negotiation, may at local level be handled by generalist personnel managers with help from specialist personnel officers at local level and centralised advice from head office specialists.

5. LEVELS OF PERSONNEL MANAGEMENT RESPONSIBILITY

The number of levels of responsibility within the personnel function inevitably varies from organisation to organisation, depending on its size and the number of locations:

1. Clerical level: Responsibility at this level is for the maintenance of personnel records, for example, individual personal files; employee statistics by skill, location, job title salary level etc; absence figures; lateness figures; labour turnover statistics; and other control and 'organisational health' data. The task may also include other clerical, and perhaps also secretarial duties under the guidance of a senior personnel officer or manager.

2. Junior operational: This may include a title such as 'Personnel Assistant'. The job may include routine interviewing and routine training, perhaps emphasising induction training. A personnel officer, who carries overall responsibility, may delegate tasks.

3. Operational personnel officer: This may be a specialist or generalist post and will carry responsibility for the day-to-day personnel function. Policies and procedures determined by more senior levels will establish the boundaries.

4. Senior operational: This may be a senior specialist post, i.e. training manager, wages administration manager, or it may carry the title of 'Personnel Manager'. It may thus include those who carry responsibility for operational functions and also advise members of line management on the implementation of broad policy guidelines, but it may include those who are responsible for the derivation of policy, especially in specialist areas. It will also include responsibility of a line nature, in directing the work of subordinate personnel officers.

5. Policy maker: If the company has a personnel general manager or a personnel director he will direct and control the activities of the personnel department. He will also be involved in the creation and evolution of policy, especially personnel policy.

It is very difficult to differentiate these operational levels from job titles as job titles are often unique to the organisation. For example, a senior personnel officer within, say, British Gas will probably fulfil the same role as someone who is given the title personnel manager within a private sector organisation.

It will aid your understanding if you examine your own organisation against the structures outlined and the operational levels described.

6. PERSONNEL OBJECTIVES AND THEIR RELATION TO ORGANISATIONAL OBJECTIVES

Strategic and operational advice on personnel matters is directed towards the attainment of the organisation's overall objectives. As we have already outlined (and will expand in the next section) it covers issues such as manpower planning, the development of harmonious employee relations and the maintenance of individual and group motivation. It does so by developing appropriate and adequate personal and career development opportunities; maintaining and deriving equitable and fair remuneration packages and policies; and providing appropriate responsibilities within tasks required to perform the organisation's function in society. In addition, it requires the development of appropriate procedures for the control of employee behaviour, taking into account the structure of tasks in the organisational hierarchy, the relevant external values of society and legislation developed to protect the individual at work.

Finally, the personnel department will be required to contribute appropriately to the development of organisation structures to ensure that the implications of changed technologies and objectives are related to the needs of individual employees.

Ultimately the actual roles carried out by personnel specialists will be determined by the attitudes of senior management to the value of the personnel activity in helping to attain overall objectives. Where personnel is recognised as having something of value to contribute, then personnel specialists will be given a key role in operational and strategic planning. Where, however, personnel is seen primarily as a service function, providing advice and guidance, on demand, from senior managers, it will be given a routine administrative role and will only be called upon to demonstrate its expertise in crisis situations. Whichever role is given depends on the knowledge and credibility of the particular personnel professionals.

This has been emphasised by Karen Legge in *Power Innovation and Problem Solving in Personnel Management,* McGraw Hill 1978, where she looks at the personnel specialists power to implement policies and operate successfully, and lists the following factors which influence that power:

'1) The organisation's dominant ideology.

2) The areas of contextual uncertainty which are defined as being of crucial importance to resolve.

3) How (the organisation) defines measures and evaluates success.'

(1—3 being organisational factors)

'4) The manager's own level of expertise in the areas of activity he undertakes, whether specifically personnel management or not.'

(N.B. If personnel managers are only prepared to develop expertise in their own functional specialism and not in a general business sense, they will lose credibility anyway.)

'5) His right of access to those he needs to influence and from whom he requires information in order to design and implement policy.

6) His ability to establish credibility with those individuals he seeks to influence and from whom he seeks support.

7) The resource power his position commands.'

(4—7 being individual factors)

7. OBJECTIVES OF THE COMMON PERSONNEL MANAGEMENT ACTIVITIES AND THE DIFFICULTY OF MEASUREMENT

The factors which have contributed to the growth of personnel management jobs and the enhancement of the status of the specialism are diffuse. We can identify two major contributors to this growth in the post-war era.

A primary influence until the mid 1970s was the simple fact that labour was a scarce resource. We had full employment and too few people chasing too many jobs. In that condition, the productivity of labour and the organisation's effectiveness in utilising its available labour force was of paramount importance. To this end it was hardly surprising that managements in both the public and private sectors of the economy paid enormous attention to any ideas and stratagems which could improve labour productivity. Thus, for example, training and development was seen as necessary; recruitment and selection skills were necessary and, as frequently turnover was relatively high and growth was occurring, there was a constant need for specialists; trade unions were powerful and hence specialists could relieve line management of many of the day-to-day pressures.

The second important feature was Government involvement in the social and economic protection of the individual employee. A succession of legislative measures were passed to increase this protection and personnel specialists were seen to be necessary as they were more able than line management to concentrate on these labour laws and ensure that appropriate policies and procedures were incorporated, leaving line management to manage the level of production or the effectiveness of the service provided.

As pressures on employment have been relieved over the last 7 years or so and legislation has become incorporated in most organisational procedures, the benefits of personnel management as a growing activity have increasingly come under scrutiny. Companies find it difficult to incorporate these benefits on a balance sheet and, unless personnel can demonstrate that it does contribute to profitability and efficiency over the next decade, there is a danger that its growth will slow down and its status may once again be questioned in the way that Peter Drucker questioned it (*Practice of management* 1955, Heinemann):

"'Personnel administration... is largely a collection of incidental techniques without much internal cohesion'. Some wit once said maliciously that it puts together... 'all those things that do not deal with the work of people and that are not management...' As personnel administration conceives the job of managing worker and work, it is partly a file clerk's job, partly a social worker's job, partly fire-fighting to head off union trouble and settle it... the things the personnel administrator is typically responsible for — safety and pension plans, the suggestion system, the employment office, and union's grievances are necessary chores... I doubt though that they should be put together in one department for they are a hodgepodge... They are neither one function by kinship of skills required to carry out the activities nor are they one function by being united together in the work process...'"

We should question our primary concern with what Herzberg has called the maintenance of hygiene needs of employees and ensure that we can demonstrate our ability to contribute towards motivation needs by involving ourselves more in job redesign, reviewing existing policies and procedures; and developing new ones to cope with the inevitable changes taking place in many UK organisations.

Let us examine each of the functions of personnel and consider the difficulties of measuring our effectiveness in real terms. At the same time we will consider the skills that personnel specialists need to develop to ensure their ability to cope with each objective. The objectives suggested are only examples and you should see if you can derive more adequate ones within the practices of your own organisation.

(a) Organisation structure

This is developed as a direct result of objectives and future policy. Organisations have to constantly monitor existing structures to ensure that they are still viable when considering future plans and the needs of the individual members. It thus requires an examination of the levels of authority, the amount of delegation and the responsibilities given to each member of the organisation.

OBJECTIVE: The objective of the personnel department is to give advice on the adequacies and inadequacies of both the formal and the informal organisation of employees into working groups and how changes should be made to cope with future needs.

REQUIREMENTS: The personnel specialist will require knowledge of social psychology in industry and commerce and knowledge of the influence of technology and other job factors and organisation structure on individual motivation. He will require knowledge of the organisation's short term and long term objectives, considerable experience of the existing formal and informal relationships, job descriptions and their relevance, and work practices.

MEASUREMENT OF SUCCESS: Success can only be measured over time and will relate to other objectives which are determined by, for example, industrial relations, training and recruitment activities. Constant monitoring is needed to ensure that the appropriate jobs are handled at the appropriate times. Success will depend on the time-span of change and on the integration of all aspects of organisational decision making and success or failure will probably be dependent on a variety of internal or external pressures which may not be easily controllable. These pressures can be illustrated as in Figure 6:1 on page 109.

It is very difficult for the personnel department to justify and evaluate the success of its contribution in the short and medium term.

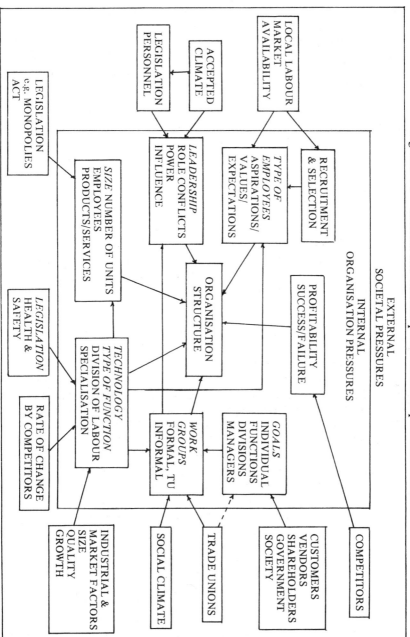

Figure 6 : 1 – Internal and external pressures on the personnel function

109

(b) Manpower planning

Manpower needs are derived from the determination of the organisation's long term objectives. This should result in the reduction of short term, crisis personnel decision making as strategems are planned with an eye to long term goals. Existing labour force numbers are analysed as well as an inventory of skills and potential patterns of voluntary and involuntary wastage.

OBJECTIVE: The establishment of realistic plans, covering the manpower needs of the organisation over the time-span of objectives to ensure that the human resources available match organisational requirements.

REQUIREMENTS: The personnel specialist involved in manpower planning will require detailed knowledge of marketing and production plans, including which products are to be phased out and which markets are to be developed, so that manpower requirements can be established both quantitatively and qualitatively. In addition, he will require a working knowledge of simple applied mathematical and statistical techniques and, in large organisations, knowledge of computer systems. He will also require reliable information about the future labour supply position, both within the organisation itself, and in the local or national labour market.

MEASUREMENT OF SUCCESS: Personnel activities should be based on short and long term objectives derived from the manpower planning process. Ideally success would be measured by examining whether the right people are working in the right jobs at the right time, performing the right functions efficiently and productively. Yet, our ability to be successful in this area of personnel work is again dependent upon a number of factors which may be difficult to forecast. Some of the influences include:

— whether new organisations move into a locality and require the skills which were forecast as likely to be available;
— whether the labour market situation changes. Suddenly, large numbers of potentially ideal employees become available due to the unexpected closure of a competitor for those skills;
— whether the economic situation reduces market opportunities;
— whether sufficient data can be obtained as to local authority plans for housebuilding and new roads;

and so on. Examine the factors which could influence your own organisation's ability to meet its future labour needs.

(c) Recruitment and selection

It is worth differentiating between these two functions. Recruitment is the process of attracting appropriately qualified candidates to the organisation in a cost-effective manner. Selection is the process of obtaining the right person from amongst the candidates, i.e. those who are most likely to fulfil the job requirements.

OBJECTIVE: This could be determined as the successful search for relevantly qualified and experienced personnel, the selection of the right individuals and the induction of the new employees to meet organisational needs.

REQUIREMENTS: The personnel professional will require knowledge of the most appropriate sources of potential employees and of the prevailing rates of pay for this category of job. He will want a knowledge of the future manpower needs of the organisation to ensure that he obtains employees who are going to be as necessary in the future as in the present. To select the appropriate candidate he will require a knowledge of interview techniques and appropriate selection tests. In addition, he will require a comprehensive working knowledge of the relevant statutory legislative requirements and of the organisation's own norms, standards and expectations regarding new employees.

MEASUREMENT OF SUCCESS: In the recruitment process the ultimate measure will be the presentation of appropriate and acceptable candidates. Care must be taken to ensure that, with the rising costs of advertising and the reduction of many advertising budgets, data is obtained and used in planning media coverage of the cost/benefit of relevant sources of candidates. Obviously the ability to attract applications is influenced by the availability of appropriate skills and experience in the labour market and the existing wages, salaries and fringe benefits package which the organisation is offering. Generally, in times of full employment, recruitment is likely to be more expensive for all levels of jobs whereas, with high levels of unemployment, costs for many jobs can be minimised.

Success in selection may be measured by examining the future performance of employees and the rate of labour turnover generally within the organisation. Yet turnover may be influenced by the state of the labour market and by prevailing competitors' wage rates. Future job performance may be influenced by the level of economic activity within the organisation concerned: an employee, for example, may be ideal when the organisation is not working at full stretch, but may be far less suitable if he is expected to work 'flat out'. Performance can also be affected by the adequacy of training activities and the speed of maturation.

These are only a few measures; look at the advantages and disadvantages of other possible measures with specific reference to your own organisation.

(d) Training and development

The level of training and development activity since the early 1960s has been affected by legislative interference which has aimed to ensure an adequate supply of properly trained men and women at all levels in industry. In those areas affected by Industrial Training Boards, this area

111

of personnel activity was one of the few in which some measure of success could be related to the amount of levy returned in the form of grant. With the reduction in the number of Training Boards, such measures will be less important, except in a few areas of the economy.

It is worth differentiating between three terms which are often applied in this area of personnel work; education, training and development.

(i) *Education:* This usually refers to the basic acquisition of knowledge and skills to enable people to make the best of life in general and it tends to be broadly based rather than specific in its coverage (in occupational terms).

(ii) *Training:* This term usually refers to the provision of specific skills, knowledge and attitudes which are related either to the current job of the person being trained or to the expected next job. It tends to be specific in its application.

(iii) *Development:* This usually suggests a much broader view of knowledge, skills and attitude acquisition than training. It is less specifically job centred and more concerned with employee potential and career orientation. It thus develops employees for future roles.

OBJECTIVE: The efficient and effective training and development of all levels of staff so that they can contribute at optimum level to fulfilling the objectives of the organisation, and adequately developing their own skills to the mutual benefit of themselves and the organisation.

REQUIREMENTS: Specialists involved in the training and development function will require a knowledge of the future manpower needs and progression plans of the organisation. They will need an understanding of the relevant behavioural scientific research applied to training, and the skills necessary to undertake training needs analysis so that training meets the priority needs of the organisation itself. Where Industrial Training Boards remain they will require knowledge of the relevant Training Board requirements. They may also have to develop the relevant instructional and teaching skills for conducting training programmes, administrative skills for the training system and the ability to relate performance appraisal to the development of suitable training programmes.

MEASUREMENT OF SUCCESS: Evaluation of training is required as part of the control process to ensure that the relevant skills are being developed to meet the shortcomings discovered by training needs analysis. To establish the value of training, measurable objectives are needed. This is relatively easy when examining training which has the objective of improving, for example, the level of output of a particular individual machine operator or training a person in a skill in which he is not currently competent. It is more difficult to evaluate where development, as defined above, is being undertaken because it is hard to separate the effects of training from the effects of maturation or increased experience.

With the reduction in the statutory involvement of ITBs the value of training can no longer be judged on the level of grant return or on the retention of exemption from levy. It means that organisations will have to use other measures of value to ensure that sufficient funds are allocated to training and development and that adequate training will occur to fulfil objectives.

(e) Employee relations

This term is used to describe the regulation of the employment relationship between employer and employee. It is concerned with the whole complex of market and institutional processes which an organisation encourages or establishes to handle both formal and informal employment relationships. It is concerned with dynamic interactive relationships which, by their nature, change over time. It includes both individual contracts and collective agreements. In general terms the key issues encompassed are those of conflict, cooperation, rule making, authority and power, information disclosure, communication, motivation and control.

OBJECTIVE: The development and maintenance, in cooperation with line management, trade unions (or staff associations), and individual employees of a fair and equitable climate of employer/employee relationships to ensure the attainment of organisational objectives.

REQUIREMENTS: To further this objective, a personnel specialist must have a sound knowledge of the policies, procedures and objectives of the organisation and an understanding of the local trade union (or other) structures, objectives and agreements. He must be competent at interpersonal skills so that a relationship of mutual trust and confidence can be established with employee representatives. He may also need to be aware of the policies of employer organisations and trade unions locally and nationally.

MEASUREMENT OF SUCCESS: Traditional measures include the number of strikes or other forms of industrial relations breakdown which the organisation suffers, and the number of grievances and the speed at which they are processed. There are problems in using such measures; strikes may occur which have nothing to do with internal breakdown in procedures or internal relationships, but which are the result of Government, employer association, or trade union pressure from outside, or they may not occur not because of good internal industrial relations, but because of the prevailing weakness of trade unions generally. The number of grievances expressed may be a result of the general economic climate and the availability of alternative work in other organisations.
   What other measures could be used and what are the problems with using them?

(f) Remuneration administration

The personnel function has an important role in the designing and implementation of an appropriate rewards or remuneration package. In some industries, e.g. electrical contracting, Local Government, the Health Service and National Government, the basic structure may be determined by national agreements made outside the organisation, but in the manufacturing sector, e.g. engineering, chemicals, rubber manufacture, organisations often need to derive a structure which is appropriate to local circumstances and the perceived value to the organisation of specific jobs. Wages can provide a source of motivation for employees to perform effectively and wage and salary rates are certainly important to people considering whether to join an organisation or not. Key influences on remuneration structures are differentials and relativities. *Differentials* can be defined as the differences in reward patterns between one job and another within an organisation. *Internal Relativities* can be seen as the differences in wages and salaries between one bargaining group and another bargaining group within the same organisation. *External Relativities* can be viewed as the differences in reward patterns comparing jobs in one organisation with another.

OBJECTIVE: To give expert advice on wage and salary policies, including fringe benefits such as pensions and sick pay schemes, to ensure that differentials are logically derived and that the organisation is paying the market rate for skills to ensure its ability to obtain labour. To ensure that the schemes are administered effectively and to reduce the potentiality of creating anomalies.

REQUIREMENTS: The specialist will require detailed knowledge of local labour market and industry rates and of the relevant local and national wage agreements. He will need to be aware of the advantages and disadvantages of the various systems of remuneration, e.g. time rates, piece rates and bonus schemes and, in larger organisations, a knowledge of job evaluation techniques. He will require the skills necessary to conduct money and fringe benefit surveys and the ability to analyse and interpret the results. He must be able to settle the problems and queries which arise from specific systems of payment. At times, he will require knowledge of any applicable incomes policies and their effects.

MEASUREMENT OF SUCCESS: One of the main problems with evaluating the success of remuneration administration is that wage and salary negotiations are a dynamic process, hence at times relativities may be maintained, whereas at other times the organisation may find itself in advance of or behind its competitors. The ability of an organisation to reward its staff adequately can also be affected by the prevailing economic situation and the existence or non-existence of a Governmental incomes policy of a statutory kind. Measures which can be used, bearing these problems in mind, are:

- the ability of the organisation to obtain labour of the appropriate calibre;
- the number of anomalies that arise;
- reductions in the number of pay queries;
- the amount of concern expressed on differentials and relativities;
- the degree to which work effort is maintained;

and so on.

Whatever measures are used, it is important to administer a remuneration package which rewards all employees in an adequate and consistent manner and which appropriately reflects market forces.

(g) Employee services

These incorporate the 'welfare' aspect of the personnel function and include responsibility for canteen or restaurant facilities, medical and other personal services, e.g. dentistry and hairdressing, recreational facilities and helping with individual personal problems. It also includes the evaluation and monitoring of the organisation's compliance with relevant health and safety legislation and the design and administration of internal company safety and work practice policies.

OBJECTIVE: To ensure that the organisation complies with prevailing health and safety legislation and develops appropriate health, safety and welfare policies to promote the general well-being of its employees and that there is adequate liaison with safety representatives and safety committees (where they exist).

REQUIREMENTS: The personnel professional will require a current knowledge of the statute laws on health and safety and the Codes of Practice and regulations which apply in the industry. He will also need a detailed knowledge of the system of statutory sick pay and of the specific organisation's sickness provisions, medical facilities and welfare services. He will also need an up-to-date knowledge of the available Governmental, local authority and private welfare facilities. He will have to develop an aptitude for committee work and knowledge of the consultative machinery, policies and procedures in his organisation.

The extent of welfare facilities varies considerably. These can include subsidised canteens and restaurants; luncheon vouchers; protective or other clothing; a laundry service; medical services; convalescent homes; special transport facilities; company houses; loans, and counselling services. There may be crêches, facilities for shopping, hairdressing facilities and leave of absence during school holidays.

MEASUREMENT OF SUCCESS: The success of personal welfare facilities to the organisation is difficult to measure, although labour turnover and general satisfaction may reflect some of their value. In terms of health and safety, measures include numbers of:

- accidents (perhaps differentiated between minor and lost time accidents);

115

— cases of industrial disease;
— cases of discipline over safety matters;
— improvement or prohibition notices issued by the inspectorate;
— days lost through illness;
and so on.

These measures can also be subject to criticism, for example, the numbers of days lost through illness are going to be affected by influenza epidemics. Lost time accidents may not adequately reflect the safety standards of the organisation, more relevant data may include the number of 'near misses'.

What measures are used in your own organisation? How useful are they?

(h) Ensuring the organisation complies with employment legislation

As previously stated, there is now a wealth of legislation in the employment field and the personnel function is often seen as the 'guardian angel' of the organisation in ensuring that legislation is implemented via rules and procedures and that line management is kept aware of the relevant provisions.

OBJECTIVE: To ensure that organisation policies are in conformance with current Government legislation and that the likely implications of proposed changes in legislation are considered.

REQUIREMENTS: The specialist requires detailed knowledge of the relevant Acts of Parliament and Codes of Practice and the effects they have on conditions of work, policies and procedures within the organisation. Where organisations do transgress rules, he should be able to write critical incident reports and possibly represent the organisation in Courts or Tribunals. He should also be able to communicate with other managers on the implications of legislation and be able to word collective and individual procedures to take legislative ramifications into account.

MEASUREMENT OF SUCCESS: Measures will include the ability to respond quickly to questions on legislation; lack of industrial tribunal or other court cases; and acceptable, easy to operate company procedures.

(i) Maintenance of personnel control and planning records and statistics

The production of meaningful manpower forecasts and planning depends largely on the availability of reliable and objective information about employees and their work records. The degree of sophistication and coverage of data will vary according to the size of the organisation. The method of collection and analysis will vary from manual systems to complicated computerised packages.

OBJECTIVE: The compilation and analysis of manpower records as a base for the optimum deployment of the organisation's human resources so that information can be retrieved efficiently and speedily to satisfy the requirements of internal decision making and external requests for information from Government departments, Government agencies, training boards, and other employers.

MEASUREMENT OF SUCCESS: the kind of analyses required to aid decision making will include employees' departmental distribution, occupational skills, age distribution, length of service, names and addresses and contact phone numbers; a register of accidents (both for statutory and control purposes); a register of disabled employees; assessment and performance appraisal reports; records of transfers and promotions; overtime levels, and labour turnover and absentee records; and sick pay records. Success can be ascertained by the availability of such data and the ease of obtaining it for the decision making process.

The list of roles, objectives, requirements and measurement of success is by no means comprehensive nor the only possible list, but it does highlight the problems of evaluating objectively the contribution which the personnel function is making to the success of organisations in the attainment of their objectives. The list also highlights the variety of roles and the skills and knowledge required to operate them. Theoretical knowledge of industrial sociology and psychology must be supported by practical skills, which can only be obtained through experience in the specialism. But what is equally important is an understanding of the environmental issues and pressures which affect organisation in the 1980s. (Some insight into these is attempted in the remainder of this book).

The current situation, which reflects the position summarised is illustrated in the written evidence of the Ministry of Labour in the Royal Commission on Trade Unions and Employers' Association which, although published in 1968, is still relevant:

'Personnel management in this country has succeeded in avoiding the criticism that it is an anti-union tool of management concerned with the manipulation of workers, which has been levelled at the profession in the United States and some European countries. However, the contribution which personnel management could have made and could make would be much greater if large sections of industry did not still regard it as something apart from the main stream of management and if the horizons of many personnel officers were not limited to the provision of limited common services or to dealing with day-to-day industrial relations questions...

...There are signs that this situation is changing. More personnel officers are assuming responsibilities in regard to clerical and administrative staff and management development, instead of confining their activities to the problems of manual workers. There is a trend towards the allocation of responsibility for personnel management to a member of the Board. Furthermore in an increasing number of cases the specialist personnel officer has been appointed to the Board.'

117

The status of personnel management has improved over the last ten to twelve years; the increasing professionalism of personnel staff has enabled them to demonstrate their contribution to overall organisational efficiency and profitability. Personnel management has expanded and is still expanding in Local Government, Central Government and the Health Service but, if the function expects to continue its importance and credibility, it must be seen to be a necessary part of all organisations. This will require the increasing adoption of a proactive role initiating change rather than a reactive role responding to problems and crises.

Those who wish to reach the top of the profession must obtain experience across the total spectrum of personnel work and cannot afford to become too narrow or specialist in outlook. Current personnel decision making requires an integration of knowledge and functional expertise across the spectrum of activities.

Amongst the issues which personnel professionals need to address to ensure their continual relevance and effectiveness are the following:

i) with trade unions being increasingly encouraged by legislation to be accountable for their actions, are existing bargaining structures and procedures relevant? Thus for example are we able to cope with moves towards decentralised bargaining in, for example, the public sector?

ii) with more demand for equal treatment in services and conditions between blue collar and white collar staff, are existing remuneration systems able to cope and do they still motivate people to perform well?

iii) do current practices and procedures enable us to cope successfully with the introduction of information technology?

iv) do we still offer an appropriate and efficient recruitment and selection service?

v) are we offering proactive advice on the range of employee relations issues?

vi) do we have adequate communication structures which encourage involvement of staff and provide them with information so that they can identify with the values of the organisation and its objectives?

vii) are our training systems adequate and related to specific identified current and future needs, or do we merely jump on the latest bandwagon?

viii) have we adequate employee records and administrative systems in order to help us plan and control our manpower efficiently?

ix) are we involved in identifying and analysing the motivational needs of employees and the design of appropriate methods of work and flexible work organisation?

x) are we developing our own skills and expertise in our chosen profession, whilst at the same time developing general management skills and knowledge so that we can communicate effectively?

Chapter 7
Personnel Management and the Law of Employment Relationships

INTRODUCTION

A massive amount of statute labour law now exists in the UK and this influences the whole of the employment relationship (in some cases even the pre-employment relationship, e.g. Race Relations Act 1976 and Sex Discrimination Act 1975). Yet, until the last 20 years or so, the distinctive feature of the UK's employment system, especially for collective bargaining, was the very small part played by the law in influencing the employment relationship and the behaviour of the parties to it.

1. SOURCES OF INFLUENCES

The employment contract is influenced by a number of sources which include:

1. Common law rights and obligations of both employer and employee.
2. UK Statute law, which has gradually built what Lord Wedderburn has termed a 'floor of rights' into the employment relationship.
3. UK Statute law, referring to collective relationships, i.e. the relationship between trade unions and employers.
4. Custom and practice arrangements.
5. The Treaty of Rome, which we signed when we entered the European Economic Community (EEC) in 1973, and the EEC legislation, which derives from the Treaty. Some of the Directives especially have had a major influence on the development of UK law and its interpretation.
6. Indirect influence has derived from the European Convention on Human Rights and Fundamental Freedoms and the European Social Charter.
7. The Conventions and Recommendations of the International Labour Organisation (ILO) founded in 1919.
8. Codes of Practice, issued by ACAS, The Department of Employment, The Commission for Racial Equality, The Equal Opportunities Commission and The Manpower Services Commission.

Let us briefly examine each of these in turn. For a more detailed analysis of the development of labour law the reader will need to consult some of the references given at the end of this book.

(a) Common law

Before 1066 and the Norman Conquest, England was split up into several kingdoms and laws were generally local in application. The Normans developed rules of law which could be common throughout the country — hence the title 'common law'. This has evolved since and, now, to a limited extent, regulates the duties and responsibilities of both employers and employees under the employment contract. The relationship between the parties is tested in the civil courts against the background of 'precedent' in determining relationships established in previous cases. This ensures uniformity in decision making. Nowadays, with the development of statute law for the contract of employment, the common law aspects have begun to take a back seat in determining obligations. Thus, where statute law and common law appear to conflict, the duties and stipulations laid down by statute law prevails. Where, however, contractual relationships are not clear or where there is no statutory intervention, then the common law rules will be applied.

Historically it can be argued that relative economic and social power in the master/servant relationship was in favour of the masters or employers. Hence the duties on the employee as determined in cases handled under common law, are more comprehensive than the duties of the employer.

The rights and obligations or duties can be summarised as follows:

(a) Duties of employer

(i)   To provide work — but only where the employee earns his wages under a payment by results scheme or obtains recognition because of the publicity he receives in a particular job.

(ii) To pay agreed wages in return for the employees' willingness to work, and to pay wages in a manner which is not unlawful.

(iii) To take reasonable care for the employee's safety.

(iv) To treat the employee with proper courtesy.

(v)   To indemnify the employee for injury sustained while in employment

(vi) To be reasonable in maintaining the employment relationship.

(b) Duties of employee

(i)   To be ready and willing (sickness or other incapacity apart) to work.

(ii) To offer personal service.

(iii) To take reasonable care in the exercise of that service, including the duty to be competent at work and to take care of the employer's property.

(iv)   To not wilfully disrupt the employer's business.

(v)   To obey reasonable orders as to the time, place, nature and method of service.

(vi)   To work only for the employer in the employer's time.

(vii) To disclose information to the employer relevant to the employer's business.

(viii) To hold for the employer the benefit of any invention etc. relevant to the business on which the employee is engaged.

(ix)   To respect the employer's trade secrets.

(x)   Generally, to be of good faith and do nothing to destroy the trust and confidence necessary for employment.

(xi)   To account for all profits received in the course of employment.

(xii) To indemnify the employer for loss caused by the employee.

(b)   UK Statute law on individual relationships

Parliament is the supreme law making body in England and the statutes it passes are interpreted by the courts. The statute must be interpreted literally, except when to do so would be offensive to reason. Thus, in some cases, individual interpretation may be used to modify the legislation. A large number of Acts of Parliament now influence the employer in his relationship with the employee. Examples include The Race Relations Act 1976; The Equal Pay Act 1970; The Sex Discrimination Act 1975; The Payment of Wages Act 1960; The Health and Safety At Work Act 1974; The Factories Act 1961; The Offices Shops and Railway Premises Act 1963; The Employment Protection (Consolidation) Act 1978 and the Rehabilitation of Offenders Act 1974. We will return to some of these and their features in the next chapter.

The function of most of these statutes is broadly to prevent those who feel that they are mistreated or feel that they are unsure of their duties and obligations from having to resort to the courts to settle a dispute. The statutes, therefore, lay down legal duties across the whole spectrum of employment and provide remedies where transgressions arise.

(c)   UK Statute law on collective relationships

Statute laws covering the rights of trade unions to operate in our society have influenced collective relationships over the last 100 years. In their early years, trade union behaviour was constrained by a combination of criminal and civil law statutes. The position has changed since the passing of two Acts in 1871, The Trade Union Act 1871 and The Criminal Law Amendment Act of 1871. Since these Acts a series of legislative changes have been made some of which have expanded trade union rights and some of which have reduced them. Currently the key pieces of legislation in this field are The Trade Union and Labour Relations Acts of 1974 and 1976 as amended by the Employment Acts 1980 and 1982, the Trade Union Act of 1984 and the Employment Protection Act 1975. These define what trade unions are; what protection they have from civil liability under the laws of tort when industrial action occurs or is contemplated; various rights to time off for officials; and disclosure of information in situations of collective redundancy and for collective bargaining purposes. In addition to those statutes, other legislation has been passed to encourage collective bargaining in those industries where, because trade unions are weak, protection is required. The Wages Councils Act 1979, as amended, by the 1986 legislation, provides some protection.

(d)   Custom and practice arrangements

These are the rules, both formal and informal, which influence the parties in the employment relationship. They include national, local and domestic arrangements made by trade unions and their representatives and employers and their representatives in the collective bargaining process. They also include the specific work rules and regulations and joint unwritten understandings between workers and various levels of management, e.g. on decisions regarding the rota for overtime; which jobs an employee will be asked to perform; the employee who regularly is asked to deliver pay-packets to those who are away sick and is paid overtime, although not on company premises; informal job and finish arrangements. Custom and practice may be used in the courts to provide the substance of implied terms in the contract of employment; it may provide the basis on which collective agreements are incorporated into an individual's contract and the contractual status of particular works rules.

(e)   The Treaty of Rome and EEC legislation

The Directives of the EEC have had an influence on the development of UK law since 1972, especially in the fields of equal pay, sex discrimination, redundancy consultation and mergers and takeovers. Certainly, a close examination of the laws in other European countries shows a marked similarity of coverage to recent UK legislation.

(1)   The collective redundancy provisions of the Employment Protection Act 1975 were designed to implement in the UK EEC Directive No 75/129 on 'Approximation of the Laws of Member States Relating to Collective Redundancies'.

(2)   The Transfer of Undertakings (Protection of Employment) Regulations Statutory Instrument No 1794, 1981 is the UK's response to the EEC Council Directive No 77/187 on 'Acquired Rights of Workers on Transfer of Undertakings'.

(3)   Article 119 of the Treaty of Rome provides for equal pay for equal work and this led to Directive No 73/117 on 'The Approximation

of the Laws of Member States Relating to the Application of the Principle of Equal Pay for Men and Women', which the Equal Pay Act 1970 covers.

(4) Article 235 of the Treaty of Rome led to the development of Directive 76/207 on 'the Implementation of the Principle of Equal Treatment for Men and Women as regards Access to Employment, Vocational Training and Promotion and Working Conditions'; the Sex Discrimination Act 1975 as amended goes far in bringing the UK into line.

(5) The scope of EEC law does not extend to the problems of racial discrimination; however the principle of the freedom of nationals of member states to work anywhere within the Community was extended by Community Regulation 1612/68 on 'Freedom of Movement for Workers Within the Community' to require equality of access to all jobs for nationals of all member states. Certainly the 1976 Race Relations Act embodies and fulfils the objects of the Regulation.

Section 3(1) of the European Communities Act 1972 states:

'For the purposes of all legal proceedings any question as to the meaning and effect of any of the Treaties, or as to the validity, meaning or effect of any community instrument, shall be treated as a question of law (and, if not referred to the European Court), be for determination as such in accordance with the principles laid down by and any relevant decision of the European Court.'

Parliament enacted that we should abide by the principles laid down by the European Court. Wherever there is conflict between the law contained in an article of the Treaty of Rome and an article in the law of a member State, the law of the Community will take precedence. This must be taken into account in any judgements made in courts in the UK, if there are precedents or case law established by the European Court.

(f) European Conventions on Human Rights and Fundamental Freedoms and the European Social Charter

The European Convention on Human Rights provides for the protection of a whole range of freedoms for individuals and for groups. Thus, for example, it protects freedom of association, freedom of assembly and freedom of religion and of conscience. These influence such matters as the right to belong to a union, union recognition and aspects regarding picketing and the closed shop. The rights established by the Convention are not enforceable in courts in the UK, but can be the subject of complaints to the European Commission on Human Rights at Strasbourg. If this body finds there is a case to answer and that no voluntary settlement can be achieved, the matter then may be referred to the European Court of Human Rights. Judgements made in favour of the applicant, as in the *Young, James and Webster* case delivered on 13th August, 1981, brought against the UK under Article 11 of the Convention which provides:

'Everyone has the right ... to freedom of association with others, including the right to form and to join trade unions for the protection of his interests.'

has no direct effect on British Law but does bring strong political pressure on the Government to change laws that are out of step with the Convention.

The European Social Charter seeks to secure protection for social and economic rights, e.g. time off and pay in relation to maternity; all workers should have two weeks annual leave; there should be rights to vocational training. The influence of the Charter is less potent than the Convention since there is no machinery for individuals to make a complaint to any European body. The only way of monitoring compliance is by biennial report on contravention giving adverse publicity to those transgressing the Charter.

(g) Conventions and recommendations of the ILO

The International Labour Organisation (ILO) was originally created by the Treaty of Versailles in 1919. It was established as a tripartite body to bring together Government, employers and trade unions to take united action to improve the social and economic well-being of all the peoples of the world by encouraging decent living standards, satisfactory conditions of work and pay and adequate employment opportunities. It is financed by contributions from its member states. In 1944 the tripartite Annual International Labour Conference meeting in Philadelphia adopted the Declaration of Philadelphia, which embodies the following principles which guide the work of the ILO:

— Labour is not a commodity.

— Freedom of expression and association are essential to sustained progress.

— Poverty anywhere constitutes a danger to prosperity everywhere.

— All human beings, irrespective of race, creed or sex, have the right to pursue both their material well-being and their spiritual development in conditions of freedom and dignity, of economic security and equal opportunity.

In order to further these principles, the ILO has the following activities:

1. The formulation of international policies and programmes to help improve working and living conditions, enhance employment opportunities and promote basic human rights;

2. The creation of international labour standards to serve as guidelines for national authorities in putting these policies into action;

3. An extensive programme of international technical cooperation to help Governments in making these policies effective in practice;
4. Training, education, research and publishing activities to help advance all these efforts.

150 nations are members of the ILO. The annual (June) International Labour Conference is the supreme policy making body and provides an international forum for discussion of world labour and social problems, and sets minimum international standards. Each member country sends a four-person delegation, two representatives from Government, one representative of the trade union movement (nominated by the TUC in the UK), and one representative of the employers (nominated by the CBI in the UK), each of whom may speak and vote independently.

Between annual conferences, the work of the ILO is funded by its Governing Body, elected every three years at the Conference, which meets in February, June and November and comprises 28 Government representatives, 14 worker representatives and 14 employer representatives. 10 of the Government seats are held by the countries of chief industrial importance. In 1985 these were: Russia, United States of America, United Kingdom, India, Japan, West Germany, France, Italy, China, and Brazil. The International Labour Office in Geneva provides the operational headquarters; the secretariat acts as the research centre and is the publishing house. Operations are also decentralised in regional, area and branch offices in more than 40 member countries.

The work of the Governing Body and of the Office in Geneva is aided by a number of tripartite committees which cover major industries by a commission of experts on such matters as vocational training, management development, health and safety, workers' education, women and young workers.

One of the ILO's most important functions is the adoption by the International Labour Conference of Conventions and Recommendations which, together, are often called the 'International Labour Code'. Through Ratifications, which are voluntary by individual states, Conventions are intended to create binding obligations to put their provisions into effect. They become an international commitment by the country concerned to abide by the provisions of the Convention. Of the 159 Conventions in 1984, 77 have been ratified by the UK. The only Convention which the ILO considers does not need to be ratified for there to be an expectation that it should be complied with is ILO Convention 87, which concerns Freedom of Association and Protection of the Right to Organise.

A Recommendation does not create any international commitments, but is designed to provide guidance to Governments on policy, legislation and practice.

A Convention comes into existence through the following stages:

1. An issue is identified which requires action. It may be drawn to the

attention of the ILO by a Government or trade union or employer, or even the ILO Office itself.

2. The Office brings the issue to the Governing Body at one of its meetings.

3. The Governing Body discusses it and may bring the issue onto a Conference agenda for discussion.

4. Concurrently, the Office consults the member nations on practice and law and draws up a report for conference debate which includes indications of standards.

5. The report is discussed at a Conference and a decision made to draw up a Convention.

6. The Office produces a draft Convention and consults with member countries.

7. A Draft Convention goes to the following Conference to be discussed, amended and agreed.

Thus, it takes at least four years from an issue being raised to a Convention being produced and, at that point, member nations decide whether to ratify it or not. In the UK the Government would produce a White Paper which sets out the Convention and discusses its status compared with existing UK law and the Government's policy. When these discussions have taken place in Parliament and a decision has been made, the Convention is ratified. The fact that the UK Government has not ratified a particular Convention does not necessarily mean that UK standards are too low. One of the main reasons used for non-ratification has been that the Government feels that existing standards are in line with or even superior to the Convention principles.

The topical Conventions the UK has ratified include:

No.87	Freedom of Association and Protection of the Right to Organise
No.95	Protection of Wages
No.98	Right to Organise and Collective Bargaining
No.151	Labour Relations, Public Services

Once ratified and in force, a Convention can be denounced every 10th year if the Government so wishes. For example, in 1982 the UK Government denounced Convention No. 94, Labour Clauses (Public Contracts) so that it could remove the Fair Wages Resolution.

In reality the ability to enforce compliance with Conventions is through publicity. Governments are obliged to communicate detailed reports to the ILO regularly and copies of these are sent to employers and trade unions in the country concerned for them to comment. Violations could be reported by trade unions to the office. These reports are examined by a committee of experts who could, if they feel there was a breach of a Convention, follow the report up by asking for clarification from the Government concerned or by conducting a formal investigatory visit, e.g. as they did to Poland over the issue of banning the trade union 'Solidarity'. The report of the committee is then published and could be discussed at the Annual Conference and the country concerned censored. There is, however, no ability of the ILO to expel a member nation, they can only use adverse publicity and castigation as a weapon.

(h) Codes of Practice

The use of Codes of Practice has developed since the publication of the Industrial Relations Code of Practice in 1972. The purpose of a Code of Practice is to provide guidelines for the development of good practices in the employment relationship, and their introduction recognises that legislation cannot hope to be totally comprehensive and that there is still a requirement to produce voluntarily-designed procedures which, whilst being suitable for the particular work-place situation, incorporate the desirable philosophies embodied in the statute laws themselves. The general procedure adopted in producing a code is that a draft is supplied and, after representations have been made by interested parties and considered, the final draft is given to the Secretary of State for approval by Parliament, before it becomes effective.

The status of the law of such codes is that, although a failure to observe the provisions in a code is not in itself likely to lead to legal proceedings before industrial tribunals or in the courts, they do have legal significance, since the relevant judicial bodies are obliged to consider in their deliberations the relevant standards required by the code in determining the rights or wrongs of the question at issue.

ACAS, the MSC, the Health and Safety Commission, the Equal Opportunities Commission, the Commission for Racial Equality and the Department of Employment, under direction from the Secretary of State, are authorised to produce Codes of Practice upon a variety of matters.

(i)   The three codes issued by ACAS are on:
    (a)   'Time off for Trade Union Duties and Activities'
    (b)   'Disclosure of Information'
    (c)   'Disciplinary and other Procedures in Employment '

(ii) The Health and Safety Commission has issued a Code of Practice on Safety Representatives and Safety Committees, and a Code of Practice on Noise

(iii) The Department of Employment has also issued two codes:
    (a)   'The Closed Shop'
    (b)   'Picketing'

(iv) The Equal Opportunities Commission & Commission for Racial Equality have each issued a code on Equality of Treatment

(v)   The Manpower Services Commission has issued a Code of Good Practice on the Employment of Disabled People.

2. INSTITUTIONS OF REGULATION

A variety of institutions have been set up to administer the collective and individual employment legislation enacted in recent years. Some of these bodies administer judgements themselves, whereas others attempt to encourage the parties to resolve disputes themselves. These institutions have not totally replaced the role of the civil courts, but they do have a significant role to play in judgements concerning statutory rights, leaving the courts to deal with common law issues and matters which are referred to them by the statutory bodies.

(a) Industrial Tribunals

Industrial Tribunals were originally established by the Industrial Training Act 1964 to determine appeals by employers against levies imposed on them by Industrial Training Boards. Since that time their jurisdiction has been considerably extended to cover almost every individual right which has been given by statute, especially with regard to claims for unfair dismissal and redundancy payments. They have been described by the Court of Appeal as a 'type of industrial jury'.

Tribunals are organised on a regional basis with about 80 different centres in Britain. They are used to provide a cheaper and less complex approach to statutory issues than the courts and their procedures are considerably less formal: neither side needs to be represented by a lawyer and thus the costs of bringing and defending an action are relatively low. Unlike other courts, hearsay evidence can be accepted and other strict rules of evidence can be waived. For example leading questions are allowed.

An Industrial Tribunal consists of a legally qualified chairman, who must have been a solicitor or a barrister for at least seven years, and two lay members drawn from two panels appointed by the Secretary of State for Employment after consultations with such organisations of employers and workers which he considers appropriate, normally, on the worker's side, the TUC and its member unions and, on the employer's side, the CBI and other employers' associations or organisations. One panel consists of workers' representatives and the other of employers' representatives. Both panels are selected to secure a spread of experience of industrial problems across the industrial sectors.

Proof does not need to be absolute when an Industrial Tribunal is considering a case. Tribunals are required to reach their decisions 'having regard to the equity and substantial merits of the case' and taking into account 'the size and administration resources of the undertaking' as the unfair dismissal laws state. Their main power, when finding in favour of an individual complainant, is to award compensation for the individual's losses. They can order reinstatement or re-engagement but (similarly to other courts) they cannot force an employer to take someone back and can only award additional compensation.

Procedure in the Industrial Tribunal is regulated by The Industrial Tribunals (Labour Regulations) Regulations 1974 (Statutory Instrument 1974 No 1386) as amended. Witnesses are normally sworn in and the chairman keeps a detailed rough-hand note of the evidence produced. The proceedings are intended to be relatively informal and a person may be represented by anybody that he wishes. A considerable number of applicants are represented by lay or full time officials of trade unions. In general, legal aid is not available if an individual prefers legal representation and costs as such are not awarded by a tribunal in favour of the 'winner', but the tribunals have the power to award costs if one party has acted 'frivolously or vexatiously'. Tribunal hearings are generally held in public and the press may attend.

Tribunals are under no obligation to adhere to the decisions of other tribunals, although they must follow the definitions of what the law means laid down by superior courts.

Appeals against Industrial Tribunal decisions are made to the Employment Appeal Tribunal (EAT) in the first instance and beyond the EAT to the Court of Appeal, and eventually, where appropriate, to the House of Lords. Appeals to the EAT, however, in the majority of cases, can only be made on points of law, not fact. The only cases where appeals to the EAT can be made on points of fact are against the decision of an Industrial Tribunal to give, or refuse, a declaration in a case of unreasonable exclusion or expulsion from a union. Even in such cases, further appeals to higher levels can only be on points of law. The EAT will only overturn tribunal decisions if their conclusions were perverse; if the tribunal misdirected itself in law, or misunderstood or misapplied the law; or where the tribunal exercised its discretionary powers, e.g. in assessment of compensation, based on the wrong principles.

An important feature relating to many of the individual claims to a tribunal is that there are attemps at pre-hearing conciliation, which is carried out by conciliation officers of the Advisory Conciliation and Arbitration Service (ACAS), who will approach both parties to try and encourage them to reach a settlement. Copies of all relevant documents, including the tribunal application form (ITI) which states the reasons for bringing the claim, and the employers' 'Notice of Appearance', which states the grounds on which the employer is contesting the claim, are sent to the ACAS conciliation officer. Any information given to the conciliation officer, when he discusses the case with the parties concerned, is confidential so that discussions are not prejudiced by risk of disclosure at the later tribunal. Thus the conciliation and judgement stages are kept firmly separate. The evidence given at the pre-hearing can, however, be admissable if the party who gave the information gives permission for its disclosure.

The conciliation officer also possesses one very important power. Cases which have been initiated cannot be withdrawn, unless the applicant formally withdraws it or agrees to a settlement of the pre-conciliation stage. No agreement which precludes a person from pursuing his claim at an Industrial Tribunal can be made by statute, except where a conciliation officer formally records an agreement made by the parties. The Court of Appeal has held that where the conciliation officer has formally recorded the terms of an agreement between the parties on an ACAS form (COT 3) and the parties have signed it, the employee is prevented from making any further complaint. In 1984, 42 per cent of cases which were initiated were settled with help from the conciliation officer and an additional 24 per cent were withdrawn (ACAS Report 1984).

It is important that both parties should take any documents to the tribunal hearings which might assist the decision making process. These documents will vary according to the type of case being considered, but are likely to include:

—   the contract of employment or any other documents which relate to the terms of employment;
—   details of pay, e.g. pay statements or wages records, in both the former and present employment;
—   documents relating to other benefits, including pensions, travelling expenses, subsidised housing, etc;
—   documents relating to statements made by either party, relevant letters etc.

The tribunal will, in many cases, announce its decision and the reason on which it is based at the close of the hearing but, in some cases, the decision and the reasons may be given later. In every case both parties will be sent a document stating the decision and the justification for it. Payment of any compensation or award will be made directly by the employer or trade union to the individual who is to be the recipient of the award.

The time limit for complaints to an Industrial Tribunal is 3 months for most matters, but is 6 months in claims of unfair exclusion or expulsion from a trade union.

Jurisdiction of Industrial Tribunals includes:

(a)   Complaints of unfair dismissal.
(b)   Applications for redundancy payments or rebate.
(c)   References regarding written terms and conditions of employment.
(d)   References regarding time off with pay for safety representatives.
(e)   References regarding time off with pay for trade union duties of officials.
(f)   References for time off for trade union activities.

131

(g) Complaints regarding the itemised pay statement.

(h) Complaints regarding guarantee payments.

(i) Complaints regarding suspension from work on medical grounds.

(j) Complaints regarding trade union membership.

(k) Complaints regarding maternity pay and maternity leave.

(l) Complaints under the Race Relations Act 1976.

(m) Complaints under the Equal Pay Act 1970.

(n) Complaints under the Sex Discrimination Act 1975.

(o) Complaints regarding the right to be paid by the Secretary of State debts owed by an insolvent employee.

(p) Complaints by a recognised independent trade union that it was not consulted by the employer about proposed redundancies.

(q) Complaints that a protective award ordered by an Industrial Tribunal has not been paid.

(r) Complaints that reasonable time off was not given in a redundancy situation.

(s) Complaints regarding action short of dismissal taken by an employer.

(t) Complaints regarding the lack of a written statement given upon dismissal.

(u) References regarding time off for public duties.

(v) Complaints of unreasonable expulsion or exclusion from a trade union.

(w) Appeals against 'improvement' and 'prohibition' notices issued under the Health and Safety at Work Act 1974.

(x) Complaints against non-discrimination notices issued under the Race Relations Act 1976 and Sex Discrimination Act 1975.

(b) Employment Appeal Tribunal

This was established in 1975. Its function is to hear appeals from the Industrial Tribunals and some appeals from the decisions on trade union independence from the certification officer. Appeals are made to the EAT on a point of law only, except in those cases where appeals are made against the findings of the certification officer and disputes over union membership under the provisions of the Employment Act 1980, where consideration can also be made on factual issues.

It consists of 7 judges drawn from the High Court and the Court of Appeal one of whom is appointed as President. It also has lay members representing both sides of industry. At each case heard there will be a judge and normally two lay members sitting. It is thus paradoxical that a court which hears appeals on points of law should contain non-legally trained members who are theoretically in the position of being able to outvote the chairman. Yet, it is argued, that their role is crucial because of their first hand knowledge of Industrial Relations matters. Most decisions are unanimous. At its hearings the EAT allows lay representation of the parties making representations to it and its deliberations are therefore informal, as compared to the higher courts. The legal aid system extends to the EAT. It has all the powers of the High Court over such matters as requiring the attendance of witnesses, discovery of documents and punishing people for contempt of court. An appeal from the EAT on a question of law, in all cases, goes to the Court of Appeal and from there to the House of Lords. The EAT is thus bound by the decisions of those higher bodies.

The majority of appeals are concerned with cases of unfair dismissal; these constituted over 80% of all appeals heard from 1976 to December 1985, and this trend has continued. The EAT laid down the guidelines of good Industrial Relations practice in the consideration of whether or not to dismiss an employee in *British Home Stores v Burchell* in 1980 — the employer must have a genuine belief in the guilt of the employee, he must have reasonable grounds for that belief and, before forming that decision, he must have made reasonable investigation.

(c) Court of Appeal

The Court of Appeal is split into two divisions (1) the Civil Division and (2) the Criminal Division. The Civil Division, which concerns us, consists of the Master of the Rolls, who is the President, and the Lord Justices of Appeal. It handles appeals on questions of legal interpretation of statutes from the judgements of the EAT in cases of employment legislation and common law and from judgements of the certification officer.

(d) House of Lords

The House of Lords is the highest court of appeal in the land and produces the final definitive interpretation of statutory legislation and common law duties and responsibilities, although appeals can be made to the European Court on some issues.

(e) Advisory Conciliation and Arbitration Service (ACAS)

This organisation was established in 1974 and given a statutory identity in the Employment Protection Act of 1975. It is run by a tripartite council composed of three nominees of the TUC; three nominees of the CBI; three independent persons; and a full time chairman. ACAS employs staff who are trained and have experience in industrial relations and employment matters generally. It is independent of Government but has to produce an annual report to the Secretary of State for Employment on its activities. It exercises a comprehensive range of functions in relation to both individual and collective employee relations. It provides the service of conciliation in claims brought by individuals before

Industrial Tribunals. It also provides a variety of facilities in collective relationships for conciliation, mediation, arbitration and inquiry which are designed to encourage the voluntary settlement of labour disputes.

(i) *Conciliation:* this is a process whereby a third party tries to help the parties in dispute reach agreement. The conciliator attempts to discover points of agreement between the parties and tries to discover the area of disagreement. By bringing a fresh mind he attempts to encourage the parties to reach an agreement themselves, either through separate or, in some cases, joint discussion.

(ii) *Arbitration:* this occurs when the parties in dispute recognise that their differences are so great that they need a third party to examine the evidence and provide them with a solution which they will normally agree to accept.

(iii) *Mediation:* this process is somewhere between conciliation and arbitration. In mediation the third party tends to be more prescriptive than in conciliation but, although he provides a settlement formula, the parties are encouraged to devise the final settlement themselves. It is not commonly used in the UK.

(iv) *Inquiry:* this is an attempt by third parties to establish the facts about a dispute which has occurred; to analyse the circumstances that have led to it; and to make a report which will lead to a settlement if one has not already been found or, at least, to provide sufficient data to prevent such a disagreement recurring.

ACAS has been given the general duty of 'promoting the improvement of Industrial Relations and in particular of encouraging the extension of collective bargaining and the development and, where necessary, reform of collective bargaining machinery.' (Section 1, Employment Protection Act 1975).

To this end it offers advice to both employers and trade unions on how to improve Industrial Relations and advice to individuals with employment-orientated questions. Finally, it has the task of issuing Codes of Practice when these are demanded.

(f) Central Arbitration Committee (CAC)

The Central Arbitration Committee, established in 1975, is a permanent body of arbitration which, although financed by the Government, is wholly independent from Government influence. The CAC, although independent also of ACAS, is served by ACAS staff. The committee consists of a chairman and members appointed by the Secretary of State for Employment after consultation with ACAS. The chairman is a lawyer and the members have academic or practical experience of Industrial Relations. The committee has a voluntary jurisdiction to arbitrate in cases referred to it by ACAS, but it also has a number of special jurisdictions under statute and its services may be invoked unilaterally by one party to a dispute. These jurisdictions generally concern collective disputes and include disputes in respect of disclosure of information by employers; and sex discrimination in collective agreements and wages structures, under the Equal Pay Act section 3.

The committee is empowered to regulate its own procedures, but it has no power to compel the attendance of witnesses, to take evidence under oath, or to order the discovery of documents. The general practice is that the parties present written evidence to the committee in advance of hearings which can be clarified at the hearing itself. The decisions of the CAC are published.

(g) Certification Officer (CO)

The Certification Officer is an independent statutory officer appointed in 1975 by the Employment Protection Act. A number of the functions now carried out by the CO were previously exercised by the Registrar of Friendly Societies. His main functions relate to the internal affairs of trade unions and employers' associations. His is the sole jurisdiction to determine whether a trade union is entitled to a certificate of independence. Only an 'independent trade union', as defined in the Employment Protection Act 1975, has the opportunity to avail itself of many of the statutory rights, e.g. to enter into union membership agreements, to demand information prior to redundancies and for collective bargaining purposes. The CO also maintains the current list of trade unions and employers' associations; receives financial returns from trade unions and employers' associations; hears complaints about the operation of trade unions' political funds and complaints regarding trade union amalgamations under the Trade Union (Amalgamations) Act 1964. Appeals about the decision of the CO can be made in the first instance to the EAT.

(h) The Equal Opportunities Commission (EOC)

The Equal Opportunities Commission was established by the Sex Discrimination Act 1975. It is independent of the Government but is funded by it. It consists of a number of commissioners appointed by the Home Secretary.

The general duties of the EOC are:- to work towards the elimination of discrimination; to promote equality of opportunity between men and women; and to keep under review the Equal Pay Act 1970 and the Sex Discrimination Act 1975. In relation to these duties, its powers are to promote research and general awareness of the advantages of equal opportunity and to improve the social climate which reduces the remaining barriers to foster equal opportunity. The main powers of the EOC in enforcing the anti-discrimination laws include the right to carry out investigations (in so doing it may require the production of documents and the giving of evidence). If, as a result of that investigation, the commission is satisfied that there has been a breach of the law, it may issue a 'non-discrimination notice' ordering the party to desist. Employers have the right of appeal against such notices to an Industrial Tribunal. This notice is retained on a register so that, if the employer continues to discriminate, the EOC may apply for an injunction against the offender in a County Court, providing an Industrial Tribunal is satisfied that the act is unlawful. The commission is also empowered to give advice on individual problems and legal assistance for representation at Industrial Tribunals or court proceedings. In most cases the Commission succeeds with informal discussions and threats of using its statutory powers. In 1985 it issued a Code of Practice on Equality of Treatment.

(i) Commission for Racial Equality (CRE)

The CRE was established by the Race Relations Act of 1976 and replaced the former Race Relations Board and Community Relations Commission. The statutory duties and powers of the CRE are identical to those of the Equal Opportunities Commission however, over its life-span, so far it has initiated more formal investigations to try to stamp out discrimination in the workplace. In 1985 it too issued a Code of Practice on Equality of Treatment.

(j) Health and Safety Commission

The Health and Safety Commission was established by the Health and Safety at Work etc. Act of 1974. It consists of a full-time independent chairman and nine part-time commissioners, which comprise three TUC nominated members, three CBI nominated members, two from the local authorities and an independent member. It is responsible to the Secretary of State for employment and must follow directions from him. The Commission has taken over responsibilities for most occupational safety and health matters. It has a number of duties which include the following:

— To assist and encourage people to further the general purposes of the Act;

— to make arrangements for, and encourage research into, occupational health and safety;

— to promote training and information connected with occupational health and safety matters;

— to act as an information and advisory service;

— to investigate needs and submit proposals for specific regulations under the HASAW etc. Act; and

— to draw up and issue Codes of Practice with the approval of the Secretary of State.

The Commission, in line with these duties, has considerable powers to direct investigations and inquiries, to appoint staff and to publish information. Although control of broad national policy is the function of the Commission, the enforcement and administration of safety standards is the job of the Health and Safety Executive.

In its *Plan of Work 1985/6 and Onwards,* the Commission outlines a number of conditions with which it wishes firms to comply to satisfy the Health and Safety Executive that they are trying to do all possible to control risks in the working environment and thus reduce the need for Health and Safety Executive monitoring, thereby making better use of inspectors.

a) the employer has a comprehensive policy on health and safety;
b) the organisational arrangements are acceptable and management is competent;
c) the appropriate resources are available for health and safety;
d) there is securely established in-house health and safety experience;
e) there is active involvement of trade unions in the health and safety system, positive commitment of employees and relevant institutions;
f) the organisation has a satisfactory recent record in relation to accidents and ill health;
g) the arrangements are acceptable to both the employer and employee representatives.

(k) Health and Safety Executive

This body was created by the Health and Safety at Work etc. Act 1974 and consists of a director and two deputies, in addition to the staff it controls. It is answerable to the Health and Safety Commission. It is an amalgamation of the independent inspectorates which existed under previous legislation, e.g. the Factories Inspectorate, the Explosives Inspectorate and the Mines and Quarries Inspectorate. The inspectors appointed by the executive have powers to enforce the safety legislation and the required standards of health and safety at work. They are entitled to enter premises at any time of the day and night to ensure that regulations are being adhered to. They also have powers to remove any substances for investigation. The main elements of enforcement open to the inspectorate are 'improvement' and 'prohibition' notices which can be served where inspectors consider the law has been broken or there is a danger to health or safety. Employers may appeal against these notices to an Industrial Tribunal. Non compliance with the notices can lead to prosecution in the civil courts and the imposition of fines or more extreme sentences. The executive is responsible for issuing Codes of Practice under the HASAWA.

3. FUNDAMENTAL LEGAL CONCEPTS

(a) Contract

The Contract of Employment is of fundamental importance in the employer/employee relationship. It is important to outline the requirements of a valid contract. Contracts are agreements with legal consequences and they are in essence voluntary transactions which happen because the parties choose to enter into them. Contracts can be made informally and are as valid when made by word-of-mouth as they are when written. It is presumed that contracts are made by parties of equal bargaining power, free to decide on the terms of their agreement — although this may not be exactly the case in the employment contract. For the formation of a valid contract, the following elements must be present:

1. *Agreement:* this is demonstrated by offer and acceptance. The agreement must be free from any stipulations which render it conditional, e.g. if an individual accepts a job offer but makes it conditional on the ability to find suitable accommodation or an employer offers a job conditionally on references being acceptable.

2. *Consideration:* this can be seen as the economic value of the relationship or the promise of a certain level of remuneration in return for a particular level of work.

3. *Intention to create legal relations:* the parties to the contract must have expressly or implicitly intended that their contract should be legally binding. This is usually presumed when a contract of employment is considered.

4. *Contractual capacity in each of the parties:* a human being generally has the capacity to enter into any contract he wants. He loses this full capacity only if he is under the influence of drink or drugs or he suffers from certain types of mental illness. Capacity will exist in the employment contract as long as the party agreeing to the contract on behalf of the employers is authorised to make that contract. A minor (i.e. a person under the age of 18) is bound by the contract if the contract as a whole is considered substantially to his benefit.

5. *No mitigating factors such as duress, undue influence, misrepresentation, mistake or illegality:* both parties to the agreement must freely consent to the terms of the contract and the proposed contract must be legal in its object and in the manner in which it is performed, e.g. a contract will be automaticaly invalid if the method of payment used is done with the intention of defrauding the tax authorities.

138

(b) Contract of service v contract for services

A person employed by an organisation can either be employed under a contract *of* services, i.e. as an employee, or a contract *for* services, i.e. as an independent contractor. It is an important distinction to make, because only those employed under a contract of service are granted the statutory legal rights of protection against unfair dismissal; rights to redundancy payments; rights to minimum periods of notice; a right to a written statement of terms and conditions of employment; and the right to pursue trade union activities etc. It is important also in considering entitlement to various State benefits, for only employees are able to claim sickness and unemployment benefit.

A number of cases have helped to clarify the differences between the two relationships of employee and independent contractor and three main tests have been used by the courts in examining relationships:

(i) *The control test:* the initial test derived by the courts was called the 'control test'. This asks whether the person alleged to be the employer, both in respect of the work done, i.e. what to do, and as regards the method or manner of performance of that work. If the employer can control these things, then the contract was said to be a contract of service, if not the individual was an independent contractor. The test was not completely satisfactory as in the modern employment relationship in large-scale organisations people like doctors, nurses and lawyers could be employed but their work was not subject to the same level of control because of their individual expertise. To try to cope with this problem, the courts developed the second test.

(ii) *The organisation or integration test:* this test was used to explain the professional's employment within organisations, e.g. doctors and nurses, and asks whether the individual is integrated into the organisation. Thus, if a person is employed as part of the business and the work done is an integral part of the business, then he can be considered to be an employee, and, if not, he is an independent contractor. Even this test was not comprehensive enough to decide all cases, and a third was developed.

(iii) *The multiple or economic reality test:* this is the most comprehensive test to date and takes into account both of the previous tests considering also the other circumstances of the relationship between the parties. It includes factors like control and the right to command; the right of selection and dismissal; whether the work was done as an integral part of the business; whether the worker was economically independent; or whether the other terms of the contract were consistent with a contract of employment. If a group of factors indicate that the relationship is one of a contract of service, then the individual can be considered to be an employee.

139

(c) Dismissal

This means that the employee has had his contract of employment terminated by an employer with or without notice. It can also refer to the non-renewal of a fixed term contract and it also applies in a situation where, because of the employer's conduct, the employee himself terminates the contract, with or without notice (constructive dismissal under the EP(C)A 1978). It also applies where a female employee is not permitted to return to work after maternity when she has fulfilled her obligations in requesting to return.

(d) Unfair dismissal

This was introduced as a concept in 1971 (Industrial Relations Act) and has been retained in subsequent legislation. Its true meaning was best described by Justice Phillips in *W Devis and Sons Ltd v Atkins* (1976) Industrial Cases Reports, 196, when he stated—

> "It is important to note, I think, that the expression 'unfair dismissal' is in no sense a commonsense expression capable of being understood by the man in the street, which at first sight one would think it is. In fact, under the Act, it is narrowly and, to some extent, arbitrarily defined. And so the concept of unfair dismissal is not really a commonsense concept; it is a form of words which could be translated as being equivalent to dismissal 'contrary to the Statute' and to which the label 'unfair dismissal' has been given."

(e) Torts

The law of economic torts is concerned with 'wrongs'. They are deeds which result in civil actions being brought by the person harmed. The most common torts in Industrial Relations are the torts of inducing breach of contract, intimidation, conspiracy and interference, trespass and public and private nuisance.

(f) Express terms

The worker and his employer may have openly stated the terms which comprise the contract of employment, e.g. relating to pay, hours of work, holidays and sick pay.

(g) Implied terms

Where the parties do not cover a particular contingency, trade usage and practice may give rise to the implication of terms. An important source of such terms are collective agreements.

(h) Trade unions

The definition of a trade union is laid down in the Trade Union and Labour Relations Act 1974 as follows:

"...'trade union' means an organisation...which either

(a) consists wholly or mainly of workers of one or more descriptions and is an organisation whose principal purposes include the regulation of relationships between workers... and employers or employers' associations, or

(b) consists wholly or mainly of

(1) constituent or affiliated organisations which fulfil the conditions specified above... or

(2) representatives of such... organisations.''

(i) Independent trade union

This is defined in TULRA 1974 as

'a trade union which

(a) is not under the domination or control of any employer... and

(b) is not liable to interference by an employer...'

(j) Union membership agreement or closed shop

Defined in TULRA 1974, as amended in 1976, as:

'...an agreement or arrangement which:

(i) is made by or on behalf of... one or more independent trade unions and one or more employers or employers' associations;

(ii) related to employees of an identifiable class; and

(iii) has the effect in practice of requiring the employees for the time being... to be or become a member of the union or one of the unions which... are parties to the agreement or arrangement.'

(k) Definition of a trade dispute

The basic definition is laid down in the Trade Union and Labour Relations Act 1974, Section 29, as amended by the Employment Act 1982

'a dispute between workers and their employer which is concerned wholly or mainly with one or more of the following...

(a) issues and conditions of employment, or the physical conditions in which any workers are required to work;

(b) engagement or non-engagement or termination, or suspension of employment or the duties of employment, of one or more workers;

(c) association of work...;

(d) matters of discipline;

(e) the membership and non-membership of a trade union...;

(f) facilities for officials of trade unions; and

(g) machinery for negotiation or consultation, and other procedures,... including the recognition by employers to employers' associations of the right of a trade union to represent workers...'

141

(l) Secondary action

This is defined in the Employment Act 1980 as a situation where a person:

'(a) induces another to break a contract of employment or interferes or induces another to interfere with its performance,

   or

(b) threatens that a contract of employment under which he or another is employed will be broken or its performance interfered with, or that he will induce another to break a contract of employment or interfere with its performance,

if the employer under the contract of employment is not a party to the trade dispute.'

Chapter 8
Key Aspects of Current Legislation

Statutory framework within which management operates

The management of the human resource is an increasingly specialised activity — over the last thirty years successive Governments have passed statutes which influence the relationships between employers and employees. Whilst some would argue that this legislation has made the business of hiring, controlling and firing employees increasingly difficult, it would be more realistic to say that, whilst on the surface the legislation is a hindrance, it does no more than provide a framework for employment that emphasises the fairness and equity of treatment which all good managers would adopt if they operated on the principle — 'do not treat your subordinates any differently from the way you yourself would expect to be treated by your superiors.' If you remember this, 99% of the time you will not fall foul of the legislation.

The extent of the legal framework which relates to employment, however, is a specialist study in itself. In this text we only have time and space to run over the major areas and, for more detailed examination, you will have to examine some of the specialist texts which are referenced at the end of this book.

The major statutes

The primary legislation of which you should have a working knowledge, can be listed as follows, in approximate date order:
1. Disabled Persons (Employment) Acts 1944-1958
2. Factories Act 1961
3. Offices Shops and Railway Premises Act 1963
4. Employer's Liability (Compulsory Insurance) Act 1969
5. Equal Pay Act 1970
6. Fire Precautions Act 1971
7. Rehabilitation of Offenders Act 1974
8. Health and Safety at Work etc. Act 1974
9. Trade Union and Labour Relations Act 1974 and 1976
10. Employment Protection Act 1975
11. Sex Discrimination Act 1975
12. Race Relations Act 1976
13. Employment Protection (Consolidation) Act 1978
14. Employment Act 1980
15. Transfer of Undertakings (Protection of Employment) Regulations 1981

16. Employment Act 1982
17. Trade Union Act 1984
18. Data Protection Act 1984

1. DISABLED PERSONS (EMPLOYMENT) ACTS 1944-58

This is one of the oldest pieces of anti-discrimination legislation. The objective of the Act was to help disabled people to find work on their own account and to secure better employment. The Act stipulates that an employer with more than 20 employees must allot at least 3% of posts to registered disabled workers. It also specifies that some jobs, such as lift and car park attendants, should be reserved for the disabled. Records must be maintained of the numbers employed, their names, and their disablement number.

The definition of a disabled person given in the Act is:

'a person who on account of disease, injury or congenital deformity is substantially handicapped in obtaining or keeping employment or in undertaking work on his own account, of a kind, which apart from that disease, injury or deformity, should be suited to his experience, age and qualifications.'

The legislation confers no rights as such on individuals; it is only the disabled, as a group of people, who are protected. The sanction for failing to fulfil the quota where an exemption certificate does not lift the obligation, is prosecution, but cases are very rare and the Act is difficult to enforce. If an employer is not fulfilling his quota, he does not have to discharge 'fit' people but, when a vacancy does occur, he should engage a disabled person. Records must be kept of people employed under permits (permits are issued to enable employers to fill current vacancies if there are no suitable disabled people available.

In November 1984 the Manpower Services Commission published its 'Code of Good Practice on the Employment of Disabled People' which makes suggestions to ensure that all disabled people receive their proper share of the available employment opportunities. The code is purely a guidance document and cannot be used in evidence before an Industrial Tribunal. Therefore, the code's approach is encouragement and it provides employers with 'a readily available means of determining how best to put their intentions into practice'. It applies to all disabled people, not only those who are registered.

The code is laid out in two parts. The first part is aimed at those managers responsible for policy divisions and recommends specific policy objectives for employing disabled people. Legislation in the form of 'The Companies (Directors' Report) (Employment of Disabled Persons) Regulations' (1980) has placed a duty on all companies employing more than 250 people to state in their Directors' Report company policy on the employment of the disabled. The statement should include policy on:

— how to give full and fair consideration to the disabled who apply for jobs, taking into account their individual aptitudes and abilities;

— how to continue the employment of employees who become disabled while working for the company, and what training arrangements could be made for them;

— generally, how to develop the training, career, development and promotion possibilities of the disabled.

The second part of the code is aimed at those responsible for putting the organisation's policy into practice and covers the following areas.

● The legal requirements regarding the employment of the disabled
● what the different characteristics of disabled people mean to employers
● an examination of employers' concerns in the recruitment of the disabled
● good practice for recruitment and selection
● good practice in relation to training and promotion treatment
● options for employees who become disabled
● the role of employer and employee representatives on practices and procedures regarding the disabled
● how to coordinate policy
● sources of financial and other help, information and advice on the employment of disabled people

2. FACTORIES ACT 1961

The Factories Act 1961 covers health, safety and welfare; the hours of work of women and young persons; and certain miscellaneous provisions.

(a) Health

(i) Temperature — at least $16^{o}C$ after one hour; a thermometer must be provided and maintained in a workroom where work is done sitting and does not involve serious physical effort. No maximum temperature.

(ii) Cleanliness — dirt and refuse removed daily; weekly cleaning of floors; wash and whitewash walls every fourteen months; painting every seven years.

(iii) Ventilation — fresh air must circulate; workers must be protected from dirt and fumes.

(iv) Overcrowding — 400 cu ft per person — a notice specifying the number of persons that may be employed in a workroom must be fixed in that room unless the factory inspector of the district otherwise rules — not counting any space above 14 feet high.

145

(b) Safety

(i) Accidents — loss of life or more than three days off must be reported to the District Inspector of Factories and noted in the General Register.

(ii) Industrial Disease — any case of industrial disease must be notified to the Factory Inspectorate.

(iii) Fencing — (or guards) to protect against moving machinery, pits or vessels containing dangerous liquids. How safe is safe? The duty to fence is absolute. One cannot use the words, 'as well as possible, conducive with use': if guarding moving parts means the machine cannot be used commercially, that is unfortunate.

(iv) Drainage — all floors liable to be wet must be efficiently drained.

(v) Inspection — of joists, lifts, chains, ropes or lifting tackle — every six months;
— of cranes every fourteen months;
— of fire alarms every three months.

(c) Welfare

Employers must provide:
— drinking water;
— washing facilities, including soap and towels;
— accommodation for outdoor clothes;
— first-aid boxes — plus 1 box for every 150 employees. Where there are more than 50 employees, the box must be in the charge of someone experienced in first-aid; (see also section on Health & Safety (first-aid) Regulations 1981.
— seating must be provided, where necessary or practicable.

(d) Employment of Women and Young Persons

(i) No woman or young person (i.e. under 18) may clean any part of a machine while it is in motion;

(ii) A young person must be instructed in the dangers of a machine before that person is allowed to use it;

(iii) Hours of work:
— Women and young persons — max. 48 hours per week;
— No woman or young person may work more than 9 hours in any day
— Young persons (16-18 years of age) must not work more than 100 hours overtime per annum or work overtime in more than 25 weeks per annum.

146

— Young persons (16-18 years of age) and women must not work nightshift without permission.

(iv) Female young persons may not be employed in those parts of a factory in which the following processes are carried out:
- melting or blowing glass — other than lamp blown glass;
- annealing glass, other than plate or sheet glass;
- evaporating brine in open pans or the storing of salt.

(v) Women and young persons may not be employed in the following occupations:
- in certain processes involving the use of lead or zinc;
- in mixing or pasting in connection with the manufacture and repair of electric accumulators;
- in the cleaning of workrooms in which the above processes are carried out.

(e) General

(i) The Inspectorate have the power to inspect every part of the factory by day and by night. They may ask for registers and certificates, question any person in the factory and may take samples for analysis.

(ii) Notices to be posted:

(a) Abstract of the Factories Act;

(b) Abstract of any statutory regulations made by the Factories Act;

(c) Notice in each workroom showing the maximum numbers permitted to work in that room (unless exemption is granted);

(d) Notice of the name of the person in charge of the First-aid Box;

(e) Notice of the addresses of local Inspector of Factories and the Company Doctor;

(f) Notice showing the hours of work and prescribed meal-times of women and young persons (under the age of 18);

(g) Notice specifying the clock, if any, by which the hours of (f) are to be prescribed;

(h) Cautionary placards under regulations of certain special processes;

(i) Placards on recommended treatment of electric shock, if voltage above 125 AC or 250 DC;

(j) Notice in sanitary conveniences used by persons handling food, requesting them to wash their hands (Food Hygiene Regulations 1960).

(iii) A General Register must be kept with particulars of:
- (a) Young persons employed;
- (b) Washing, whitewashing and painting;
- (c) Every accident and case of industrial disease reported to the Inspectorate;
- (d) Any exception to the clauses of the Act availed of by the employer;
- (e) Inspection of hoists and lifts etc.

3. OFFICES, SHOPS & RAILWAYS PREMISES ACT 1963

This Act mirrors the provisions of the Factories Act.

— all furniture, furnishing and fittings shall be kept in a clean state;
— there must be no overcrowding — each person in a room shall have at least 40 square ft of floor space (NB — does not apply in rooms to which members of the public have access);
— temperature: at least $16^{o}C$ (after 1 hour) and a thermometer must be available and conspicuously displayed;
— sufficient ventilation for every room;
— adequate lighting;
— washing facilities — hot and cold running water, soap and towels;
— drinking water;
— toilet facilities for each sex;
— accommodation for outside clothes;
— if employees in shops eat their meals on the premises, suitable facilities must be provided;
— fire alarm and means of escape;
— floors, passages and stairs must be properly maintained;
— first-aid box and, where more than 150 employees at any one time, more than one box;
— seating facilities must be provided.

4. EMPLOYERS' LIABILITY (COMPULSORY INSURANCE) ACT 1969

This act aims to prevent an employee, who is owed compensation for injuries he has suffered while at work, being unable to claim the compensation due to the insolvency of his employer. Every employer must insure against liability for bodily injury or disease sustained by an employee in the course of his employment — failure to do so could lead to a £500 fine. Copies of the insurance contract must be displayed — failure to do so can lead to a fine of up to £200. Copies must also be sent to the Health & Safety Executive who enforce the Act. An offence is committed by any responsible person in the organisation who consents to, or connives at, violating the Act's provisions.

5. EQUAL PAY ACT 1970.
As amended by the Equal Pay (Amendment) Regulations 1983 (S.1. 1983 No 1794)

The object of the Act is the elimination of discrimination on grounds of sex (i.e. both for men and for women) in regard to pay and terms and conditions of employment. The Act came into effect in December 1975 and was amended by the Regulations in 1983 due to a judgement against the UK in the European Court of Justice in 1982 under the EEC 1975 Equal Pay Directive.

(a) *Section 1* provides for equal treatment for men and women where they are engaged in the same or broadly similar work, or where a woman's job has been rated as equivalent to a man's job, e.g. through job evaluation, although the nature of the job is different; or where the work is considered to be of equal value to that of a man or woman even though the work might be completely different. The comparisons used can be, for example, effort, skill and decision making. Industrial Tribunals may call on an 'independent expert' appointed by ACAS to determine the equality of value of work.

(b) *Section 2* places the onus of proof on the employer to show, in cases of dispute, that the differences in the terms and conditions of employment between the woman claiming equal treatment with a man is genuinely due to material difference between her case and his.

(c) *Section 3* refers to collective agreements; if these contain discriminatory clauses, they may be reported to the ACAS.

(d) The woman may draw comparisons with men or with men's jobs only where the men in question are employed by her employer or by an associate employer. However, comparisons may be drawn with men at another establishment, if the terms and conditions of employment are *common* to the two establishments for men and for women.

(e) Exceptions
— Hours of work of women under the 1961 Factories Act are retained.
— The Act does not require the equal treatment of men and women, to the extent that women may enjoy special terms and conditions of employment in connection with the birth or expected birth of a child.
— Equal treatment is not required as regards terms and conditions 'related to retirement, marriage or death'.

149

Where a woman feels that the Act is not being complied with, she can complain to an Industrial Tribunal.

6. FIRE PRECAUTIONS ACT 1971

This Act governs fire safety in all places of work. Fire safety is now supervised by the fire authorities who control the issue of fire certificates. It is an offence to put premises to use as a place of work without a fire certificate, if Regulations have been passed bringing these premises into the Act. Fines can be up to £400 and up to two years' imprisonment.

(a) Premises affected

The following premises are covered by this Act:
— factories, offices, shops
— railway premises.

It is an offence to put premises to a use for which no certificate exists or to contravene the requirements of fire certificates.

(b) Exemptions

For small factories, offices, shops etc. where:
— less than 20 people are employed (unless part of a large complex of units which employ in all 20 +);
— less than 10 people work above ground floor level (unless part of a larger complex).

If factory, office, shop or railway premises are outside the main Act's provisions, they will still have to comply with other regulations laying down minimum fire precautions, even though no fire certificate is required (under Fire Precautions Non-certified Factory, Office, etc. Regulations 1976 SI No. 2010). These are:

(a) Doors from the building, or from any room where more than 10 people are employed, must open outwards.

(b) Fire escape doors and windows must be clearly marked and must be easily opened, and passageways kept clear.

(c) Fire fighting equipment must be readily available for use.

(c) Certificates

Existing certificates under Factories Act or Offices, Shops and Railway Premises Act continue in force and are treated as issued under the 1971 Act. Applications for new fire certificates are made to the fire authority.

This will involve giving details of the use of the premises, together with a plan, following which the fire authority will inspect to see if the fire precautions are as good as circumstances reasonably require.

The certificate will specify:

— the use of the premises which it covers;
— means of escape;
— ways by which the means of escape should be kept available;
— fire fighting equipment;
— fire alarm systems;
— other requirements, where deemed necessary.

Penalties, for not having an appropriate certificate or contravening fire certificates, are up to £400 fine and/or two years' imprisonment. Any company director, manager or secretary will also face these penalties, if the offence is done with their consent or connivance.

(d)   Enforcement

Fire authorities appoint inspectors who, in enforcing the Act, have the power to:

— enter and inspect premises;
— make necessary enquiries;
— require production of a fire certificate.

(e)   Special premises

Special premises, where processes and the use of certain chemical compounds have a particularly high level of fire risk, are looked after by the Health and Safety Executive who supervise them and issue fire certificates under the Fire Certificate (Special Premises) Regulations 1976 (SI 1976 No. 2003).

7.   REHABILITATION OF OFFENDERS ACT 1974

The purpose of this Act is to allow offenders, who have not been reconvicted of any offence for a period of time, to apply for jobs and take up job offers without the embarrassment of having to admit to past convictions. Thus, after a period of time from the date of conviction, providing another serious offence is not committed, the conviction can be counted as 'spent' and, except in certain, specified cases, the individual cannot be forced to disclose that conviction, nor can it be used to dismiss the employee. Some sentences never become spent — life sentences of imprisonment, sentences of preventative detention and prison sentences of more than 30 months.

Exempted occupations and professions

Persons employed or seeking employment in any of the following categories are not at liberty to conceal details of spent convictions under Statutory Instrument 1975 No. 1023, the Rehabilitation of Offenders Act 1974 (Exceptions) Order:

— registered teacher (in Scotland)
— medical practitioner
— barrister, advocate, solicitor
— chartered accountant
— certified accountant
— dentist, dental hygienist, dental auxiliary
— veterinary surgeon
— nurse, midwife
— opthalmic optician, dispensing optician
— pharmaceutical chemist
— any profession to which the Professions Supplementary to Medicine Act 1960 applies
— certain judicial, local authority and education posts.

8. HEALTH & SAFETY AT WORK, etc. ACT 1974

Introduction

Employers' duties under existing legislation, e.g. Factories Act 1961, Offices, Shops and Railway Premises Act 1963 etc. will continue for the time being. The aim of the 1974 legislation is to try to rationalise the position regarding safety and health at work.

The most important aspects occur in the first 26 sections. The guiding principle of the Act is *involvement*. The intention is to alter the emphasis of law from compensation after injury (as previously) to one of enforcement of acceptable standards, by mutual agreement.

Prior to the Act, legislation was piecemeal. Enforcement machinery differed and also the defences which were available against an ultimate criminal sanction. One of the reasons for the generality of the legislation in 1974 was the fact that the more narrowly-defined a legal duty, the more narrowly that duty will operate, and the more opportunity there will be for legal loopholes. Excessive reliance on legal technicalities is the antithesis of true safety.

(a) Purposes of 1974 Act

1. Covers the whole working environment, without the need to differentiate between different premises.

2. Produces generalised definitions of those duties of the widest possible scope; details will be filled in by regulations issued under the Act.
3. The Act seeks to involve everyone — the employer *and* the employee who has to take reasonable care for his own safety and also that of his colleagues and other persons.
4. Seeks to improve enforcement machinery, e.g. Improvement and Prohibition Notices.

(b) General duties

It is simply provided in the Act:

'it shall be the duty of every employer to ensure as far as is reasonably practicable the Health, Safety and Welfare at work of all his employees'.

Without prejudice to this general duty, the section then goes on to apply it to more specific functions, but again in a generalised form. Duty extends to:

'provision and maintenance of plant and systems of work and to arrangements ensuring safety and absence of risks to health in connection with use, storage, handling and transport of articles and substances'

and

'taking steps for the provision of such information, instruction, training and supervision which is necessary to ensure the safety and health at work of his employees'.

He must:

'maintain any place of work... in such a condition that it is safe and without risks to health and provide means of access to and exit from it that are safe and without such risks'.

Finally, he must provide a working environment that is safe and adequate as regards facilities.

Systems of work are well defined in Common Law. It means the whole organisation of the job, management and layout.

Courts will always lean in favour of action rather than excuses. It remains to be seen whether lack of money can be pleaded, but this is doubtful.

The duty is there to take reasonable practical steps to train employees to ensure health and safety. The employer cannot blame the employee if he has not taken these steps.

The employee is required to cooperate with the employer.

(c) Manufacturers and suppliers

There is, under the 1974 Act, a duty on all those who manufacture, supply or import equipment and substances to ensure that safety and health standards are reached and information on operation is supplied. This does not mean that the employer can rely on this; he needs to check himself. But there will be cases where the manufacturer will be prosecuted, not the employer, providing the employer has used the machine the way the manufacturer intended.

There is a problem in the interpretation of the word 'supplier'. It means not only the furnisher of the machine, but also the employer who supplies the articles or machine to his employees.

(d)   Self employed

> 'It shall be the duty of every self employed person as of every employer to conduct his undertaking in such a way as to ensure that it is, in so far as is reasonably practicable, free from risks to the health and safety both of himself and of other persons who may be affected by it.'

(e)   Controllers of premises

Under the 1974 Act, *controllers* of premises must take reasonably practical steps for the safety of people employed in their premises.

(f)   Enforcement

Enforcement powers under the old legislation will remain, but there are new enforcement procedures under the 1974 Act for the inspectorate.

(i)   Section 21 of the Act, on the use of Improvement Notices, reads:

> 'If an inspector is of the opinion that a person:
>
> (a)   is contravening one or more of the relevant statutory provisions (i.e. of this Act and preceding legislation) *or*
>
> (b)   has contravened one or more of these provisions in circumstances that make it likely that the contravention will continue to be repeated:
>
> he may serve on him a notice requiring that person to remedy the contravention within such period as may be specified in the notice.'

A notice requires the statutory standard to be reached. The only limit on the time is that it shall not be shorter than the time of appeal. The machine can be used in the meantime.

(ii)   Prohibition Notices — if the inspector is of the opinion that there will be, or may be, serious injury, the activities must cease until the matter has been remedied. Any activity can be prohibited — this is the surest way to reach the highest standard of safety. If a machine is unsafe and cannot be modified, the use will be prohibited. Appeals can be made to an Industrial Tribunal; however the activity will have to cease, unless the IT finds otherwise.

Fines for failure to comply with Prohibition and Improvement Notices accrue on a daily basis.

(g) Information

An employer should give:

(i) A written statement of his general policy and attitudes to safety and health to each employee.

(ii) Information to persons who are not his employees who are likely to be affected.

(iii) Training, warning notices and follow up.

(h) Safety representatives

The Secretary of State may provide for the appointment of safety representatives from amongst the employees, in prescribed cases, either by direct appointment from amongst trade unionists or elections amongst the employees in general. But, even with safety representatives and safety committees, responsibility for ultimate decision making is that of the employer. The Health and Safety Executive has issued a Code of Practice on *Safety Representations and Safety Committees.*

(i) Regulations

The general duties of the Act will be supplemented by regulations which will modify and extend the scope of the Act. Three important regulations, which have been issued under the Act, are the Health & Safety (First-aid) Regulations 1981, and the Control of Industrial Major Accident Hazard Regulations 1984 and the Reporting of Injuries, Diseases and Dangerous Occurrences Regulations 1985.

(j) Codes of Practice

Regulations will only be made where Codes of Practice are inadequate. Consultation with those industries concerned will take place and they will be worded in everyday language. Codes of Practice have been issued on Safety Representatives & Safety Committees and on reducing the exposure of employed persons to noise.

(k) Health & Safety (First-aid) Regulations 1981

The duty to provide adequate first-aid is specifically dealt with by the Health & Safety (First-aid) Regulations 1981.

The Regulations together with an approved Code of Practice and Guidance Notes replace a number of old, often outdated requirements, to a wider spectrum i.e. virtually all employers.

The Regulations lay down three broad duties. These are:

— the duty of the employer to provide first-aid;

155

- the duty of the employer to inform his employees of the arrangements made in connection with first-aid;
- the duty of the self-employed person to provide first-aid equipment;

Employers can exempt themselves from the Code of Practice where they provide a full-time occupational health service which is in the charge of a medical practitioner or qualified occupational health nurse. The code acknowledges a medical practitioner or nurse will have made suitable first-aid arrangements. The service does not have to be a permanently staffed one as long as there is coverage for all employees during working hours.

The Code of Practice lays down what criteria employees should adopt to determine what equipment, facilities, personnel, etc. they require. These are:

a) the number of employees;
b) the nature of the undertaking;
c) the size of the establishment and the distribution of the employees;
d) the location of the establishment and the locations to which the employees go in the course of their employment.

depending on a company's degree of hazard upon the number of first aiders to employees. In general, an employer should provide a first-aid room if more than 400 people are employed.

The goal of employers is to see that every employee has reasonably quick access to first-aid. A centralised provision may suit a compact office but not a sprawling factory.

Special guidance is given by the Guidance Notes for small establishments, a travelling first-aid box is advised as being necessary.

Employers are under a duty to provide:

'such number of suitable persons as is adequate and appropriate in the circumstances for rendering first-aid to his employees if they are injured or become ill at work; and for this purpose a person shall not be suitable unless he has undergone such training and has such qualifications as the HSE may approve for the time being in respect of that case or class of case, and such additional training, if any, as may be appropriate in the circumstances of that case'.

An employer also has to inform his employees of the arrangements that have been made in connection with first-aid facilities.

A miscellaneous item, an employer has no obligation to provide first-aid to anyone other than their employees, however, a provision could be worked out for regular visitors.

9. TRADE UNION AND LABOUR RELATIONS ACTS 1974/76

The Trade Union and Labour Relations Act passed in 1974 was amended in 1976 and has subsequently had some of its provisions amended by the Employment Acts 1980 and 1982.

(a)   Its main purposes were:

To repeal the Industrial Relations Act of 1971, but to re-enact most of the provisions relating to unfair dismissal (now incorporated in the EP(C)Act 1978). To restore the status of trade unions' and employers' associations to the pre 1971 position.

To restore the basic right of employees to legal immunity for certain actions taken in 'contemplation or furtherance of a trade dispute' (now modified by the Employment Act 1980).

(b)   TULRA defines a trade union as follows: (S 28 (1))

'An organisation (whether permanent or temporary) which either (a) consists wholly or mainly of workers of one or more descriptions and is an organisation whose principal purposes include the regulation of relations between workers of that description, or those descriptions and employers or employers associations; or... '

(c)   Trade unions are imbued with certain corporate features in section 2; thus:

— they are capable of entering into contracts
— they are capable of suing or being sued in their own name
— criminal proceedings may be brought against them in their own name
— all trade union property must be vested in trustees who hold the property in trust for the union
— court judgements, orders or awards are enforceable against its trust property.

(d)   The Act defines an independent trade union as one which is not under the domination or control of an employer or a group of employers. Only once a trade union has been certified as an independent trade union do the following rights pertain, once it has been recognised by an employer:

— the power to request the employer to disclose information for collective bargaining purposes
— the right to be consulted on proposals for collective redundancy
— the employee has the right to join in and take part in its activities
— the right to time off for trade union duties and activities for its officials and its members
— the ability to negotiate a union membership agreement (closed shop)
— the appointment of safety representatives

(e)   The Act contains the definition of a trade dispute which as amended by the Employment Act 1982 reads as follows in S 29 (1). 'In this Act' trade dispute means a dispute between workers and their employer which relates wholly and mainly to one or more of the following, that is to say:

157

(i)   terms and conditions of employment, or the physical conditions in which any workers are required to work;

(ii)   engagement or non-engagement or termination of suspension of employment or the duties of employment of one or more workers;

(iii) allocation of work or the duties of employment as between workers or groups of workers;

(iv) matters of discipline;

(v)   the membership or non-membership of a trade union on the part of a worker;

(vi) facilities for officials of trade unions; and

(vii) machinery for negotiation or consultation, and other procedures relating to any of the foregoing matters...

(f)   Section 13 of the Act, as amended and influenced by the Employment Acts 1980 and 1982, states that any person acting in contemplation or furtherance of a trade dispute who induces or threatens a breach of any contract or interferes with the performance of any contract cannot be sued for damages, provided that the actions are:

— reasonably capable of furthering that dispute *or*

— taken predominantly in pursuit of that dispute and not for any reasons unconnected with it.

Subject to the secondary action provisions and the acts to compel trade union membership provision of the Employment Acts 1980 and 1982.

(g)   Under S16 of TULRA it is made clear that employees cannot be ordered to work or attend at their place of work by a court.

10. EMPLOYMENT PROTECTION ACT 1975

The Act had two major objectives — to introduce machinery to promote the improvement of industrial relations; and to introduce a new series of rights for employees and provide greater job security.

Most of this Act has either been repealed or its provisions transferred to the 'Consolidation' Act of 1978. However, some significant elements remain, as follows:

(a) Statutory bodies

This Act created and lays down the general duties of the Advisory Conciliation and Arbitration Service (ACAS), the Central Arbitration Committee (CAC), the Certification Officer (CO) and the Employment Appeal Tribunal (EAT).

(b) Disclosure of information

This Act imposes a general duty on employers to disclose to independent trade unions, on request, information which would lubricate the process of collective bargaining. This should be 'information which it would be in accordance with good industrial relations to provide' and which is in the employers possession. An ACAS Code, issued in August 1977, suggests the sort of information which should be provided. If an employer fails to disclose information, the union can appeal to the CAC who would ask ACAS to conciliate. If the CAC upholds a complaint from a union, it has the power to enforce the employer to release that information.

There are limits set on the information which must be disclosed; the employer cannot be forced to disclose information:

— which would be against the interests of National Security;
— which would cause substantial injury to an undertaking;
— which has been communicated in confidence;
— which was about an individual, unless the individual gives consent;
— which was relevant to legal proceedings, or which it would be illegal to disclose;
— which would involve cost or an amount of work out of proportion to its bargaining value.

(c) Consultation regarding proposed redundancies

An employer planning redundancies is required to consult the appropriate recognised independent trade union about their implementation at the earliest possible moment. The employer shall disclose the information about the redundancies in writing and this information should include:

— the reasons for the redundancies;
— the numbers and descriptions of employees whom it is intended to dismiss as redundant;
— the total number of employees of any such description in the establishment in question;
— the proposed method of selection;
— the proposed procedure for carrying out the redundancy dismissals.

Where 10-99 employees are to be made redundant, the consultation period is a minimum of 30 days prior to the first of the terminations; for 100+ employees, the period is at least 90 days. Employers must also notify the Department of Employment within the same period.

Where an employer fails to consult with a relevant trade union, the trade union or unions may apply to an Industrial Tribunal for a 'protective award' which will require the employer to pay normal wages to the employees covered by the award for the specified period.

(d) Statutory Joint Industrial Councils

The Act also established the possibility of creating statutory joint industrial councils as a 'halfway house' between wages councils and free collective bargaining.

11. SEX DISCRIMINATION ACT 1975

This Act makes discrimination unlawful in employment, training and related matters; in education; in the provision of foods, facilities and services; and in the disposal and management of premises. The Act also:
— established the Equal Opportunities Commission (EOC)
— applies to discrimination against both men and women
— applies to discrimination against married persons.

(a) Exceptions

Excluded from the Act are:
— employment which is wholly or mainly outside GB
— provisions made in respect of pregnancy, death or retirement
— private households
— religious orders
— mineworkers who work mainly underground
— where a person's sex is a genuine occupational qualification (GOQ)

(b) Definitions of discrimination

The SDA defines two types of action which are discriminatory:
(i)   Direct discrimination occurs if on grounds of sex or marital status a woman is treated less favourably than a man and vice versa.
(ii)   Indirect discrimination occurs if an action is discriminatory in effect, as opposed to deliberate intention, so that even if the same treatment is applied equally to both men and women, the proportion of women (or men) who can comply is smaller than the number of women (or men), unless the requirements are justifiable irrespective of the sex of the person to whom it is applied.

(c) Discrimination in recruitment

The four ways in which this can occur are:
— in the way decisions are made on who should be offered the job. A

160

person who feels discrimination is taking place in an organisation does not need to have applied for a job in order to make a complaint;
— in relation to the terms and conditions offered
— by refusing or deliberately omitting to offer a person employment
— in the recruitment advertising literature and job descriptions.

(d) Discrimination in treatment of present employees

(i) It is unlawful to discriminate by refusing or not allowing access to:
— Promotion, transfer or training:
However, it is permissable in training to treat one sex more favourably than another in areas where it is necessary to overcome the effects of past discrimination against a particular sex.
— Provision of benefits, facilities and services subject to the provisions of pregnancy, death benefits or retirement pensions.

(ii) It is unlawful to discriminate in dismissal, redundancy or lay offs directly or indirectly because of density of male or female employment.

(e) Genuine Occupational Qualifications (GOQ)

A person's sex is a GOQ for a job:

(i) Where the essential nature of the job calls for a man or woman for reasons of physiology (excluding physical strength or stamina), modelling clothes, dramatic performances (for reasons of authenticity).

(ii) Where considerations of decency or privacy require the job to be held by a man (or woman), perhaps because of the likelihood of physical contact between the job holder and colleagues, or where the job holder is likely to work in the presence of people who are in a state of undress.

(iii) Where the nature or location of the establishment makes it impracticable for the job holder to live in premises other than those provided by the employer and the only available premises do not provide separate sleeping or sanitary accommodation — unless it would be reasonable for the employer to suitably equip or provide other premises.

(iv) Where the job is in a single-sex establishment or in a single-sex part of an establishment, it will need to be shown, in relation to any particular job, that the character of the establishment requires that job to be held by a person of a particular sex.

(v) Where the holder of the job provides individuals with personal

161

services providing their welfare or education e.g. some women might respond best to help offered by a female welfare officer.

(vi) Where the job needs to be held by a man because of restrictions imposed by the laws regulating the employment of women, e.g.factories legislation and night work.

(vii) Where the job involves work outside the UK in a country whose laws or customs are such that a job can only be done, or done effectively, by a person of a particular sex.

(viii) Where the job is one of two to be held by a married couple.

(f) Enforcement

In the employment field an individual may make a complaint of unlawful discrimination to an Industrial Tribunal within 3 months of the alleged discrimination. Where an Industrial Tribunal has decided in favour of an employee it can issue an order:

(i) declaring the rights of the parties

(ii) requiring the employer to pay the complainant damages.

(iii) make a recommendation that the employer follows a particular course of action, e.g. promote the complainant, desist from using a particular test etc.

Where a complaint is too complex for an individual to deal with alone or an issue is raised which is relevant in the wider public interest, the EOC:

(i) could conduct formal investigations into any matter and, if it does discover behaviour which contravenes the SDA, it is empowered to issue a 'non-discrimination' notice.

(ii) could institute legal proceedings if the organisation persists in its discrimination.

(g) Code of Practice

'The Code of Practice for the elimination of discrimination on grounds of sex and marriage and the promotion of equality of opportunity in employment.'

In April 1985 the EOC received Parliamentary approval for its Code of Practice on the elimination of sex and marriage discrimination in employment. The Code which, though it does not have the force of law, will be taken into account by Industrial Tribunals, has three main purposes.

— To eliminate discrimination in employment

— To provide guidance on steps that employers might reasonably take to ensure that their employees do not, in the course of their employment, act unlawfully contrary to the SDA

— To promote equality of opportunity between men and women in employment.

162

The Code is divided into two parts; the first part is concerned with the role of good employment practices in eliminating sex and marriage discrimination and the second of the role of good employment practices in promoting equality of opportunity.

The Code sees as the key feature in promoting true equality of job opportunity the establishment of a sound and realistic policy of equal opportunity which:

'should be clearly stated and where appropriate be included in a collective agreement; overall responsibility for implementing the policy should rest with senior management; and the policy should be made known to all employees...'

The policy and its implementation should be monitored regularly so that the organisation can at any moment justify that the policy is operating properly. The Code also recommends the use of positive action programmes to encourage training and promotion.

12. RACE RELATIONS ACT 1976

The Race Relations Act 1976 strengthens the law against racial discrimination in:

— employment;
— education;
— housing;
— the provision of goods, facilities and services; and
— extends the law to cover discrimination by private clubs.

The Act closely follows the form of the Sex Discrimination Act 1975.

(a) General intentions

(i)   To replace the existing Race Relations Acts of 1965 and 1968.
(ii)   To harmonise the powers and procedures for dealing with sex and race discrimination so as to ensure genuine equality of opportunity in both fields.
(iii) To provide individual victims of discrimination with fuller redress through the Civil Courts and Industrial Tribunals.
(iv)   To establish a Commission for Racial Equality, which will fulfil a strategic role in tackling discrimination and promoting equality of opportunity; to help individual victims of discrimination; and to support and coordinate the work of local Community Relations Councils.

(b) Definition of discrimination

Part 1 of the Act defines two kinds of conduct which constitute racial discrimination:

(i)   *Direct Discrimination* — This arises where a person treats another person less favourably *on racial grounds* than he treats or would treat someone else. 'Racial Grounds' includes colour, race, nationality (including citizenship) or ethnic or national origins. Such discrimination may be done not only openly, but also by inference.

(ii) *Indirect Discrimination* — This involves practices which (whether or not intentionally so) are discriminatory in their effect on a particular racial group and cannot be shown to be justified. It thus prohibits anyone from applying a condition or requirement which, although also applied to people not in that racial group, meets all the following conditions:

— It is such that the proportion of that racial group who can comply with it is considerably smaller than the proportion of other people who can comply.

— The discriminator cannot show the condition to be justifiable, irrespective of the origins of the person to whom it is applied.

— It is to the detriment of that person because he cannot comply with it.

(c) Victimisation

The definition of discrimination is also broadened to include victimisation of a person because he has asserted his rights under the legislation. However, victimisation does not apply if people are being badly treated because they have made allegations which are false and in bad faith.

Any employee, who gives evidence before an Industrial Tribunal or Court on behalf of another who is alleging racial discrimination, is also protected against any consequential discrimination.

(d) Employment

Part II of the Act applies to employment and related matters. Thus:

— It is unlawful for employers to discriminate on racial grounds between job applicants or employees. For example, in selection procedures, employment terms, job offers, access to promotion and training, dismissal, earnings, and redundancy.

— The employer is liable for any act done, with or without his approval, by his employee. Thus, the employer and the employee are liable for an unlawful act.

(e) Exemptions

There are some exemptions:

— where racial identity is a genuine occupational qualification (GOQ);

- private households;
- small partnerships with less than 6 partners;
- for employment providing training in skills for people not ordinarily resident in GB, intending to use those skills outside GB;
- in cases of positive discrimination, where previously there were no members of a particular nationality in a specific job.

(f) Positive discrimination

The Government was also concerned that the principle of non-discrimination should not be applied inflexibly so that the disadvantage experienced by some members of racial minority groups in employment and related fields is ignored. The Act, therefore, allows action to be taken to meet the special educational, training and welfare needs of members of particular racial groups. Employers and certain training bodies are allowed to provide training for and encouragement to, members of particular racial groups to take advantage of opportunities for doing jobs in which they have been under-represented. There are similar provisions for positive action by trade unions employers' associations and professional bodies (Section 53).

(g) Advertisements

Discriminatory practices (even where there is no victim), discriminatory advertisements and instructions and pressure to discriminate are all unlawful. An advertisement which indicates an intention to discriminate will generally be unlawful — a person who feels discriminated against does not need to have applied for a job in order to make a complaint.

There are, however, exceptions where for example a 'Genuine Occupational Qualification' applies. It will also not be unlawful to advertise for a person of a particular nationality to be employed outside GB.

(h) Genuine occupational qualification

The GOQ is not an automatic exception for general categories of jobs; in every case it will be necessary for the employer to show, if the exception is to be claimed, that the criteria set out to apply to the particular job.

(i) Where the job involves participation in a dramatic performance or other entertainment in a capacity for which a person of the racial group in question is required for reasons of authenticity.

(ii) Where the job involves participation as an artist's or photographic model in the production of a work of art, picture or film, for which a person of the racial group in question is required for reasons of authenticity.

(iii) Where the job involves working in a place where food or drink is provided to, and consumed by, members of the public or a section of the public, in a particular setting, for which in that job, a person of that racial group is required for reasons of authenticity.

(iv) Where the job-holder provides persons of the racial group in question with personal services promoting their welfare and those services can most effectively be provided by a person of the same racial group.

(i) Other organisations

Other organisations specifically brought within the scope of the law are:

— trade unions
— the police
— professional qualifying bodies
— vocational training bodies
— employment agencies
— careers service
— the Manpower Services Commission.

Discrimination is also unlawful in education, the provision of goods and services and clubs.

(j) Enforcement

Whereas, under the 1968 Race Relations Act, all complaints about discrimination had to be made to the Race Relations Board which had the sole right to institute legal proceedings, under the new Act individuals will have direct access to the courts or, in education, training and related cases, to Industrial Tribunals within 3 months. For Educational bodies, complaints will go direct to the Education Minister.

The remedies available from the courts will be damages (including damages for injured feelings), a declaration of rights or an injunction.

Complaints of discriminatory practices, advertising or instructions or pressure to discriminate can only be brought by the Commission for Racial Equality.

Industrial Tribunals will deal with complaints about racial discrimination in the same way as complaints of sex discrimination and unfair dismissal etc.

Complaints of discrimination in the employment field will be referred initially to ACAS conciliation officers, who will try to promote a settlement of the complaint without the need for recourse to an IT.

Where a complaint remains unresolved, normally arrangements will be made for the IT to include a lay member with knowledge or experience of race relations in employment as well as the required knowledge or experience of employment in industry or commerce.

(k)   Code of Practice

In April 1984 the CRE issued a Code of Practice

'for the elimination of racial discrimination and the promotion of equality of opportunity in employment'.

The Code quotes from the Race Relations legislation but, like all Codes of Practice, does not impose any legal obligations itself; however breaches of the Code could result in breaches of the law and the provisions of the Code are, therefore, admissable in evidence in proceedings before an Industrial Tribunal.

Like the EOC Code the most important feature to develop equality of treatment is the initiation of policy which is endorsed and backed by senior management. The Code recommends that employers should:

'make an... analysis of the workforce and regularly monitor the application of the policy with the aid of analyses of the ethnic origins of the workforce and of job applicants'

i.e. what has been termed 'ethnic monitoring' in order to ensure the success or improvement of equal opportunity policy.

13.   EMPLOYMENT PROTECTION (CONSOLIDATION) ACT 1978

This Act has brought together into one piece of legislation the individual rights of employees previously contained in the Redundancy Payments Act 1965, the Contract of Employment Act 1972, the Trade Union & Labour Relations Act 1974 and 1976, and the Employment Protection Act 1975. The Act does not alter or amend any of the previous enactments, but merely incorporates the provisions in one document. Some amendments have been made by the Employment Acts of 1980 & 1982.

(a)   Written particulars of employment

The opening sections of the Act deal with the issuing of particulars of terms and conditions of employment, within 13 weeks of the commencement of work. The particulars should broadly include the following:

— employers' name, employee's name, date of contract and job title;
— scale or rate of pay and intervals at which payment will take place;
— the hours of work;
— terms and conditions relating to holidays and holiday pay, sickness and accident arrangements and payment for these, pension arrangements (and whether a contracted out scheme is in force);
— the length of notice to be given on either side, i.e. the employer must give, under the statute, one week after four weeks continuous

service, two weeks after two years, three weeks after three years and so on up to a maximum of twelve weeks after twelve years or more service; the employee need only give one week's notice;
— steps to be followed in any grievance which the employee might have;
— details of the disciplinary rules which apply to the employee;
— where necessary, the date on which a fixed term contract is due to end.

Trade union membership and activities

An employee has the right not to have action short of dismissal taken against him to prevent him from being or seeking to be a member of an independent trade union; preventing him taking part in the activities of an independent trade union at an appropriate time; forcing him to become a member of a non-independent trade union; or compelling him to become a member of a trade union with a union membership agreement, if he has grounds of conscience or deeply-held personal convictions against membership of a trade union or a particular trade union. Dismissal in those cases is automatically unfair under the later provision of the Act.

(c) Time off for trade union duties

Employees who are officials of recognised independent trade unions are entitled to reasonable time off with pay, to pursue trade union duties or to receive industrial relations training applicable to their duties. Arrangements should take account of the provision of the ACAS Code of Practice *Time off for trade union duties and activities,* which came into force in April 1978.

(d) Time off for trade union activities

Employees, who are lay officials or who are members of recognised trade unions, have the right to take time off during working hours without pay to take part in the activities of the union.

(e) Time off for public duties and to look for work

Employers are required to allow employees time off without pay to carry out public duties as a Justice of the Peace; a member of a local authority; a member on a statutory tribunal; a member of a regional health authority; a member of a governing or managing body of an educational establishment maintained by a local authority; a member of a water authority; and to attend meetings or work on sub-committees of such bodies.

An individual employee is also entitled to reasonable time off with pay (if he has been employed for over 2 years), or without pay (if less than 2 years), to look for work or seek training on being made redundant, before the expiry of his notice.

(f) Maternity provisions

The EP(C) Act 1978 consolidated the benefits for expectant mothers which were introduced in the EPA 1975. These rights have been modified by the Employment Act 1980, and amendments are incorporated in the notes. The basic rights are as follows:

(i)   A woman who stops work because of pregnancy, who has worked continuously with the employer for 2 years and remains with the company up to the 11th week before the expected date of confinement, is entitled to be paid for the first 6 weeks of her absence at 90% of her average pay, less State maternity allowance. She does not have to state that she wishes to return to work to be entitled to receive maternity pay. Employers can claim a refund of the full amount of maternity pay from the Maternity Payments Fund.

(ii)   The Employment Act 1980 added a further right, that to paid time off for ante-natal care.

(iii)   An employee who is off work because of pregnancy, who works for an organisation which employs 6 or more people and who has worked continuously for it for 2 years, is entitled to ask (in writing) at least 21 days before she leaves work, to return to her job (or a similar job with the same terms and conditions) at any time up to 29 weeks after her baby has been born. This return can be postponed for up to 4 weeks by either the employer or the employee. Under the amendments made by the Employment Act 1980, the employer has the right to ask for written confirmation of the continued intention to return to work after 49 days of the expected date of confinement. The reply must be made within 14 days of the request from the employer; if not, she loses her statutory right to return to work. The employee must give 21 days notice (in writing) of her intention to return to work.

(g) Unfair dismissal

The employee's right not to be unfairly dismissed was first introduced in the Industrial Relations Act 1971.

Some groups of employees are not protected by the unfair dismissal provisions, regardless of the reason for dismissal:

—   Part-time employees (see (i));
—   persons working under contracts for services;
—   the husband or wife of the employer;

- those who ordinarily work outside Great Britain;
- members of the armed forces, police, share fishermen, merchant seamen and registered dock workers.

(i) There are, however, certain groups of employees who, although not protected from unfair dismissal, are protected when the reason for dismissal is inadmissable (i.e. the reason for dismissal was because of membership of a trade union or taking part in trade union activities at an appropriate time, or on race or sex or maternity grounds). These are:

- people over the statutory age of retirement;
- part-time employees who work for less than 16 hours per week, unless they have worked for 5 years or more, when they are entitled to claim unfair dismissal;
- part-time employees who work less than 8 hours per week;
- employees who have not completed 104 weeks continuous service.

Industrial Tribunals will not consider cases where dismissal was incurred during an industrial dispute.

(ii) A dismissal may be justified on the following statutory grounds:

- for reasons of capability or qualifications of the employee;
- for reasons relating to the employee's conduct;
- for reasons of redundancy;
- where to retain the employee would contravene a statutory enactment or criminal law;
- some other substantial reason.

(iii) The 'reasonableness' of the employer's behaviour, taking into account the size and administrative resources of the undertaking, will be considered. Guidance is given in the ACAS Code of Practice *Disciplinary and Other Procedures in Employment,* which came into force in 1986.

(iv) Dismissal relating to refusal to join a trade union, where a union membership agreement is in force:

(a) The Employment Act 1980 makes it unfair to dismiss an employee who objects to joining a trade union on 'grounds of conscience or other deeply held personal conviction'.

(b) Also it is unfair to dismiss an employee for refusing to join a trade union where a union membership agreement (UMA) is in force:

- the UMA is a 'new' one (i.e. came into effect after 15th August 1980) and the individual was not a member of the trade union when it was agreed, and has remained a non-member ever since;

170

— where the UMA is a 'new' one and has not been approved by a secret ballot among all relevant employees (with not less than 80% of those entitled to vote voting in favour of a UMA).
— from 1.11.84 where the UMA has not been reaffirmed by ballot (either with not less than 80% of those entitled to vote voting in favour of the UMA *or* 85% of those voting affirming in favour of the UMA) within 5 years prior to the date of dismissal.

If an employer does dismiss an employee for refusing to become a member of a trade union, on the above grounds, as a result of union pressure, the employer may 'join' a trade union or representatives acting on behalf of that trade union, which means that any Industrial Tribunal finding a case of unfair dismissal can order that compensation awarded to the dismissed employee can be reclaimed whole, or in part, by the employer from the trade union forcing him to take that action. The individual also has the right to 'join' the trade union before the IT.

(v) An employee is also protected from the employer taking action short of dismissal against him under the circumstances outlined in (iv) above.

(vi) Remedies for unfair dismissal:

Where an individual considers he has been unfairly dismissed or he is subjected to action short of dismissal, he may bring a complaint before an Industrial Tribunal within 3 months. The Tribunal has the power to make an award of compensation or to demand that the employer *re-employ* (in the employee's original job) or *re-engage* (i.e. in some other post similar to the original one) the individual concerned. Unreasonable failure to obey such an order from a Tribunal can lead to additional compensation being given to the dismissed employee.

(h) Redundancy

The Act does not amend in any way the Redundancy Payments Act 1965 provisions. The objectives are to reduce the impact of unemployment by compensating workers who have over 2 years' service for job loss; to reduce the hardship that results from unemployment; and to encourage job mobility. An employee is dismissed for reasons of redundancy if:

'the dismissal is attributable wholly or mainly to —
(a) the fact that the employer has ceased, or intends to cease, to carry on the business for the purpose for which the employee was employed by him, or has ceased, or intends to cease, to carry on the business in the place where the employee was so employed; or
(b) the fact that the requirements of the business for an employee to carry out work of a particular kind, or for an employee to carry out work of a particular kind in the place where he was so employed, have ceased or diminished or are expected to cease or diminish...'

171

The rights do not apply to those who are over the normal retiring age at the time of the redundancy or employees who work less than 16 hours per week, unless employed for 5 years or more and working in excess of 8 hours per week. In addition, registered dock workers, share fishermen, crown servants and husbands of wives of the employer are not covered.

The provisions for redundancy pay represent a minimum standard. The legal minima are as follows:

18-21   years of age — ½ week's pay for each year of service in that age range.
(Service up to the age of 18 does not count as reckonable service. Therefore, an individual will have to be 20 before he can benefit from the provisions.)

22-40   years of age — 1 week's pay per year of service in that age range.

41-65   (men) 60 (women) — 1½ week's pay per year of service in that age range.

The maximum reckonable service for statutory redundancy pay purposes is 20 years and there is a statutory limit on the amount of a week's pay. Between 59 and 60 for women and 64 to 65 for men, the total redundancy pay is reduced by 1/12th per month over the age of 59 or 64. Employees do not have to pay tax on statutory redundancy pay.

(i) Employees' rights on the insolvency of an employer

Under the provisions of the Act, if and when an employer becomes insolvent, payments owed to his employees are to be given priority over all other debts covered by the Bankruptcy Act 1914 and the Companies Act 1948. Application for sums owing should be made to the Receiver or Liquidator and authorised by the Secretary of State for Employment. The debts may initially be paid from the Redundancy Payments Fund and include:

— guarantee payments;
— payments for suspension on medical grounds;
— maternity pay;
— payment for agreed time off;
— arrears in pay of up to 8 weeks;
— payment for statutory notice;
— arrears in holiday pay up to 6 weeks;
— compensation under an Industrial Tribunal award;
— reimbursement of apprenticeship or articled clerks' fees;
— an employer's payments into an occupational pension fund.

(j) Guarantee payments

An employer is required to guarantee a payment to his employees who lose pay because of short-time working or lay-offs, providing the employee is willing and able to work and has been employed for 4 continuous weeks. A guarantee payment will not, however, have to be made if the shortage of work is due to a trade dispute involving other employees of the employer or an associated employer, or if suitable alternative work is refused. The maximum amount of a guarantee payment is limited by statute to only 5 days in any rolling three-months period and the employer is only required to make the payment when a full working day is lost.

(k) Medical suspension

An employee who has been suspended from working under statutory regulations concerned with jobs involving exposure to ionising radiation, lead and certain other chemicals, by an Employment Medical Adviser or an appointed doctor, will be entitled to be paid normal wages for the time of the suspension up to a total maximum of 26 weeks. He is not entitled to this pay if: he has been offered suitable alternative work; he fails to fulfil reasonable conditions set by his employer, regarding availability; he has not been continuously employed for 4 weeks; or he is incapable of work because of other sickness or injury.

(l) Itemised pay statement

Every employee has the right to an itemised pay statement which contains the following particulars:

— the gross amount of his wages or salary;
— the amounts of any variable or fixed deductions;
— the net amount of his pay or salary.

14. EMPLOYMENT ACT 1980

The purpose of this Act was to 'readjust the balance' between management, trade unions and individual employees. It attempts to regulate some of the activities of trade unions and to relieve small businesses of some of the provisions of employment protection legislation.

(a) Secret ballots

The Act permits public funds to be made available via the Certification Officer to enable independent trade unions to conduct secret ballots for specific purposes including:

- obtaining a decision on calling or ending a strike, or other industrial action;
- carrying out elections provided for in trade union rules;
- election of trade union officials;
- amending trade union rules;
- decisions on trade union amalgamations or transfers of engagements;
- other purposes which the Secretary of State for Employment specifies.

Where more than 20 workers are employed, the employer is obliged, when requested to do so by the union or unions concerned, to provide a place where a ballot can take place on the premises.

(b) Picketing

Picketing usually involves attempting to persuade employees to break their contracts of employment by not going to work and, because it disrupts the business of a picketed employer, the breaking of commercial contracts.

Lawful picketing may occur, providing the following conditions are met: it must be in contemplation of furtherance of a trade dispute; its purpose must be to peacefully obtain or communicate information, or to persuade a person to work or refrain from working; the person doing so may only picket at or near his own place of work.

Under the Act, three exceptions are made to the requirement that the person picketing can only do so at his own place of work:

- a trade union official may accompany a member of the union whom he represents and who is picketing at his own place of work or another acceptable place;
- persons who do not normally work at one particular place, or for whom it is not practicable to picket at the place of work, may picket at the premises of the employer or from where his work is administered;
- unemployed people can picket at their former place of work.

Picketing apart from these exceptions, is not protected from liability in tort. The Act also restricts the immunity from tort in cases of 'secondary picketing' where the employees picketing are not in dispute with their own employer, unless it fulfils the acceptable standards of secondary action. Pickets however remain subject to the laws of obstruction, nuisance, trespass, conspiracy, assault and the pickets stand the risk that they may face action for 'obstruction of the highway' or 'obstruction of a police officer in the lawful execution of his duty'. Further guidance on picketing is given by the Department of Employment Code of Practice on *Picketing*.

(c) Secondary action

The Act limits the immunities from tort provided by the Trade Union & Labour Relations Act 1974 in cases of secondary action, e.g. sympathy strikes or blacking of goods or services. If a person persuades employees, of an employer who is not a party to the trade dispute, to break their contracts of employment, this is secondary action; if it interferes with commercial contracts, the organiser of the action has no immunity and can be sued for an injunction to prevent him taking the action or for damages. To qualify for immunity, the principal purpose of the secondary action must be to put direct pressure on the employer in dispute by preventing or disrupting supplies, during the dispute, to or from the employer. It must not affect other supplies to or from other employers, and there must be a current contract for those supplies between the employer in dispute and the employer where secondary action is taking place. Special provisions allow action to be taken in cases where the employer in dispute transfers work which would otherwise be done on his premises to the premises of a subsidiary or associated employer, providing that the action only disrupts that work which has been transferred. Immunity is granted to the organisers of the secondary action.

(d) Acts to compel trade union membership

The Act removes immunity from prosecution for the employees of one employer who 'black' the work of employees of another employer, where the purpose of the action is to put pressure on the second group of employees to join a particular trade union. This does not apply where both groups of employees work for the same employer at the same premises.

(e) Closed shop

In addition to the protections given to employees where 'new' union membership agreements are formed, i.e. ballot provisions which must be adhered to in order to confirm a union membership agreement (applicable since August 1980, and mentioned under the Unfair Dismissal section of the Employment Protection (Consolidation) Act 1978), additional rights are given to those affected by union membership agreements.

Any person, who is employed or is seeking employment in a job which is covered by a closed shop arrangement, has the right to appeal to an Industrial Tribunal (within 6 months) if he feels that he has had an application for membership of the trade union unreasonably refused or if he feels he has been unreasonably expelled from a trade union. He can make a complaint against the trade union directly and demand compensation at the tribunal. A Code of Practice on the *Closed Shop,* issued by the Department of Employment, clarifies these provisions related to union membership agreements.

Changes to other matters, such as unfair dismissal, maternity benefits and guarantee payments, have been considered in the previous section on the EP(C)A 1978.

(d) Exclusion or expulsion from a trade union

The Act also provides that, where a closed shop exists, individuals have a statutory right not to be unreasonably excluded or expelled from membership of a relevant trade union.

On admission policy the Closed Shop Code of Practice requires unions to have clear and fair rules on membership qualification which should include data on who has power to make decisions regarding membership; on what grounds can membership be refused; what appeals procedure is available to an individual seeking a redress from a decision; and the power to admit applicants when an appeal is upheld. Union rules on expulsions are expected to conform to the rules of natural justice, i.e. an individual must be informed of the charge against him in reasonable time; he must have the opportunity of being heard before an impartial Tribunal; and he must have a right of appeal to a higher authority in the union or the TUC.

Individuals, where they feel their rights have been abused, can appeal to an Industrial Tribunal within 6 months of the exclusion or expulsion.

15. TRANSFER OF UNDERTAKINGS (PROTECTION OF EMPLOYMENT) REGULATIONS 1981

The basis of the Regulation is to protect the employees' rights if the business for which they work is transferred from one company to another company. The Regulations introduce the principle of automatic transfer of:

— contracts of employment
— collective agreements and trade union recognition

in the case of certain transfers of organisations from one owner to another as a going concern and render automatically unfair dismissal for a reason other than an economic, financial or organisational one, connected with the transfer. The Regulations in addition impose a duty to inform and consult representatives of recognised trade unions.

16. EMPLOYMENT ACT 1982

This Act:

(a) Makes unions liable to be sued if they have organised unlawful industrial action. Thus the union will be held liable for any unlawful act, such as industrial action outside the S.29 TULRA definition, or secondary action, which is authorised or endorsed by any of the following:

— the National Executive Committee
— the General Secretary or President
— any other person given power under the union's rules to call industrial action
— any official employed by the union
— any committee of the union to whom an employed official regularly reports.

However, in the following circumstances, a union will not be held liable

— where the official or committee who authorised or endorsed the Act acted against the union rules
— or the authorisation or endorsement is disowned as speedily as possible by the responsible officials of the union.

Where an employer considers the union is taking unlawful industrial action, he can seek an injunction to prevent the action taking place or have it stopped and can claim damages from those responsible for the unlawful acts. There are however upper limits on the amounts which can be awarded in damages. These are linked to the size of the union, thus:

up to 4,999	members —	£10,000 maximum
5,000 — 24,999	members —	£50,000 maximum
25,000 — 99,999	members —	£100,000 maximum
100,000 +	members —	£250,000 maximum

(b) Amendments to the definition of Trade Dispute i.e. S.29 TULRA (see under TULRA 74/6)

(c) Amendments to the rules on dismissal in connection with industrial action. An employee who is dismissed while participating in a strike or any other form of industrial action cannot claim unfair dismissal if the following conditions prevail:

(i) his employer has dismissed all who were taking part in the action at the date of the dismissal

(ii) his employer has not offered re-engagement to any of those dismissed taking part in the industrial action, within three months of the dismissal date without making him a similar offer.

The individual has six months to claim at an industrial tribunal.

(d) Union membership or recognition requirements in contracts.

The Act prohibits companies, local authorities etc. from imposing union labour only or recognition requirements on their contractors, i.e. requirements which make it a condition of getting onto a tender list or of obtaining a contract. The Act also covers industrial action intended to put pressure on employers to maintain union only or recognition only contracts by withdrawing TULRA immunity from such Acts.

(e) Closed shops. The Act laid down the requirements for 'review ballots' for closed shops where dismissal results for non-membership. Unless there has been a review ballot or a ballot establishing a closed shop within five years of the date of the dismissal for non-membership, the dismissal will be automatically unfair.

In addition it is unfair to dismiss for non-membership:

— an employee who has genuine grounds of conscience or deeply held personal convictions;

— an employee who was employed before the union membership agreement came into effect and has never been a member since;

— if proceedings are pending before an Industrial Tribunal or where an IT declaration is in force;

— if the individual holds a professional qualification relevant to his position, and is subject to a written Code of Conduct of that profession, and has refused to become a member of the trade union or has been expelled for refusing to take part in a strike and other industrial action and, in either case, he would have been in breach of the Code of Conduct.

The Act, in addition, nullifies the ability of employers to insist on the practice of paying subscriptions to charity (what has been called Agency Shop Agreements) from employees who wish to be excused from compulsory membership.

(f) Compensation for dismissal for union membership and non-union membership. The Act specifies a minimum basic award for such cases; clarifies the circumstances when an employee's basic award can be reduced i.e. men between 64 and 65 and women between 59 and 60 by 1/12 per month over the age of 59 or 64:

— where the employee's conduct before dismissal merited a reduction

— where the employee has unreasonably prevented a reinstatement or re-engagement order being complied with or refused an offer;

and establishes a high special award where reinstatement or re-engagement is requested by the individual or ordered by the industrial tribunal or unreasonably refused by the employer concerned.

(g)   The Act requires that companies employing an average of more than 250 employees in a financial year must include a statement of employee involvement in their annual report. This statement must describe the action which has been taken during the financial year to:

— provide employees systematically with information on matters of concern to them as employees
— consult employees or their representatives on a regular basis so that the views of employees can be taken into account in making decision which are likely to affect their interests
— encourage the involvement of employees in the company's performance through an employees' share scheme or by some other means
— achieve a common awareness on the part of all employees of the financial and economic factors effecting the performance of the company.

17.   TRADE UNION ACT 1984

(a)   Election of voting members of Union Executive Committees

Part I of the TUA imposes on unions a requirement that voting members of a union's executives should be elected and specifies how the elections should be carried out. However the requirements can only be activated if an individual member brings an action. The members of the executive should be elected every five years.

— in a secret ballot
— by making a voting paper without interference or constraint.

(b)   Ballots before industrial action

The Act removes the TULRA immunities from both individuals and trade unions where a strike has been initiated or endorsed without receiving majority support in a ballot, which must be:

— of all those likely to be affected
— held in secret
— by the making of a ballot paper
— within a period of four weeks before the date the strike starts.

(c)   Revisions to the 1913 Trade Union Act on Political Funds.

Trade unions are now required to review the operation of their political funds at least once every ten years and, if the ballot is not re-established, the political fund resolution trade unions can no longer spend money on political objects.

18. DATA PROTECTION ACT 1984

The purpose of the Act is

'To regulate the use of automatically processed information relating to individuals and the provision of services in request of such information'

The Act does not cover data which is processed by manual methods: it regulates the use of data by a system of Registration with the Data Protection Registrar.

Registrations last for three years and need to contain the following information:

(i) The name and address of the data user;

(ii) A description of the personal data held by the data user and of the purpose or purposes for which the data is held or used;

(iii) A description of the sources of the data;

(iv) A description of the person or persons to whom the data user intends or wishes to disclose the data;

(v) The names or descriptions of any countries outside the UK to which data is to be directly or indirectly transferred;

(vi) One or more addresses for data subjects who may wish to access the data.

It is a criminal offence to hold personal data without being registered or to knowingly use, obtain, disclose or transfer personal data in a manner inconsistent with the descriptions in the register entry.

The DPA lays down eight Data Protection Principles which must be complied with. These are:

(i) The information to be contained in personal data shall be obtained and personal data shall be processed fairly and lawfully;

(ii) Personal data shall be held only for one or more registered specified and lawful purposes;

(iii) Personal data held for any purpose or purposes shall not be used or disclosed in any manner incompatible with the purpose or those purposes as registered;

(iv) Personal data held for any purpose or purposes shall be adequate, relevant, and not excessive in relation to that purpose or those purposes;

(v) Personal data shall be accurate and, where necessary, kept up to date;

(vi) Personal data held for any purpose or purposes shall not be kept longer than necessary for those purposes;

(vii) An individual shall be entitled:

(a) at reasonable intervals and without undue delay or expense:

    — to be informed by any data user whether he holds
      personal data of which that individual is the subject
    — to be supplied with any such data held by a data user.

(b)   where appropriate, to have such data corrected or erased.

(viii) Appropriate security measures shall be taken against any unauthorised access to, or alterations, disclosure or destruction of personal data and against loss or destruction of personal data.

Chapter 9
Role of Government and Government Policies in the UK

The attitude and behaviour of Government plays a very important part in stimulating and controlling the economic and social environment within which organisations operate. It is hard to get Government behaviour into perspective, because inevitably individual policies are influenced by political affiliations. Before we examine the current political affiliations of the UK population, we should examine the influence and objectives of Government. Governments operate in a number of ways which affect the economic stability and growth of an economy.

Governments can be said to have the following roles in our society:

(1) PROVISION OF PUBLIC SERVICES

They have a responsibility for the provision and maintenance of public services, which either may be uneconomic when left to private organisations, or which are so essential to the community at large that Government must, of necessity, control them. In our society we expect the Government to be involved in the maintenance of law and order; the provision of roads, schools and a public health system; to provide and run the basic transport system; to direct the provision of power through the Gas and Electricity network; and to provide basic water and sewerage facilities through the Water Authorities. Thus, the output of some organisations and the work they do may be considered important enough to be centrally controlled, because they yield benefits for the community in terms of overall health and welfare which are in excess of their potential monetary returns. Governments over the last ten to fifteen years have become increasingly concerned with the profitability and efficiency of nationalised industry and the public sector in general.

On the one hand, it has been suggested that the public sector is producing vital goods and services and that the community should not be asked to pay excessively for those services; they should be subsidised through taxation. On the other hand, it is argued that the public sector is consuming too much of our gross national product and that this is preventing the private sector from developing in the way that it should, because the tax burden on industry is too heavy. Thus, the public sector should become more efficient and those parts of it which actually provide a saleable good or service should be expected to conform to profit or monetary targets so that public sector investment is self-funded. The public sector is a major employer, employing almost 27% of the UK labour force as the following table illustrates:

Table 9:1 Employment in the UK public sector 1985

	Numbers (000's)	% of total UK Labour Force
Central Government	2360	9.7
H.M. Forces	326	1.3
N.H.S.	1223	5.0
Other Central Government Dept.	811	3.3
Local Authorities	2891	11.9
Education	1429	5.9
Health & Social Services	376	1.5
Police	187	0.8
Other Local Authority Depts.	899	3.7
Public Corporations	1262	5.2
Total UK Public Sector	6513	26.9
Total UK Private Sector	17732	73.2
Total UK Labour Force	24245	100.0

Source *Economic Trends* December, 1985.

(2) INFLUENCE THE ATTITUDES AND BEHAVIOUR OF BUSINESS AND THE POPULATION

Attitudes to work, to saving, to family size, to foreign trade, to equality of treatment, to social mobility, to new technological methods can all be influenced by Government action through the provision of services; the encouragement and provision of finance; and through legislative protection.

Every Government has to be concerned with questions as to whether it favours large scale or small scale enterprise; a competitive or monopolistic market; public or private enterprise etc. The legal system will inevitably reflect societal attitudes and consequently there are laws which relate to contract, to companies, to partnerships, to protection against monopolies and restrictive practices, to property and to the employer/employee relationship. The Government also administers a framework of agencies and departments which either regulate business activity, e.g. the Monopolies Commission, or assist with money, advice or guidance for enterprises (e.g. Department of Trade and Industry, ACAS), or individuals and organisations within the society (e.g. Training Services Division (TSD) or the Manpower Services Commission (MSC)). Common attitudes and approaches can be developed through organisations like the National Economic Development Council (NEDC).

Role of National Economical Development Council (NEDC)

The Council is composed of the Chancellor of the Exchequer, who is the Chairman, the Secretaries of State for Trade and Industry, Energy and Employment, six management representatives, six nominated by the TUC, six independent, and the National Economic Development Office's Director General.

The combination of the NEDC, the Economic Development Committees (EDCs) and the National Economic Development Office — forms the economic advisory group to the Government of the day with the nomenclator of NEDDY. The functions of NEDDY are to:

— consider the country's economic performance and industrial and commercial prospects.

— to discuss the problems hindering faster economic growth.

— to find ways to improve industrial efficiency through consultation between management, trade unions and Government.

The NEDC meets monthly and reviews the medium and long term industrial, commercial and economic situation. It does not concern itself with day-to-day matters formally. In order to arrive at the overall picture, it may request the Economic Development Committee for specific sectors, e.g. Agriculture, or Electronics to carry out particular studies for it. In addition, the NEDC may set up working parties to examine particular subjects.

The EDCs and their sub-committees meet on a regular basis to review the progress and potential threats and opportunities in the industries with which they are concerned.

Each one has a Chairman, who is from outside the industry which is its predominant concern, representatives of the industry, including management and employees, and Government appointed officials.

The National and Economic Development Office is an independent body which is financed by public funds — controlled by a Director General. It is divided into three operating divisions.

— The Economic Division examines issues concerned with economic growth, prepares papers for NEDC discussions and gives advice and statistical support data to the EDCs.

— The Industrial Division does support work where necessary for the NEDC and provides a secretariat for the EDCs.

— The Administrative division does the administrative work of NEDDY, including providing a secretariat for the NEDC and involves itself in public relations functions.

(3) CONTROL OF THE MONEY SUPPLY

When money consisted primarily of precious metals, there was little need for the Government to control the money supply. This was limited by the supply of those precious metals and its value was based on theirs. In Britain, up to 1914, the supply of extra currency depended on the amount of gold coined at the Mint. From that time, money has been made of materials whose intrinsic value is far less than their face value and, although up until about 1931 the amount of money in circulation was based on the holding of reserves of gold bullion into which notes could be converted, from that time the link has been broken and the Government now regulates the amount of money in circulation through the Bank of England. Other banks are required to operate within a certain liquidity ratio, which issues Government securities to increase the money supply. The Government also controls the money supply by its taxation and transfer payments. e.g., the form of social security and policies. If the quantity of money is not controlled, inflation tends to be fuelled. This is the fundamental belief expressed in monetarism today.

A current political issue is the international movement of capital and whether there should be more controls on investment overseas. The recent position on capital movement is as follows:

Table 9:2 Import/export of private capital 1977—1985

Year	Export (£m)	Import (£m)	Net balance (£m)
1977	5599	2978	-2621
1978	5845	3677	-2168
1979	6220	4437	-1793
1980	8150	5206	-2944
1981	10389	3447	-6942
1982	10910	3487	-7423
1983	11596	5093	-6513
1984	15377	3584	-11793
1985	22247	7480	-14767

Source: Various

(4) TO INFLUENCE THE USE AND DEVELOPMENT OF RESOURCES

Governments have some influence on the use and development of resources to ensure that they are economically used and dispersed in a socially acceptable way. Society may demand that some resources are conserved for the benefit of future generations, e.g. land, water, oil and other minerals. To this end governments have established conservation areas and green belts, and have passed anti-pollution laws to protect the community against ruthless exploitation.

Some productive systems may not be economically viable in a free market economy and it may be necessary to protect these activities by means of subsidy or, perhaps, nationalisation, or through the placing of

Government contracts to ensure their continuance. This may be done either for strategic or defence purposes, e.g. British Aerospace.

Other organisations may require Government investment or loans to encourage them to develop resources or products which would otherwise be too expensive for them to fund themselves.

Generally, governments will attempt to create an economic environment which encourages investment in technological changes and improvements in business and managerial efficiency. Small firms and large firms face different problems in coping with the prevailing economic situation.

Small firms

The small firm, if it is efficient in meeting the demand for its products or services, will require access to capital in order to expand. In most cases this will require it to go into debt. Governments can help firms by means of their control of the level of interest rates and the availability of grants of one sort or another. Throughout the 1960s and 1970s, governments provided generous tax-based investment incentives to British industry to stimulate growth and maintain full employment. On the other hand, growth can be hindered by increases in taxation or any other policies which require firms to hold high levels of liquid funds. Thus, for example, it has been argued that the Incomes Policy operated by the Edward Heath Government, which was based on threshold payments, had just that effect because of uncertainty about rises in the cost of living index. This triggered the threshold payments and reduced the propensity of small firms to invest in new productive assets, mainly because of uncertainty over how much cash they would require for wages and salary bills on a month-to-month basis.

Large firms

Large firms, on the other hand, which are an increasingly familiar feature of the UK economy, are usually more able to cope financially with short term difficulties because they can adapt their policies to changed political and economic conditions. Yet, longer term economic uncertainty and lack of economic control can lead to a preoccupation with 'survival' planning to the detriment of innovation, technological progress and growth. Survival can be bought by reducing high risk investment in new products, new production technology and the development of new markets at home and abroad and by not increasing their core labour force but by using overtime and part-timers to meet their needs.

Governments thus have a responsibility to reduce economic uncertainty in the market place and to attempt to encourage demand by the operation of appropriate economic and fiscal policies.

186

(5) MAINTENANCE OF THE STABILITY OF FOREIGN EXCHANGE

The UK lacks many of the natural resources which are essential for the nation's survival. There is coal and, in recent years with the development of technology and investment in the North Sea, we have been able to extract oil and gas. We produce some of our basic foodstuffs. Yet, for many years, we have become increasingly reliant on imports of raw materials and other items which we either do not possess at all or cannot produce in sufficient quantities. The effects of this were especially evident during the Second World War when overseas assets, like Argentinian Railways and Malaysian rubber plantations, had to be sold off to pay for the essential goods we required for our survival. We thus need to export to produce sufficient foreign currency to pay for those things we need to import. Britain is now far more dependent upon her own industrial and commercial ability that it was a century ago when the Empire produced exclusive sources of raw materials and, in return, had tied markets for the disposal of the goods and services made from those raw material imports. Two world wars and emergence of powerful new competitors, the USA, Japan and Germany in particular, plus the demand for political and industrial autonomy from most countries in the old Empire, which has broken many of the old trade relationships, has required British governments over the last twenty years to involve themselves consciously in helping the direction of our trading efforts to prevent balance of payments difficulties. Key influences on all governments since the mid 1950s have been our regular balance of payments deficits, inflation and the consequential effects on the value of sterling.

To facilitate trade in earning foreign exchange and maintaining the value of the pound, governments have adopted various policies to try to contain prices at home and to ensure our competitiveness abroad. Until 1972, when the £ was allowed to float, governments tried to maintain the value of the currency at a fixed rate. In the immediate post-war era this was $4 to £1; then later $2.80; and then, from the devaluation of 1967, $2.42 to £1. Although, since 1972, the pound has floated, the Government has tended to maintain the value of sterling at certain levels by dealing in the international money markets through the Bank of England.

Table 9:3 Sterling exchange rates — annual averages

	US Dollar	Deutschmark	Sterling Rate Exchange Index 1975—100
1979	2.12	3.89	87.3
1980	2.33	4.23	96.1
1981	2.03	4.56	95.3
1982	1.75	4.24	90.7
1983	1.52	3.87	83.3
% charge between			
1979—1983	-29	—	-5

Source: *Economic Progress Report* No. 172 — October 1984.

(6) INFLUENCE THE DISTRIBUTION OF INCOME

A balance must be found between protection for those groups whose bargaining power is low relative to other groups whilst, at the same time, attempting to ensure that incentives for effort are available. We can identify three sources of income for individuals and families in the UK:

(a) **earned income,** which can include all income from the employment relationship and from self-employment, including fringe and non-monetary benefits (e.g. pensions, free housing, use of a company car);

(b) **unearned income,** which comes from ownership of assets and includes rent from the ownership of land or property and interest from investments;

(c) **transfer income:** this is not paid in return for work or the use of an individual's assets but consists of benefits paid by the State, e.g. State pensions, family allowances, supplementary benefits, unemployment benefits, etc.

All households pay both direct and indirect taxation. *Direct* taxes are paid through income tax and national insurance contributions, and *indirect* taxes are paid through value added tax (VAT) and duty and through local rates. Companies also pay taxes both directly and indirectly. Those taxes are used in Government expenditure from which the community as a whole benefits through the national health service, housing and food subsidies and payments of benefits and allowances in cash.

The main intention of expenditure on items such as pensions, supplementary benefits and unemployment benefits is to support people during periods of reduced earning, and their net effect is to redistribute earnings to the less well-off with low income families benefiting most. Similarly, the net effect of direct taxation, which rises as income rises, is that the better-off households pay more tax and income is redistributed to the less well off. In addition, in theory, indirect taxes take more from the higher income groups who spend more, and less from the lower income groups.

Evidence from the Royal Commission on the Distribution of Income and Wealth, 1975, shows that the combined effect of the tax system, with the receipt of cash benefits, subsidies on rents and other benefits, does create some redistribution of income.

Table 9:4 Wealth distribution

Marketable wealth owned by wealthiest	1971 %	1976 %	1982 %	1983 %
1%	31	24	20	20
5%	52	45	40	40
10%	65	60	55	54
50%	97	95	96	96
Total wealth (£ billions)	140	263	602	745

Source: *Social Trends*, January 1986

(7) TO MAINTAIN FULL EMPLOYMENT

Government policy, from the White Paper *Employment Policy* (Cmnd 6527), 1944, was to stimulate economic growth to maintain 'a high and stable level of employment' and this remained a priority of all governments until the mid 1970s, when unemployment began to increase substantially. However, the ability of a government to pursue a policy of full employment is influenced by the general world trade situation.

One of the major problems which all governments have to face is that the prosperity of each nation is linked to the world economy and, throughout the western world, unemployment is increasing. The movement of prices for international commodities has a significant impact on the prosperity of all economies, however large. This was particularly evident in the steep rise of international oil prices in the mid 1970s.

In addition, increasing independence of the emerging nations in producing their own consumer goods, often financed by large multinational organisations who are taking advantage of relatively low labour costs and the availability locally of raw materials, has posed a threat to the security of employment of large sectors of the population in the traditionally-industrialised nations. Workers especially affected are those in vehicle manufacture, iron and steel production, the textile and electrical manufacturing industries.

In March 1985 the Government published the White Paper *Employment: The Challenge for the Nation* which was the first White Paper for forty years on employment, but reflected that the following words in the 1944 White Paper were still true.

'Employment cannot be created by Act of Parliament or by Government action alone. Government policy will be directed to bringing about conditions favourable to the maintenance of a high level of employment... but the success of the policy... will ultimately depend on the understanding and support of the community as a whole and especially on the efforts of employers and workers in industry; for without a rising standard of industrial efficiency we cannot achieve a high level of employment combined with a rising standard of living.'

The following points were emphasised in the White Paper:

— Jobs come from customer demand, i.e. when businesses produce goods and services that people want at prices they can afford;
— Public Sector Employment, however valuable, has to be paid for through taxation of both businesses and individuals;
— Adaptation to change is inevitable and something to which every part of society has to contribute;
— The role of Government, however crucial, is unfortunately limited. Its role is:

(i)   To provide a sound and stable framework of economic and industrial policy; to encourage sustained economic growth through an industrial environment in which organisations can flourish and industry and commerce can compete successfully and raise output. Thus a primary aim has to be to control inflation.

(ii) Within the economic framework the Government has to encourage jobs by removing obstacles which hinder employers taking on workers or prevent individuals using and developing their potential, and to modernise training so that job seekers are able toacquire the necessary skills for the future.

(iii) To take direct action to tackle problems of unemployment especially amongst those groups affected by changes in industry.

The White Paper lists the steps which are being taken or need to be taken to improve the movement in the labour market. The task it suggests is to improve the workings of the labour market in several ways.

(a)   In quality and incentives, so that people are neither prevented from pricing themselves into jobs (possibly by accepting lower wages than currently paid) nor deterred from taking them up.

(b)   In flexibility, so that employers and employees adapt quickly to new circumstances.

(c)   In freedom, so that employers are not so burdened by regulations that they are reluctant to offer more jobs.

Thus:

— The educational system has to recognise the importance of the wealth creating business and improve the level of vocational training for young people and adults. To this end the White Paper Education and Training for Young People 'April 1985 — *Better Schools*' suggests further modernisation of the school curriculum and the examination system, e.g. through the MSC initiative Technical and Vocational Education Initiative (TVEI) and developments in in-service training. In higher education development of plans for producing more graduates in the technological industries is needed.

— Improvements needed to be made in the Youth Training Scheme initiated in April 1983. Therefore, this was expanded from a one year duration to two years in 1985.

— More adult training initiated by the MSC should be created in the remainder of the decade.

— Industry needs to examine its training requirements with Government help, in the form of pump-priming funds, being made available where necessary through the MSC.

— Flexibility needs to be developed in patterns of work with trade unions and employers cooperating with each other to change procedures and attitudes.

— Care should be taken to avoid pay rises which are potentially damaging to competitiveness or not linked with productivity.

— More help was needed to encourage the development of new organisations. Thus, for example, schemes like the Enterprise Allowance Scheme were expanded.

— Further improvements should be made where necessary in other Government training initiatives, e.g. an expansion in the number of 'mobile trainers' working for the MSC Skill Centre Training Agency.

(8) GOVERNMENT AS A CONSUMER OF GROSS DOMESTIC PRODUCT

The problems of the British economy over the last twenty-five years or so have led to increasing concern about the levels and distribution of public expenditure. In 1900, of the £10,380 millions of Gross Domestic Product the public authorities spent £1164 millions, or 10% of GDP. In 1981, of the £260,000 millions the Government spent £129,000 millions, or 42% of GDP.

Table 9:5 Public expenditure as a percentage of gross domestic product 1978—1988

Source: White paper on Public Spending 1984—1985

1978/79	40.5%
1979/80	40.5%
1980/81	42.5%
1981/82	44.0%
1982/83	43.5%
1983/84	43.0%
1984/85	42.5%
1985/86	41% est
1986/87	40% est
1987/88	39.5% est

This represents a major influence upon the economic and financial policies within industry and commerce. The Government obtains its funds primarily by forms of direct and indirect taxation; by selling goods and services; and by borrowing. In 1984/85, taxes accounting for about 81% of the total receipts of the Government were obtained as follows (£1 billion = £1000m) in per cent items and cash terms.

	%	Approx £ Billion
Income Tax etc.	22	33.8
Corporation Tax	5	8.2
Petroleum revenue tax and oil royalties	7	8.0
Value Added Tax	12	18.4
Customs & Excise Duties	11	7.9
National Insurance Contributions	15	23.6
Interest & Dividends	4	5.3
Local Rates	9	12.8
Other sources including vehicle excise duty, capital taxes from trading surplus and rent, all contributions	9	13.0
Other revenue was raised from borrowing by Central and Local Government	6	10.1

Some examples of planned Government expenditure were as follows for 1985/86:

	in £ billion
Health and Personal Social Services	14.1
Social Security	37.2
Education	13.6
Law and Order	5.2
Defence	18.1
Industry, Energy, Trade and Employment	4.7
Environment, Housing and Transport	10.3

Table 9:6 Changes in public expenditure in real terms, 1979/80 to 1984/85

All figures in £ million	1979/80 outturn	1984/85 estimated outturn	Increase from 1979/80 to 1984/85
Defence	13,405	16,467	+22.8%
Education and science	12,994	13,125	+1.0%
Health	12,933	15,087	+16.7%
Social security	28,204	36,221	+28.4%
Industry, energy, trade and employment	5,822	6,856	+17.8%
Housing	6,569	2,979	-54.6%
Other environmental services	3,833	3,592	-6,3%
Law, order and protective services	3,746	4,837	+29.1%
Scotland	6,613	6,817	+3.1%
Northern Ireland	3,615	3,875	+7.2%

1983/4 price base

Source: *The Government's Expenditure Plans*

With revenue and expenditure levels this high, and in many cases growing, it is inevitable that there will be differences of opinion as to how far the development of the public sector has affected the competitiveness of British industry generally and how we should use our overall resources to regenerate our ability to compete in world markets.

(9) SOLVE ECONOMIC PROBLEMS

The solutions to our economic problems are varied. Some would suggest that the only way that British industry can become more efficient in the long run is to protect it for a considerable period by a combination of import controls and tariffs. Meanwhile, the Government should intervene in the economy financially and by encouraging the development of planning agreements, through the operation of a National Enterprise Board. This will require more public ownership to protect the weaker but essential industries, and more central control and intervention. The other extreme position sees the future in the development of an economy which encourages competitiveness to improve overall efficiency; reduces taxation to encourage innovation, investment and profitability; and thus reduces the restrictions on enterprises, especially high income taxes which are said to demotivate the creation of additional effort, and corporation taxes which reduce potential efficiency. The change in the impact of taxation and national insurance on a married man with two children earning the average weekly wage was illustrated by the Royal Commission for the Distribution of Income and Wealth in 1973, as follows:

Year	Tax & National Insurance Contribution as proportion of income
1955	3.0%
1975	25.0%
1983	22.5%

If one considers the effects of all taxation and includes Income Tax, National Insurance and VAT etc. as a drain on income, figures produced by the House of Commons library in July 1985 show that the proportion of earnings taken by tax in 1978/79 was 37.4% for the average family man and 41.2% in 1985/6. In order to reduce the tax burden most argue that this would require a reduction in public expenditure and a shift in the balance of resources from the public to the private sectors of the economy. Part of the reduction in public expenditure can be achieved by improving the management of resources within public sector organisations and changing the objectives of public corporations from cost minimisation to project maximisation.

Which of these strategies will be adopted from time to time will depend on the political leanings of the Government in power. One difficulty which is faced by governments generally is that they have to work within a five-year timetable, although many of the problems they face are so complex that the answers require a longer time scale. Governments

Table 9:7 Annual rate of change of wage rates, retail prices gross domestic product 1946—84

Year	Hourly wage rate Oct—Oct (Male married)	Retail prices — all items (Oct—Oct)	GDP at cost (year on year increase)
1946	9.4	—	—
1947	9.0	—	0.8
1948	8.0	7.0	4.4
1949	1.8	3.6	3.6
1950	1.2	2.5	3.7
1951	10.1	11.9	1.8
1952	7.5	6.9	-0.7
1953	4.4	1.7	4.2
1954	4.8	2.8	4.1
1955	7.0	5.3	3.3
1956	7.9	3.9	1.1
1957	5.8	4.3	1.7
1958	3.7	2.1	-0.2
1959	1.1	-0.2	4.6
1960	5.4	2.0	5.4
1961	6.4	3.9	1.8
1962	4.0	2.9	1.4
1963	2.8	2.3	3.2
1964	5.7	4.1	6.1
1965	7.2	4.8	2.7
1966	5.4	3.8	1.8
1967	5.4	2.0	1.8
1968	5.5	5.6	4.3
1969	5.6	5.4	2.0
1970	11.6	7.4	1.6
1971	11.7	9.4	1.5
1972	15.5	7.9	3.2
1973	11.3	9.9	6.1
1974	22.1	17.1	-1.8
1975	25.4	25.9	-1.9
1976	15.8	14.7	2.1
1977	5.1	14.1	2.5
1978	18.0	7.8	3.0
1979	NA	NA	NA
1980	20.7	18.0	-2.3
1981	13.0	11.9	-1.3
1982	9.4	8.6	2.1
1983	8.4	4.6	3.3
1984	7.3	6.1	2.5

Source: Various

often, however, feel it necessary to take action of temporary effectiveness to achieve immediate results. Several post-war governments, representing both political parties, have introduced incomes policies which have a short term effect but tend, in the longer term, to create higher wage demands as people try to recoup what they think they have lost.

Whatever strategies are adopted in the 1980s, it is inevitable that governments will take economic action to facilitate employment and influence business activity: as the manager of the economy as a whole and the watchdog of our overall competitive economic position, it has no choice. Ultimately it has the responsibility for creating an industrial economic environment to ensure adequate and sustained growth for the benefit of all. It must, therefore, be concerned with education, manpower planning, regional development and technological innovation and with helping organisations to cope with the problems of rapid change. Progress in our type of economy should not mean profits and benefits for the few and hardships for the many. Thus, it is also a duty of governments to ensure that there is an equitable distribution of the nation's wealth and that there are basic safeguards against hardship for those who are affected adversely, despite planning. The Government should also ensure that legislation provides the framework required to make the employment relationship equitable and should ensure that those areas where collective bargaining power is weak should not suffer too much in comparison with those whose collective bargaining strength enables them to improve their standard of living.

A Government should encourage economic activity and increase Gross Domestic Product whilst, at the same time, attempting to control the retail price index so as not to increase the pressure on wages caused by inflation. The annual rate of change in wage rates, retail prices and GDP from 1946—1984 can be seen in Table 9:7.

Chapter 10
The UK Political System

1. INTRODUCTION TO THE UK POLITICAL SYSTEM

It has long been recognised that if individuals are going to live together in a community some rules must be developed to lay down the acceptable parameters of behaviour. In order to derive those rules and control their application, some sort of leadership or government has to be established. Politics exist because individuals and groups have different interests and hold different beliefs and attitudes towards the aims, objectives and rules of their society. In order to turn the expression of their views into the reality of practice, individuals, as members of groups, have to acquire the power necessary to achieve their political objectives. It is through power that things can be done and power can be obtained by the force of the gun on the one hand or the cut and thrust of reasoned debate leading to success in a democratic election on the other.

The nature of political institutions and the manner in which they operate is influenced by the culture in which they have developed and reflect and embody the beliefs and mores of the society over time. Britain, it must be remembered, has a long history of independence and national unity and its institutions have not been affected by the wars and revolutions which have significantly influenced other societies: it has been protected from foreign invasion since 1066. Britain uniquely amongst the world nations does not have a written constitution or body of rules and practices which regulates its Government. There are, however, numerous statutes which influence the composition and powers of particular institutions. Thus for example:

— The Magna Carta of 1215 provided certain rights. Article 39 reads:

'No free man shall be taken or imprisoned or deprived of his lands or outlawed or in any way destroyed, nor will we go upon him nor put upon him, except by the lawful judgement of his peers or the law of the land'.

The free men of the Magna Carta did not include serfs but the principle was the same. The King had rights, free men had rights and even serfs had rights and no one might infringe those rights.

— In 1628 the Petition of Right prescribed that taxation could only be levied by Parliament;

— The powers of the Monarchy were limited by the Bill of Rights of 1689 and the Act of Settlement of 1701;

— The powers of the House of Lords were defined by the Parliament Acts of 1911 and 1949;

— The modern electoral system was regulated by the Representation of People Acts of 1948 and 1949.

Other individual rights have developed through a process of evolution, enforced by the judges in the Courts, based on the principles of Common Law.

Additional rights are laid down by other Acts of Parliament which establish fundamental rights and freedoms and limitations on behaviour.

The British system of Government has authority resting in a single legislative organisation — Parliament, which comprises the House of Commons, the House of Lords and the Monarch. Supreme power lies with Parliament which has direct control over legislation and indirect control over the actions of the Cabinet and the Civil Service (EEC membership has imposed some limitation on the sovereignty of Parliament, if UK legislation is found to be in conflict with EEC rights and freedoms). No Parliament can bind a future Parliament and in the UK the Government is ultimately accountable to the people and can be removed by the people.

In theory, the powers of the Sovereign to use the Royal prerogative and act without consulting Parliament are very wide. In practice, that power is restricted and the Monarch only acts on the advice of the Government members. The Monarch has power to summon, prorogue and dissolve Parliament but normally does so on the advice of the Prime Minister. Technically, the Monarch has power to select and appoint all Ministers, including the Prime Minister, but these decisions are invariably made within the Party winning an election and the appointments are confirmed by the Monarch. Thus, the influence of the Monarch these days is only indirect through the weekly meetings with the Prime Minister of the day and her reading of State Papers. All Acts of Parliament however have to receive the Royal Consent.

The House of Lords is the upper house or second chamber within Parliament and comprises hereditary peers, life peers and the Archbishops and Bishops; in essence the House of Lords is the successor of the Great Councils of the Monarch in the 11th Century. Until 1911 the House of Lords had virtually the same powers as the Commons and it could veto legislation, but by the Parliament Act of 1911 the upper house had its rights limited to delaying Bills for two years and this was reduced to one year in 1949. There are three functions of the House of Lords:

(i) It revises Bills sent to it by the Commons and sends them back to the Commons for reconsideration. This is useful because many Bills are not given a full enough debate in the Commons because of pressure of time on the discussion, and amendment and tidying up of legislation by the Upper House is generally welcomed by the Commons.

(ii) It saves the time of the Commons by giving a first hearing to non-controversial Bills introduced by the Government.

(iii) It constitutes a chamber in which major issues of national policy can be debated without the pressure of time that influences the Commons.

The House of Commons consists of 650 elected members of Parliament whose major role is to scrutinise and criticise the activities of the Government. This role can be split down into three parts:

(i) Parliament provides a system where Government can explain its policies to the electorate and where the policies can be questioned and discussed so that they can be amended, approved or rejected.

(ii) Parliament can also influence and restrain the Government by its ability to control the raising of money, primarily through taxation and its spending of that money.

(iii) Parliament is a forum through which individual members of the electorate, via their MP, can air their grievances.

One of the major functions of Parliament is, of course, to pass legislation. Every law starts as a Bill and only becomes an Act when it has been read, debated and approved three times in both the Commons and the Lords and has received the Royal Assent.

Because the MPs in their formal debates cannot give detailed consideration to all aspects of Bills and public administration in general, there are within the House of Commons a variety of sub-committees:

(i) **Standing Committees,** which are appointed for each Parliamentary session. They consist of 30/40 MPs from all political parties chosen to try to reflect the distributions of the Parties, with a Chairman apointed by the Speaker. These committees discuss and investigate the Bills proceeding through Parliament.

(ii) **Select Committees,** which inquire into specific aspects of Government can be of two types:

— *ad hoc committees* set up to inquire into specific issues, which are disbanded once the investigation and report is complete;

— *permanent committees* 14 of whom are set up to monitor the work of Government departments and others which, for example, look after matters such as privileges, European legislation, House of Commons services, Public Accounts and Statutory Instruments.

Not all legislation is totally comprehensive and many Acts of Parliament confer powers on Ministers or local authorities to make further rules, regulations and orders within the limits and purposes of the statutes. These laws, when made by Ministers, are generally known as Statutory Instruments and can be drawn up through consultation to meet changing situations or to comply with EEC legislation without having to go to the lengthy process of amending Acts through new Bills. They are known as 'delayed legislation' because they are made through the authority given by Parliament and there are some 2000 or more Statutory Instruments a year. The Select Committee on Statutory Instruments, chaired by a member of the opposition, and which includes members from both the House of Lords and the House of Commons, monitors these before they are laid before Parliament whence they become Law, if they are not challenged, after 40 days.

The relationships of Government can be represented as follows:

Figure 10:1 Relationships of Government bodies/roles

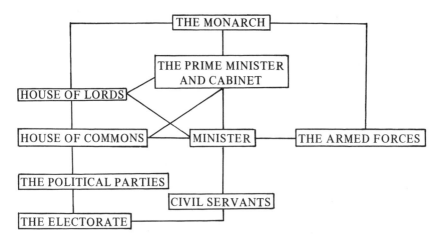

The British system of Government is referred to as a liberal democracy in that:

— Limitations are put on Government action and the power of the State by the constitutional obligations that have been established.

— Individuals and groups are tolerant of the political views and opinions of others and those views can be expressed openly as there is a recognition that society is pluralist (i.e. consists of divers views) and conflict of ideas is seen as creative.

— Periodic elections are held at least once every five years in accordance with the 1911 Parliament Act.

— There is universal franchise; since 1969 everyone over the age of 18 has the right to vote and any individual in society over the age of 21 can stand for election.

— Basic civil liberties — freedom of association, freedom of speech and freedom from arrest — are protected.

— Elected representatives, whatever their political allegiance, have to be accountable to, and represent, all members of their constituency.

The Government consists of some 100 or so ministers (a maximum number of 95 of whom can sit in the Commons); of these ministers 20 or so are the Cabinet which is headed by the Prime Minister and which meets regularly once or twice a week. It is the Cabinet which formulates and establishes Government policy. It is, therefore, the responsibility of the Cabinet which is chosen by the Prime Minister:

— To reconcile the demands of ministers and coordinate the work of departments;
— To establish the priorities of Government action;
— To further the objectives of the party in power's manifesto;
— To modify policy in the light of the current situation;
— To deal with unforeseen problems and crises, *and*
— To generally look after the well being of the nation.

A number of Cabinet Committees of either an ad hoc or a permanent nature are set up to help expedite the business of Government. These enable non-Cabinet ministers to influence policy decisions.

The ability of Parliament to control the Government is limited for the following reasons:

(i)   MPs of the Government party very rarely, in divisions of the House of Commons, vote against their party. This is particularly important where a Government has a slender majority.

(ii) Amendments to legislation are often fought by the Government, unless the objectives complement the proposed legislation, as they may be seen as ministerial defeats.

(iii) The procedure of the House requires that at Question Time each MP is restricted to one supplementary question which enables Government ministers to evade problem question's to give themselves time to respond in a more informed way.

(iv) The Government controls the Parliamentary timetable.

(v)   Government ministers are much more able to be better informed on matters than the average back bench MP, which gives them a greater edge in Parliament.

2.   VOTING PATTERNS IN POST-WAR BRITAIN

Until relatively recently, political commentators on British post-war politics have argued that we have a two party political system and that the dominance by one party in Parliament — the House of Commons — is crucial to the idea of responsible Government and the ability of the Cabinet to run the country. This belief can no longer be maintained as a general trend has been discernible away from the two-party domination of politics since June 1951 and the formation of the SDP and the SDP/Liberal Alliance in 1981/82 produced a threat to Labour/Conservative domination. This can be illustrated by tables 10:1 and 10:2.

TABLE 10:1 — PARTY VOTES AS PERCENTAGES OF ELECTORATE 1951—1983

	1951	1955	1959	1964	1966	1970	Feb. 1974	Oct. 1974	1979	1983
Conservative	39.6	38.2	38.9	33.5	31.7	33.4	29.9	26.1	33.3	30.8
Labour	40.3	35.6	34.5	34.0	36.4	31.0	29.3	28.6	28.0	20.0
										Lib/SDP
Liberal	2.1	2.1	4.6	8.6	6.5	5.4	15.2	13.3	10.5	18.4
Other	0.6	0.9	0.7	1.0	1.2	2.2	4.4	4.8	4.4	3.4
Abstentions	17.4	23.3	21.3	22.9	24.2	28.0	21.2	27.2	23.8	27.3

TABLE 10:2 — VOTES CAST AND MEMBERS ELECTED AT GENERAL ELECTIONS 1951—1983

Year	Conservative Votes	Seats	Labour Votes	Seats	Liberal Votes	Seats	Others Votes	Seats	Total Seats
1951	13718199	321	13948883	295	730345	6	198966	3	625
1955	13310891	345	12405254	277	722402	6	321182	2	630
1959	1350875	365	12216172	258	1640760	6	254845	1	630
1964	12002642	304	12205808	317	3099283	9	349415	0	630
1966	11418455	253	13096629	364	2327457	12	422206	1	630
1970	13145123	330	12208758	288	2117035	6	873882	6	630
Feb 1974	11872180	297	11645616	301	6059519	14	1762847*	23*	635
Oct 1974	10462565	277	11457079	319	5346704	13	1922756	26	635
1979	13697753	339	11509524	268	4313931	11	1799582	17	635
1983	13012612	397	8456504	209	Lib/SDP Al 7793778	23	1320590	21	650

Source: FWS Craig *British Electoral Facts* London, 1976 and *The Guardian* 5.5.79. and R. Fraser *ed.*, *Keesings' contemporary archives* Longman, 1983.

(*NB: due to realignment of the Northern Ireland Unionists.)

The argument that electoral support for the two major parties — Labour and Conservative — has reduced, can be made for a number of reasons:

(a) these two parties now win fewer votes and seats;

(b) The turnout at elections has generally declined. Turnout at elections is however generally higher in rural areas than in urban areas and is particularly low in the inner cities.

(c) bye-election results specifically show evidence of disenchantment with the two major parties;

(d) opinion polls underline the loss of support for the major parties;

(e) surveys have shown that voters are less inclined to identify themselves as Conservatives or Labour.

Despite these statements, the majority of people still tend to vote for one or other of the two major parties, but their share of the vote has steadily declined over the last 30 years. Thus, for example, in 1951, 97% of those who voted, voted either Labour or Conservative, yet in October 1974 only 75% voted for either of these two parties, and by the General Elections in 1979 and 1983 70% showed allegiance to the two major parties.

The proportion of the electorate who turn out to vote at a General Election has also declined from 82.6% in 1951 to 76.2% in 1979 and 72.7% in 1983. This has paralleled the decline in the Labour/Conservative party vote share. For example, in October 1974 the largest party vote was for the Labour Party and the second largest group were those who abstained. The Conservatives effectively came third in popularity.

There has also been an increase in those voting for other parties. In 1951 only 2.7% of the electorate voted for other parties, in February 1974, 19.6% voted for other parties and in 1983 30.1% voted for the other parties. The increase in the number of Members of Parliament representing parties other than Labour or Conservative has acquired increasing importance because it has occurred at a time when the difference in the numbers of MPs returned by the two major parties has been declining. Hence, the smaller parties are increasingly liable to hold the Parliamentary balance.

In the aftermath of the indecisive election of 1974, Ted Heath sought an agreement with the Liberal Party, but his offers were rejected and in 1977, when the Labour Party lost its overall majority in Parliament, the Labour and Liberal parties agreed to the LIB—LAB pact of March 1977, which lasted until the end of the 1977—78 Parliament and enabled the Labour Party during that time to retain Government.

This increase in electorate voting for other parties has opened the debate about our current method of electing representatives. Our method at present is 'first past the post', but other methods debated have included 'preference voting' where the votes of the weakest candidates are transferred to other candidates according to the preference of the voters and the one which has been argued should be adopted by the Liberals — proportional representation — in which the seats won are proportional to the votes cast. These arguments have occurred because the votes captured by the parties other than the major two have increased much more dramatically than their number of Parliamentary seats. This is especially evident in the February 1974 election when the Liberals gained the support of 15.2% of the population, but only obtained 2% of the Parliamentary seats. It is also evident on a regional basis for, in 1979, the Scottish Nationalist Party — the SNP — obtained 17.2% of the Scottish vote, but only returned two MPs to Parliament and, in 1970, the Welsh Nationalist Party — Plaid Cymru — obtained 11.5% of the Welsh vote, with no MPs returned.

No party since 1945 has won 50% of the votes cast and in March 1974 the Labour Party was able to form a single party Government with only 37% of the votes cast.

Bye-election results have also shown loss of support for the two main parties. Since 1964 bye-elections have shown that the party of Government is likely to lose even safe seats with large electoral swings, although the seats may return in the next General Election; for example, between 1964 and 1970 the Labour Government lost 16 of the 31 seats it defended, and between 1974 and 1979 it lost 7 of the 21 seats.

In an article 'Partisan Realignment in Britain 1964—74' in the *Scottish Journal of Political Science* Vol 7, 1977, Ivor Crewe, using survey data gathered over a 10 year period from 1964—74, found a weakening of the willingness of manual workers and workers in general to think of the Labour Party as their party, and an increase in the proportion of the electorate who consistently voted for the minor parties as an alternative to the main parties. There was also evidence of a substantial growth of those who switched from voting to abstention and the article hinted that this could be the result of an increased scepticism amongst the electorate about politicians.

Evidence also suggests that the two major parties are each moving to their own ideological extremes. Thus, the Conservative Party under Mrs. Thatcher is to the right of its predecessors and, although the Labour Party leaders identify themselves with the centre, their annual conference has tended to elect a left-wing National Executive Committee and has tended to pass left-wing resolutions.

Despite the election results of 1983 many commentators would argue that the alternation of the two major parties in office alone is becoming a more arguable presumption, especially with the formation of the Social Democratic Party in January 1981, and the SDP—Liberal Alliance which was so formidable in the total share of the votes in 1983. The Labour Party has apparently lost the old working class traditons of loyalty and solidarity which once gave them so many safe seats and the Conservatives have lost the confidence of many of the influential institutions which once backed the party. Both parties are unable to rely on the loyalty of large numbers of supporters. Particularly influential have been the geographical influences on the Parties of the Scottish and Welsh Nationalists and also the influence of the realignment of Northern Irish Unionists who, until 1974, voted in Westminster with the Conservatives. The Conservative Party is stronger in the South East including East Anglia, the Midlands and Southern England, whereas the Labour Party is stronger in the North West, Scotland, Wales and Northern England. The 1983 election has produced the following results:

Seats	Conservative	Labour	Others
N.W. Britain	103	150	18
S.E. Britain	294	59	13

One of the problems which occurs with our political system is that elections must be held at least every 5 years. The dominance of the two parties has tended to produce adversary politics with the opposition party criticising and attempting to replace the existing governing party.

This electoral system results in discontinuities in Government policy between both parties, and constant attention to the opinion polls from halfway through office. This can lead to decisions being made with the next election in mind, rather than necessarily what is required for the long-run benefit of the economy and the population in general.

Neither of the two main parties appears able to generate the conditions for overcoming Britain's economic decline or managing the recession in a way that will restore faith in Parliamentary Government and the parties themselves. So long as the central economic problems of a low annual growth rate obtains, compared with our major competitors, there will be a readiness of electors to switch their votes and party allegiancies. Annual rates of growth are given in table 10:3.

TABLE 10:3 — REAL GROSS DOMESTIC PRODUCT — ANNUAL PERCENTAGE GROWTH RATES 1960—1982

TOTAL

	1960—68	1968—73	1973—79	1979—82
USA	4.5	3.3	2.6	0.1
Japan	10.5	8.8	3.6	4.1
West Germany	4.2	4.9	2.4	0.2
France	5.4	5.9	3.1	1.0
UK	3.1	3.1	1.4	-0.5
Italy	5.7	4.6	2.6	1.2

PER HEAD OF POPULATION

	1960—68	1968—73	1973—79	1979—82
USA	3.2	2.2	1.6	-0.9
Japan	9.4	7.3	2.5	3.3
West Germany	3.3	4.0	2.6	0.1
France	4.2	5.0	2.7	0.5
UK	2.5	2.8	1.4	-0.6
Italy	5.0	4.0	2.1	-0.9

Source *OECD Historical tables* 1960—1982 OECD Paris

2. THE CONSERVATIVE PARTY

The Conservative Party structure can be represented as in Table 10:4. The Conservative Party has been more often and longer in Government in the 102 years since the extension of the voting franchise in the 1884 Third Reform Act than any of the other parties who have held Government in that time. Either alone or in coalition, they have held office for 67 years and have won fourteen of the twenty-seven elections. In order to maintain this record Conservative leaders have had to operate an electoral strategy which appeals to all sectors of the community and which ensures a substantial number of working class votes, although office holders within the Party tend to be primarily middle class. Estimates by D Butler and P Kavanagh, in *The British General Election 1983*, MacMillan, 1984, have suggested that in 1983 55% of management and professional classes (A,B + C1), 40% of the skilled working class (C2) and 33% of the unskilled working class and others (D and E) voted Conservative. Thus, in 1983, nearly 40% of the voters did not vote for the party of their social class. It was also estimated that 32% of trade unionists voted Conservative (Data from MORI polls).

Figure 10:2 Structure of the Conservative Party

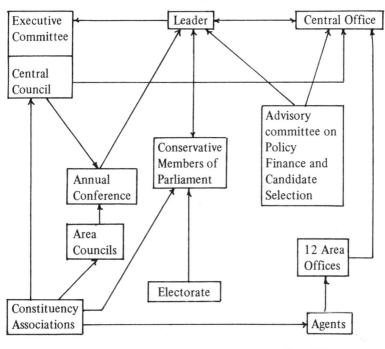

Source: A R Ball *The British Political Parties* Macmillan, 1981

Conservative leaders have tried to ensure that the party does not consider itself to be an instrument of any particular part of the electorate. There is a tendency to identify it as the party of big business finance but it has a following amongst all class groups thus, for example, in 1983 members of the relatively affluent working class who were car owners, employed in the private sector, and buying their own houses, tended to vote Conservative.

Home-ownership was especially significant. MORI found that, whereas council house tenants voted 49% Labour and 29% Conservative, the figures amongst working class voters owning or buying their own homes were 26% Labour and 47% Conservative voting.

All important powers in the party are concentrated in the hands of the Leader to whom all the major Committees, Central Office departments and area offices report. The Cabinet is appointed by the Leader as is the Chairman and all the other leading officials of the party. Financially it is the wealthiest of the political parties.

Members of Parliament are in class and social terms unrepresentative of their electorate. According to Butler and Kavanagh (op.cit) in 1983 71% of MPs were university educated (48% from Oxbridge) 70% attended Public Schools, 45% were professionals and 36% were businessmen.

Since the election of Margaret Thatcher as Leader of the Party in 1975, the Conservative policy has moved more to the right than previously. The party has now adopted economic policies which owe more to nineteenth century laissez-faire values than to the corporatist principles that were developing during the 1960s and early 1970s under both of the major parties.

The chief policy bases of the Conservative Party are:-

(a) Inflation is a consequence of too much money in circulation, so a reduction in the money supply will reduce inflation and stimulate a more efficient economy. It is recognised that the adoption of such a policy leads to higher unemployment in the short and medium term but, in the long term, this is merely a temporary phenomenon.

(b) There should be a reduction in the role and emphasis of the State, especially in the provision of social and welfare services.

(c) There should be greater reliance on the market mechanism and a reduction of State intervention in the economy. The sale of Government holdings in British Telecom, BP, National Freight Co. Ltd., the proposed privatisation of British Airways, British Gas, British Transport Docks Board are examples. As a consequence, major State aid to ailing sectors of the economy should be reduced.

(d) There should be a shift from direct to indirect taxation to encourage the individual enterprise necessary for industrial reorganisation.

(e) Trade unions should be controlled so that they do not use their monopolistic position to hinder free market economic forces and impinge on the freedom of individual citizens. To quote from the Conservative election manifesto, Conservatives are 'committed to redressing the balance in industrial relations by curbing the abuse of Trade Union power wherever it occurs and by tackling some of the uniquely privileged positions of Trade Unions under the law'. The 1980 and 1982 Employment Acts go some way towards protecting individuals against the collective power of the Trade Unions and the Trade Union Act 1984 is aimed at increasing democracy in Trade Unions.

(f) There should be continued reduction in public spending.

Summary of Tory Party Policy:

—   free market economy;
—   trade union reform;
—   cuts in public expenditure and taxation;
—   sale of nationalised industry (privatisation);
—   economic liberalism to create a climate of profitability and enterprise to encourage small businesses;
—   rigid monetary targets;
—   no interference in wage negotiation;
—   no help to lame ducks;
—   the unity of the UK.

There are inevitable conflicts between the different wings of the Party on these economic policies, but these differences tend to represent differences of emphasis rather than differences of fundamental ideology. The so called 'wets' are heirs of those who believed in Keynesian economic policies and who are less sure of the validity and desirability of allowing free market forces to operate. Broad agreement exists over the need for public spending cuts, reform of trade unions, and inflation control, but they disagree about the primary reliance on monetarism as the way to bring these objectives to fruition.

4. THE LABOUR PARTY

The structure of the Labour Party can be depicted as in Figure 10:5.

The Labour Party Constitution is formal and elaborate and attempts to control the Leader. It is based on the assumption that the Leader is in office to carry out the wishes of the members of the party. In practice, policy is decided by the National Executive Committee which the Annual Conference elects. The Leader must be re-elected every year when the party is in opposition. The party franchise in the selection of the party leader and the deputy leader has been extended and the choice is not left entirely to MPs. More power has been given to the NEC and the Constituency parties. More power has also been given to the NEC in the drafting of the election manifesto and re-selection of MPs takes place by constituency parties between General Elections, thus giving more power to the rank and file. Trade unions control 40% of the votes for Leader, the constituency parties 30% with the Parliamentary Labour Party the other 30%.

The Labour Party was founded in 1900 and grew out of the political

Figure 10:3 Structure of the Labour Party

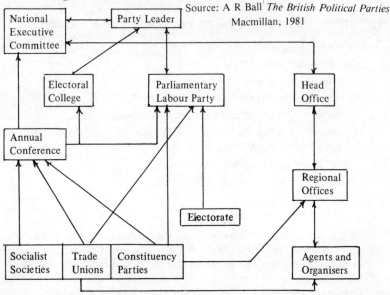

Source: A R Ball *The British Political Parties*
Macmillan, 1981

desires of the trade union movement. After its foundation in 1900, it was more of a pressure group than a political party and its hopes of political success rested on its ability to persuade other parties to legislate on its behalf. Both in 1924 and 1929, the party took office without having a majority in the House of Commons and, as a result, it found it had the responsibility of governing without the power to govern.

The Labour Party is a coalition of socialists and was formed to express the views of the trade union movement. The unifying beliefs of the groupings within the party can be said to be the use of Parliamentary means for achieving power; the goal of economic equality of opportunity in income, wealth and living standards; the elimination of poverty; protection of working class interests; and a vision of society as one in which the means of production, distribution and exchange are publicly owned. Divisions exist over the range of policy options and the extent to which socialist ideals should be promulgated in Government.

Labour Party support is broad but its greatest support comes from amongst the working classes in general, especially amongst the unskilled. Thus, in 1983, according to Butler and Kavanagh (op. cit.) 16% of the social classes AB + C1 voted labour, 32% of the C2's, and 41% of the D's and E's voted for the party. Labour therefore reflected only a portion of the working class, only 38% of manual workers and 39% of trade union members — blue collar and white collar — voted Labour.

Crucial to the strength of the Labour Party are the trade unions in 1983. They provide the party with 79% of its finance. In 1983 6.0 million of the Labour Party's 6.4 million members were affiliated to the party as members of trade unions. The unions dominate the seats on the National Executive Committee. Unions also sponsor MPs and, in 1983 there were 115 union-sponsored MPs in the Parliamentary Labour Party, out of a total of 209 Labour MPs in all. The figures from 1900—1983 can be seen in Table 10:4.

Table 10:4 1983 election — union sponsored candidates

Union	Total	Elected
TGWU	30	25
AUFW	27	17
NUM	14	14
GMBATU	14	11
ASTMS	11	10
NUR	12	10
NUPE	10	4
APEX	3	3
COHSE	3	3
ECTPU	7	3
POEV	3	3
SOGAT '82	2	2
USDAW	2	2
UCATT	2	1
SLADE	2	1
OTHERS	9	5
TOTAL	154	115
COOPERATIVE PARTY	17	8

Unions influence Labour Party voting by their participation in the annual conference and their influence on the election of the National Executive Committee, where they have 12 direct representatives out of the 26 seats, and are heavily involved in the election of the 5 women representatives, the leader of the party, deputy leader and treasurer. They thus have influence over 20 of the 26 seats. The union's voting system at the conference for NEC places is often criticised because the block vote system is used which allows the unions to ignore minority opinions.

Communication takes place with those unions who are not affiliated to the Labour Party but who are affiliated to the TUC by the existence of a Labour Party — TUC Liaison Committee, which comprises 9 members of the Parliamentary Labour Party, 10 representatives of the NEC and 7 representatives of the TUC.

The social background of the Labour MPs elected in 1983 was more cosmopolitan than that of their Conservative colleagues, according to the Nuffield election studies; 53% went to University, 14% had been to Public School; 42% were professionals and 9% businessmen, 33% were working class and 16% were miscellaneous and white collar.

Table 10:5 Union sponsored MPs 1900—1983

Election year	No of Labour MPs	No of Union Sponsored MPs	% of MPs who were Union Sponsored
1900	2	1	50
1906	30	21	70
1910—1	40	38	95
1910—2	42	39	92.8
1918	57	49	85.9
1922	142	86	60.6
1923	191	102	53.4
1924	151	88	58.2
1929	287	115	40.1
1931	46	32	69.5
1935	154	79	51.3
1945	393	121	30.8
1950	315	110	34.9
1951	295	105	35.6
1955	277	96	34.6
1959	258	93	36.0
1964	317	120	37.9
1966	364	132	36.3
1970	287	114	39.7
1974 Feb.	301	127	42.2
1974 Oct.	319	129	40.1
1979	269	133	49.6
1983	209	115	55.0

Source: *Various*

Not all trade unions are affiliated to the Labour Party and, in 1984, only 54 trade unions had a political fund. This does not mean that, of those 54, all their members are affiliated to the Labour Party, as many members go through the process of contracting out of the political levy. Thus, for instance, in 1977 only 44% of SOGAT (82) members were affiliated, whereas 98% of ASLEF members were.

Table 10:6 Political allegiances of Trade Union members

White Collar Trade Unionists (3.6m)

	June 1983	Jan/March 1984
Labour	27%	36%
Conservatives	38%	39%
Liberal/SDP	33%	22%

Blue Collar Trade Unionists (6.4m)

Labour	46%	56%
Conservatives	27%	25%
Liberal/SDP	26%	15%

Overall Position (Blue Collar and White Collar)

	Oct. 1974	May 1979	June 1983	June 1984
Labour	55%	51%	39%	51%
Conservative	23%	33%	31%	26%
Liberal/SDP	16%	13%	29%	21%

Source *MORI* 1984

The main features of Labour Party policies could be summarised as follows, as stated in their 1983 manifesto *The New Hope for Britain*:

— increased public investment including transport, housing and energy conservation;
— increased investment in industry especially in new technology with some steering of jobs and industries to areas of high need. Creation of a National Investment Bank;
— new job subsidies and allowances to encourage employment and training;
— a new Department of Industrial and Economic Planning with a 5 year National Plan in consultation with employers and trade unions. As anounced by Roy Hattersley and Labour Chancellor in April 1985, a new social contract with the unions;
— repeal Conservative legislation on industrial relations and make provision for introducing industrial democracy;
— common pension age of 60 to be introduced;
— return to public ownership of public assets sold off by the present Government;
— improve social services;
— increase spending on education;
— introduce positive action programmes to promote women's rights and opportunities and the rights and opportunities of racial minorities;
— on defence — new initiatives to promote peace and development;
— cancel Trident, refuse to deploy Cruise Missiles and begin discussions on the removal of Nuclear bases from Britain;
— prepare for Britain's withdrawal from the EEC.

Conflict often occurs between the left of the party, organised around the Tribune Group, and on the right of the party, those organised around the Manifesto Group. There are frequent claims that the party is being infiltrated by various militant groups. The close relationship with the trade unions does not, however, ensure an ability to obtain total cooperation from the unions, as the events in 1969 over '*In Place of Strife*' and 1979 over Incomes Policy show, although agreements like the Social Contract and the Concordat of 1979 are more likely with Labour than the Conservatives. Tensions within the Labour Party as to policy can influence its share of the vote, which dropped in 1983 to 20% of the electorate — the smallest poll percentage since 1931. The most recent arguments between the left and the leadership over the selection of MPs and the involvement of those with militant tendencies, have still left the party with a poor position in the opinion polls. The party lost an unprecedented 119 deposits in 1983 and returned 209 MPs, 49 less than in any post-war election.

5. THE LIBERAL PARTY

The Liberal Party was strong in British politics from the mid-nineteenth century to the outbreak of the First World War, but it declined to a minor position in the 1930s, 1940s and 1950s. Liberal policy for a long time has talked of a partnership between capital and labour and some form of industrial democracy; it has long advocated membership of the Common Market.

Since the Second World War the number of Liberal MPs at Westminster has varied between 6 and 14, yet the actual share of the votes which the Liberals have gained has been increasing and Liberals have judged their performance on this ability to gain votes rather than the winning of Parliamentary seats. Their share of the vote has been as low as 2.5% in 1951, and as high as 19.3% in February 1974 (see Table 10:7). Yet only at one election in October 1974 has the party fought all the Parliamentary seats. During the 1960s it tended only to fight 50% of them. Normally seats are fought or left unfought depending on local decisions, which reflect organisational preparedness and the political confidence of the local constituency. For the first time in 1983 all the Parliamentary seats on the mainland were fought by the Liberal/SDP Alliance.

Evidence suggests that there is a hard core Liberal vote which spans all the social groupings but with an emphasis particularly in the lower middle classes, especially professionals, and then a much larger group of Liberal sympathisers. According to Alt *et al's* survey (J Alt *et al* Angels in plastic — the Liberals surge in 1974 *Political Studies* XXV, 1977) the Liberal core voter is less concerned with such matters as prices, unemployment, taxation and social services, and more concerned about industrial democracy and equality of treatment for minority groups and with environmental problems like nuclear power stations. Most evidence suggests that the floating Liberal vote is a result of dissatisfaction with the other major political parties and especially those with a central (as distinct from left or right) belief on many economic and social issues. Thus, the emphasis on moderation rather than extremism by the Liberal Party attracts votes. Interestingly enough evidence suggests that the Liberal Party does best when the Conservatives rather than Labour have been in power, especially at bye-elections. This has tended to reinforce the view amongst many Liberals that it is more in opposition to the Conservatives than to the Labour Party and explains the Lib-Lab pact of 1974.

Liberal candidates tend to pursue a policy of 'community politics' and concentrate on local issues which are of direct concern to the local voters.

Liberal Party Policies

The main features of Liberal Party Policies could be outlined as follows:

— worker participation and profit sharing (in firms of 50 +) are seen as important. Thus, every company of 20 + employees should have a Works Council with a statutory right to information, consultation and joint decision making;

— supervisory Boards would be introduced in all companies of 200 + employees, with no requirement that the only channel for elections would be through the union;

— trade unions should be encouraged to improve communications and consultation with their members;

— an agreed system should be developed for determining public sector pay;

— civil liberties and fundamental freedom should become a constitutional right;

— decentralisation in decision making to the Regions with Regional and Community Enterprise Boards;

— stronger statutory protection of the environment;

— expansion of public spending, especially in the development of new technologies, training and retraining, new building programmes;

— retention of membership of the EEC;

— support the NATO alliance, the establishment of a Nuclear free zone, abandon the concept of an independent nuclear deterrent.

Liberal MPs are overwhelmingly middle class — of the 17 Liberals returned to Parliament in the 1983 election, 11 came from the professional middle class and there was one farmer, one businessman, 3 publishers and 5 journalists. Generally, the Liberals fail to get consistent working class support.

Table 10:7 Liberal election results 1950—1983

Election	Seats won	% vote	No of candidates	No of lost deposits
1950	9	9.1	475	319
1951	6	2.5	109	66
1955	6	2.7	110	60
1959	6	5.9	216	55
1964	9	11.2	365	52
1966	12	8.5	311	104
1970	6	7.5	332	184
1974 Feb.	14	19.3	517	23
1974 Oct.	13	18.5	619	125
1979	11	13.8	577	284
1983	17	13.8	322*	7

*Seats split with SDP

Source: D E Butler and A Sloman *British political facts 1900—1979*, 1980, Macmillan; D E Butler and D Kavanagh *The British general election of 1983*, 1984, Macmillan.

6. THE NATIONALIST PARTIES: SCOTTISH NATIONALIST PARTY (SNP) AND PLAID CYMRU (PC)

The fortunes of the Liberal Party in the 1960s and 1970s have to some extent been mirrored by the SNP and PC, who experienced increased electoral participation in local and national elections. There followed a slow ebbing of support with defeats in the 1975 EEC referendum, while the devolution referendums of March 1979 constituted a reversal for the SNP and disaster for PC. Table 10:8 gives vote shares for SNP and PC. The nationalist parties in 1983 obtained 1.5% of the UK vote.

10:8 Vote shares for the Scottish Nationalist Party & Plaid Cymru 1959—1983

	SNP		PC	
	Seats	% Scottish vote	Seats	% Welsh vote
1959	0	0.8	0	5.2
1964	0	2.4	0	4.8
1966	0	5.0	0	4.3
1970	1	11.4	0	11.5
1974 Feb.	7	21.9	2	10.7
1974 Oct.	11	30.4	3	10.0
1979	2	17.3	2	8.1
1983	2	11.8	2	7.8

The Nationalist Parties have been the recipients of a negative protest vote and have reflected the reactions to regional economic difficulties — both Scotland and Wales have a feeling of neglect at Westminster. The SNP case was helped enormously by the development of North Sea oil, for it can be argued that an independent Scotland would not suffer enormously from a break up of the UK. PC has no such advantage but its support is rooted firmly in the principality's culture and language, and is greatest in the Welsh speaking areas.

7. NORTHERN IRELAND PARTIES

Before 1972 Northern Ireland enjoyed a measure of self government and therefore the elections to the Stormont Parliament were more important than Westminster elections. Economic and class factors play an unimportant role in Northern Ireland. Political allegiance and voting behaviour occurs because of religion: Protestants vote for the various Unionist parties and for the maintenance of links with Britain, whereas the Catholics (33% of the population) tend to vote for Unification Parties.

Until the 1970s the Unionist parties in Northern Ireland were indistinguishable from the Conservative Party, but with the 1972 suspension of the Stormont Parliament, these old alliances broke up and the Ulster Unionist Party fragmented into different units. The old

Nationalist Party disappeared and its place was taken by the Social Democratic and Labour Party (SDLP). After 1974, the Protestant MPs refused to follow the Conservative Party whip and there are now 12 independent MPs who do not specifically align themselves with any of the other majorparties.

In contrast to the position in the rest of Great Britain, turnout in the 1983 General Election rose compared with 1979.

Northern Ireland voters had the choice of 6 political parties for the 17 seats which were contested in 1983 — the results were as follows:

— the Official Unionist Party (OUP) — 11 seats — 34% of the vote;
— Provisional Sinn Fein — 1 — 13.4% of the vote;
— Alliance Party MSLGASS — 8% of the vote;
— Democratic Unionists Party (DUP) — 3 — 20% of the vote;
— Social Democratic and Labour Party (SDLP) — 1 — 17.9% of the vote;
— Ulster Popular Unionist Party — 1.

8. SOCIAL DEMOCRATIC PARTY

A new party was formed in January 1981 by some disaffected Labour MPs and ex MPs who were concerned with the increasing involvement of the 'left' in the design of the Labour Party's policies, especially the arguments for unilateral disarmament and to discontinue membership of the EEC. The initial founders of the party — the 'gang of four' were ex MP (at that time) Shirley Williams, Bill Rodgers, David Owen and the ex Labour MP and President of the EEC, who in the Dimbleby Lecture in November 1979 had argued for a party of the 'radical centre', Roy Jenkins. In March 1981 the party was formally established supported by 14 ex Labour MPs and one Conservative. By 1982 the SDP MPs numbered 29 and opinion polls showed the SDP in alliance with the Liberals as a powerful embryonic force in British Politics. In the 1983 General Election, 23 out of the SDP MPs were not re-elected.

The SDP produced thirteen green papers in 1982—83 which outlined their policies. A manifesto *Working together for Britain* was published in 1983 in liaison with the Liberals. Its main features were:

— to reduce unemployment by means of Government borrowing, more public investment in programmes of housing, and environmental development and improvement;
— no further nationalisation or de-nationalisation;
— in industrial relations, secret ballots for the election of trade union national executives;
— strike ballots, if required by 10% of those likely to be affected;
— control of wages through tripartite agreement annually by Government, trade unions and employers with an assessment board to deal

with public sector bargaining, providing there is agreement not to strike, and a prices and pay commission which could refuse price rises to those organisations which did not follow the 'norms';

— pre-entry closed shops should be illegal, but workers should have the right to a closed shop if a majority vote in favour;

— each workplace should have a Works Council which should have the right to share decisions on day-to-day matters and information on future plans, e.g. mergers, location changes, closures, investments;

— electoral reform on a single transferable vote system;

— decentralisation or sharing of power, proposals include: directly elected assemblies for Scotland and Wales and twelve English regional assemblies which would be able to plan and finance industrial development in their regions. A move towards local income tax;

— continued membership of the EEC;

— Defence Policy to include remaining in NATO and, whilst retaining some nuclear weapons, to reduce reliance on them by strengthening conventional forces. The establishment of nuclear free zone of 95 miles in Western Europe in each side of the East/West divide;

— the establishment of a Human Rights Commission to replace the Equal Opportunities Commission and the Commission for Racial Equality — the basic rights and freedoms of the European Convention on Human Rights should be incorporated in UK law;

— education policy includes an aim to move towards smaller classes, more opportunities in higher education (especially for 'late developers'), and to renew the tax advantages of independent schools;

— In a policy paper 'Focus on the Future, a strategy for Innovation' published in August 1985, proposed a five year programme to end the skills crisis in high technology electronics with cash incentives to stimulate new technology ventures, and tax incentives, among the proposals is a 'mobilisation programme' to train more graduates and technicians in skills in short supply and to broaden the educational base so that those under 18 would be obliged to take a combination of mathematics, science, technical vocational subjects in addition to any arts and humanities subjects. A further SDP/Liberal document published and accepted at the SDP conference in September 1985 entitled 'Facing the Jobs Challenge' proposes spending an extra £5,000 million to create jobs.

At the General Election in 1983, the SDP — Liberal Alliance polled 25.4% of those voting. However the SDP share was as follows:

Table 10:9 SDP election results 1983

	Seats	% rate	Number of Candidates	Lost Deposits
1983	6	11.6	311	6

Of the 6 MPs elected, 3 came from the professions and the other 3 came from middle class white collar jobs; 4 went to university (3 Oxbridge) and 2 had attended Public Schools.

The SDP's Alliance could, in the long term, be a success at least in holding the balance of power between the two (historically) major parties; on the other hand, internal inconsistencies in policy, who fights what constituencies and who would be Prime Minister designate could cause problems for both parties — Liberal and SDP. An important factor also in the cooperation over seats in elections is that, although they are fighting seats in 'Alliance', there is no guarantee that those who do not identify themselves with one party's policies, Labour or Conservative, will see the Alliance candidate as an alternative.

9. EFFECT ON PERSONNEL MANAGEMENT

With the reduction in the vote for the two major parties over the last 25 years or so, it is increasingly likely that the balance of power in future Parliaments will be held by the minority parties. This could have the effect of reversing the trend where one party, when it gains power, either repeals, in entirety employment legislation passed by the other party, or amends the legislation to limit what are seen as the excesses of the previous Government. It thus will be less easy to forecast the likely effects on legislation with changes in Government. This was illustrated in the period of the weak Labour Government, under Harold Wilson in 1964, which only had a majority of 3 over all the other parties after 2 months of office. Priority was given to winning the next election and policies were therefore much less radical than people would have expected.

If the Nationalist parties were to hold the power balance, we could expect to see an influence on regional policies and perhaps some form of devolution, which would bring their own advantages in the form of grants and subsidies, but could also interfere with the existing features of particular labour markets as firms transfer in to provide competition in the labour market for existing firms. At the same time, personnel managers may be faced with the problems of transferring key labour to new units in order to start up production processes or the provision of services.

If the Liberal/SDP Alliance were to be successful in forming a Government, we are likely once again to be faced with the problems of incomes policies and the pressures that result from trade unions and also the consequential effects on differentials and relativities in organisations.

The issues would be clearer if either of the two major parties were returned to power, although how far they could fulfil their manifesto promises would depend on the levels of economic activity and the pressures of inflation, the balance of trade and the value of sterling and levels of unemployment. Only if we can increase the growth in our gross domestic product, whilst at the same time, holding down increases in retail prices (which are inevitably affected by the price Government charges for its services), can we reduce pressures on wage rates and allow organisations and their personnel staffs to devote their time to the other crucial issues of productivity and the introduction of technological innovations.

The increasing involvement of Government in the public sector and the consequential financial and manpower cut backs have adversely affected relations between the employers and the trade unions in those industries. Disputes in recent years in the local authorities, the coal mines, the railways, the NHS, education, fire service, water industry, etc., have left scars which, in the present economic climate, will be slow to heal. Issues like control of wages and privatisation will continue to cause problems into the next decade.

Chapter 11
The Labour Market in the UK

In 1985 there were 33½ million people in Great Britain who were of working age. This is 1.6 million more than in 1976, due to a rise in the birth rate in the 1960s and the drop in retirements due to the low birth rate during the 1914—18 era. There were 26½ million people either in employment or seeking employment, which was 4 million more than in 1951 and 1 million more than in 1976. The number of men in the labour force was around 15½ million and the number of females around 11 million.

It is estimated, in the White Paper *Employment: The Challenge for the Nation,* that over the next few years the population of working age will rise by about 500,000 to just over 33.9 million in 1989 and will then remain broadly unchanged until the year 2000.

Although the focus of personnel management is upon individuals and groups of people in organisations, it is important to remember that these individuals and groups are members of a much larger number of people — the UK labour force as a whole. Over time, changes occur in the total labour force, both in terms of its age and sex distribution and in the skills available within the community. This is partly due to the level of demand from companies for certain skills and partly to the willingness of individuals to develop certain skills and to enter particular jobs. Manpower is a key resource in society and there is thus a need for governments to consider manpower in the forefront of their industrial and commercial strategy and planning.

Although it may appear callous, labour can be considered to be the same as other factors of production, e.g. materials and machines, in that it is bought and sold for a price. Features like unemployment, non-discrimination by race or sex in pay, and the effects of incomes policies in attempting to control the price of labour, must be examined within the context of the general social and economic forces which inevitably affect the working of the market.

1. WHAT IS A LABOUR MARKET?

A labour market is a complex system with people offering themselves for work and with employers seeking to recruit and retain the workers they need by offering rewards or pay for services rendered. We tend to talk generally about *the* labour market, but the labour market in fact operates as a series of distinct markets with boundaries determined by geographical, occupational, industrial, and organisational boundaries. Whilst the boundaries of these markets tend to overlap in places, they can be regarded as separate entities. Sometimes there is little or no movement between labour markets, for example, the labour market for steeplejacks is different to, and separate from, the labour market for dress designers. We can expect little or no movement at all between them, even if there were vacancies for steeplejacks and an over-supply of dress designers. Conversely, other markets overlap considerably; so you will get semi-skilled car workers moving from the car industry into, for example, the electrical components industry.

The major influences on demand for labour within the market include the demand for products and services produced by the organisations which employ the labour; the technology which is used for producing those goods and services and whether it is labour intensive or not; the type of labour, in terms of skills that are available; and the degree to which organisations operate, what has been termed the internal labour market by Doeringer and Piore in *Internal Labour Markets and Manpower Analysis,* (1971), i.e. the extent to which employers try to insulate themselves from the pressures in the external labour market by favouring the employees inside their own organisations for higher level jobs in terms of skill, pleasantness and responsibility.

2. INTERNAL LABOUR MARKETS

The factors which influence the extent to which organisations will operate internal labour markets include the cost of labour turnover, i.e. recruitment, selection and training costs; the influence of trade unions and staff associations in protecting the job security of their members; the custom and practice arrangements on seniority rights which have developed; and the degree to which training is specific to the organisation. As labour turnover is most likely to occur in the early months of employment, organisations will tend to prefer to utilise existing employees who can be retrained for more senior or more responsible jobs. They can reduce the costs of hiring labour (which could be scarce) by training existing staff who are already felt to be committed to the organisation. This provides an incentive for those people who wish to develop their skills further to remain with an organisation. Thus organisations will attempt to leave themselves with a situation where they only incur the costs of hiring, i.e. advertising and screening, for those skills which are more readily available in the open market and where the costs are likely to be lower.

In some industries, e.g. steel manufacture, where trade unions perhaps operate a closed shop and attempt to protect the job security of existing employees, they will only allow management to promote employees who have a certain length of service. Over the years custom and practice reduces the tendency of such an organisation to go into the labour market.

We can recognise an internal labour market at work by the following features:

— All jobs, except the lowest in certain skills categories, are filled through internal advertising, which leads to promotion and retraining for existing workers. There are thus what are called specific *entry ports*;

— The wage system will be based on rigid differentials, according to an internal grading system, and the wage differentials will have little relationship with external forces. Thus wages are linked to the job, not the workers themselves;

— Seniority rights are widespread. For example, labour reductions are often based on the concept of last in first out (LIFO); there are overtime possibilities for long service workers.

Good examples of internal labour markets exist in the public sector, e.g. for teachers, civil servants, nursing staff and hospital doctors. Internal labour markets can be said to have developed partly because within organisations skills, whether they are transferable or not, become developed within specific jobs and require training which is specific to the particular job or organisation and often acquired on the job. Experience with particular technologies can tend to be 'firm specific' because of the particular idiosyncrasies within each plant. Equipment use can generate training which has value only within one organisation, especially where particular rules, regulations and standards operate.

3. DUAL LABOUR MARKET

Some people argue that the total labour market, apart from being divided on geographical, occupational, industrial and organisational or internal labour market lines, can also be sub-divided into two generally separate sectors, primary and secondary.

(a) Primary labour markets

These markets contain the skilled and professional workers. Jobs tend to be performed within large firms; unionisation tends to be generally strong; wages are high; working conditions are good; job security and employment stability are high; and there are good prospects of advancement and training for promotion and to retain workers.

(b) Secondary labour markets

These markets contain the less attractive jobs which tend to have a low skill or knowledge requirement. There tend to be few training or promotional opportunities; working conditions are poor with long hours and relatively low levels of payment for work done. Organisations in these markets tend to suffer from high levels of labour turnover because there is little economic and psychological satisfaction from employment. Individuals employed in the secondary labour market find it difficult to move into the primary market because their education and skills are of a low level. Doeringer and Piore, in *Internal Labour Markets and Manpower Analysis* (1977) argue that, within the primary labour market, workers are judged in relation to their skills and potential productivity, considering their employment. Lower skilled workers are less likely to obtain employment because organisations will require a basic level of skill and experience. Those workers who are unsuccessful in obtaining work in the primary sector will, therefore, be forced to seek work in the secondary sector, but this sector does not allow them to increase their marketability by increasing their skills because of the nature of work in the secondary labour market. They are forced to remain in that sector. Examples of the secondary sector include unskilled work in the hotel and catering and the construction industries.

4. MOBILITY OF LABOUR

It can be argued that as employers, regions and occupations prosper and increase their labour demand, the chance of stable earnings and employment prospects will lead to an increased supply of people in those successful sectors or areas and reduced supply in less prosperous sectors as individuals adapt their skills and change their place of residence to take advantage of job opportunities. There are, however, many imperfections and regidities in the overall labour market which prevent the demand being supplied by those with appropriate skills, knowledge and experience. This is partly caused by inadequate mobility of labour from one region to another, even though jobs may not be available to individuals in their current region. The following factors are likely to influence labour mobility:

(a)   Inefficiency in information flow — jobs may be available in a particular organisation, area or occupation but recruitment methods are such that suitable workers do not know about them and are thus unable to take them. Although the MSC argues that the job centre system is efficient in matching jobs to suitable employees, their report *The Employment Service in the 1980s* showed that the Employment Service only handled 18% of total engagements in 1976—1977, increasing to 20% in 1979.

(b)   People may hear about vacancies, but may not have the relevant qualifications and skills to be eligible for them. At current levels of economic activity, organisations may not be prepared to give them the chance of acquiring skills, unless the jobs are those for which there is an acute shortage.

(c)   Individuals may not be able to afford the cost of moving house to work in another area, especially those who own their own homes and who are moving from an area which is hit especially hard by the depression and find it difficult to sell their existing house.

(d) Psychologically, people may not be willing to move from an area where most of their friends and relatives live and where their roots are.

(e) Higher skilled, managerial and professional workers are more likely to move than semi-skilled and unskilled workers, who may not be prepared to take the risk of moving.

(f) Younger workers with few family ties may be more prepared to move or more able to afford to purchase or rent property, especially if they currently live in a high cost property area.

(g) Employers and trade unions may impose restrictions on entry to specific jobs, which means that those technically qualified to fill them may not be able to do so.

5. SUPPLY OF LABOUR

The total supply of labour in the UK is of major significance in determining the success of the economy. The supply is limited by the total population and its age and sex distribution and what is known as the participation rate or activity rate of those of working age. In addition, the legal framework of society determines the minimum age at which people leave school (at present at 16) and it may also influence the retirement age. Most men are entitled to a State pension at the age of 65 and most women at the age of 60. Social attitudes, often underpinned by legislation, can also influence the ability of minority groups, especially women, to obtain employment.

The size of the total population, which was around 54.3 million for the UK in 1981, sets the upper limit on the supply of labour. Within this figure are 26.3 million males and 28 million females (1981 census data). The population size is influenced by three major factors — the death rate, the birth rate and the level of migration, i.e. immigration and emigration.

6. PARTICIPATION RATES

The *participation rate* or activity rate measures the percentage of those who can work, are of working age and who actually offer themselves as available for work to their appropriate labour market. The 1983 labour force survey shows that the over 60s have been leaving the work force rapidly during the 1980s. Thus, figures in the July 1984 *Employment Gazette* showed that economically active men aged 60—64 declined from 69.6% in 1981 to 59.6% in 1983. Overall, too, the proportion of men over school age who were economically active declined between

223

1981—83, whereas the proportion of women marginally increased, especially in the 25—34 age group. The survey also reported that 51.1% of Britain's employed in 1983 were in non-manual occupations, the swing from manufacturing to service industries also being maintained with the retail trade, banking, finance, insurance, other services and hotel and catering showing the biggest increase. Economic activity by age group was as follows:

Table 11:1 Economic activity by age — 1983 labour force survey

% economically active i.e. employed or looking for work

Source: *1983 Labour Force Survey*

Age	Male	Female	Total
16—19	69.3	64.4	66.9
20—24	90.1	70.1	80.2
25—34	95.9	57.4	76.7
35—49	96.1	69.1	82.7
50—59	88.8	57.8	73.0
60—64	59.6	21.2	39.3
65 +	8.7	3.8	5.8

Labour economists would argue that most individuals decide to offer themselves for work through a household decision. A household allocates its labour resources and makes a choice between what can be called market work or non-market work, which includes housework, leisure and time spent in education. The decision on what proportion to allocate to market versus non-market work is influenced by a number of factors which can be listed as follows:

— The total household's financial resources and its perceived needs — some households will be able to purchase the necessities of life, based on one income, whereas some will have a higher level of needs or may not be able to manage on one income and will require two or more.

— The non-work sources of income, e.g. State social security benefits investment income and property income.

— The economic and social values placed on non-market activites and leisure. Some may be able to work but may prefer to use their time in other ways.

— The availability of work in the labour market.

In the UK the participation rates of males have fallen over this century due to increased education, voluntary early retirement and the lowering of the retirement age. The highest rate of participation occurs amongst males in the age group 20—60; between these ages almost all those who are not in full time education, and are not seriously physically or mentally handicapped, are working or registered as unemployed.

Although legislation, in the form of the Equal Pay Act 1970 (as amended by the Equal Pay Amendment Regulations 1983) and the Sex Discrimination Act 1975, has reduced the degree of sexual discrimination in the UK, there are still a number of jobs which can be identified as typically male or typically female. In addition, attitudes are slow to change as we can see if we chart some successes in the history of equal opportunity. For example:

1893	first female factory inspectors
1898	first female architect
1920	first female magistrate
1929	first female Cabinet minister
1945	first female prison governor
1958	first female bank manager
1966	first female racehorse trainer

(Source *Employment News* March, 1985)

The participation rate of unmarried females has fallen over this century due to increased education and earlier retirement. This decline has been offset by the increased participation rate of married women. Table 11:1 gives the percentages of the participation of married women drawn from official census figures:

Table 11:2 Participation rate of married women 1911—1982

Year	Percentage of those in work or actually seeking work
1911	9.6
1921	8.7
1931	10.0
1951	21.7
1961	29.7
1971	42.3
1982	40.0

Source: Various

The reasons for this are complex, because the decision on married women's participation is often taken in a family context. Evidence suggests that the higher the level of the husband's wage, the lower the labour force participation of a married woman. Notwithstanding this evidence, wives' participation increases the higher the potential wage they can earn themselves. Additional factors, which also influence the work/non-work decision, can be listed as follows:

1. The availability of work locally: in some parts of the country there is very little work available. Married women tend to work closer to home than men because of family commitments.

2. The level of educational attainment of the individual woman: the higher the level of educational attainment the more likely a women is to work.

3. The level of family income: Mincer, in *Labour force participation of married women : a study of labour supply* (1962), argued that when family income was low in relation to the normal or permanent level, thus when overtime is cut or husbands become or are likely to become unemployed, wives tend, where possible, to enter

the labour force, at least in the short term, to supplement family income. This effect was noticeable over the 1970s when high levels of inflation were reducing the levels of 'real' wages.

4. The ages of any children and the availability, either in the public sector or in the private sector, of child-care facilities.

5. Appropriateness of hours of work: when there were labour shortages in the 1960s and early 1970s, some organisations attempted to encourage the employment of married women by introducing special shifts and other acceptable arrangements for part-time work, including the right to take time off during school holidays.

6. As women tend nowadays to have their families later, their level of work experience tends to be greater. This helps in the job search process.

7. Improvements in household technology and the availability of labour-saving devices such as washing machines, automatic ovens and pressure cookers, plus the availability of fast foods and late night supermarket shopping, have reduced the time necessary for housework. Women have found it easier to substitute market work for housework.

8. There has been greater social acceptance for women working over the last thirty years. This has been underpinned by anti-discrimination legislation. As Tom King emphasised when the EOC code on equality of opportunity was launched in April, 1985 (quoted in *Employment News* May, 1985):

> 'For Britain to succeed we do have to make the most of all the resources that we have; and one of the most neglected resources we have in the country is the skill, and intelligence of many women. What is needed is a revolution in public attitudes — a recognition that what matters is not whether an employee is a man or a woman but their skill and aptitude and acceptance that there is virtually no job that a woman cannot do. That cannot be achieved by changes in the law. It requires a constant process of persuasion and example by employers, employees and trade unions.'

In the UK, after a decade of steady growth, the female labour supply began to fall in 1980. This represented a fall in the numbers of women offering themselves for employment; women's employment tends to be heavily concentrated in certain occupations. Of all women workers:

29.1% are clerical workers, e.g. secretarial and typing;

23.2% are in service, sports and recreation, including canteen assistants, and office cleaners;

11.9% are professional, technical or artistic workers, including teachers, and nurses;

10.7% are in sales and distribution.

Within occupations women account for:

96.8% of all canteen assistants, counter hands etc.;

91.7%   of all charpersons, office cleaners, etc.;
91.6%   of all nurses.

If we accept that the demand for labour is derived demand, which is based on the level of economic activity, we can recognise that significant changes have occurred in the type of employment undertaken in the sectors which employ women. We can discern in the UK a shift in employment patterns from manufacturing to service employment. Since 1951 this has been especially represented in a decline in those manufacturing sectors which employ women. For example, there are now less permanent part-time jobs in the manufacturing sector generally, because of the increase in technology and the fall in demand for goods produced due to the economic recession. In addition, the textile and clothing industry, which has long been female dominated, has reduced in size. Two-thirds of all working women are in the service sector where there is extensive part-time employment. For example, in the distributive trades with extensions in the opening hours of shops and garages due to the need for employers to reduce variable overhead costs at low levels of demand, the use of part-time labour has increased.

Services associated with the Welfare State increased during the 1950s, 1960s and into the 1970s, at a time when male unemployment was low, so female labour was drawn into many white collar and blue collar jobs within the public employment sector.

Although unemployment increased from 1966 onwards, due to the decline in the manufacturing sector, women tended not to be employed in that sector in large numbers and were cushioned from this decline. Men did not move into the 'female' jobs in the service sector because many were deterred by the low pay and relative lack of skills and training required and because many of the jobs were traditionally considered to be 'female', e.g. shop assistants, typists, secretaries, nurses.

From 1974 onwards the economic recession became more severe and began to hit even the service sector, especially as concern increased over the levels of public and local authority expenditure. The total numbers of full-time female employees fell, yet this continued until recently to be offset by the continued availability of part-time jobs for women, as the service sector could see the benefits of employing part-timers rather than full-timers to reduce costs. At the same time, as there was a slowing down of the demand for female employees, the supply of women wishing to work increased. This was partly due to the lower birth rate; the availability of child-care facilities; the significant changes in the social attitudes to working women, evinced in the Equal Pay and Sex Discrimination Acts; and the effects of inflation on real incomes, combined with the decline in husbands' employment opportunities. These influences have led to a rise in registered unemployment amongst women, due partly to an increased propensity of women to register in order to be able to enter Government skills education programmes, e.g. the Training

Opportunities Scheme.

With the likelihood of increasing technological incursions into clerical and allied jobs, especially with the advent of the microprocessor, the prospects for female employment, if organisations decide to take advantage of such technologies and can afford to install it, are likely to be even gloomier over the remainder of the decade. A report by Tannenbaum *Technology : the issues for the distributive trades,* (1982), shows that microprocessors are rapidly permeating through the distributive trades and affecting existing and future job numbers significantly. A further influence will be the likelihood of the male unemployed, faced with few opportunities in traditionally male-dominated activities, competing for those jobs traditionally held by women.

An MSC report published in March 1985 showed that from 1981—1983 the number of self-employed women had risen by 24% to around 500,000.

In July 1982 about 6½ million, or 40% of the workforce, were married women, this is 40% of all married women and 60% of women at work. Around 3 million of the married women work part-time. In fact females comprise 85% of all part-time workers.

7. FACTORS INFLUENCING THE WORKINGS OF THE LABOUR MARKET

The efficient working of the labour market can be said to be impaired by the following:

(a)   Employment legislation which, in protecting the individual, fails to enable employers to shed labour immediately where necessary and has put up the cost of termination with rights to paid notice, redundancy pay, index-linked pensions, transferable and frozen pensions, unfair dismissal penalties etc.

(b)   Pay relativities — the existence of local, regional and industrial pay structures, which are quoted and defended by trade unions in their negotiations, affect the ability of employers to adjust payment rapidly.

(c)   Increased fixed labour costs — the cost of employing extra labour is said to be high because of the various national insurance contributions, pension schemes, increased holidays (including bank holidays) etc.

(d)   Reliance on sub-contracting and overtime — because of the high costs of employing labour with the above expenses (plus the range of other fringe benefits which are frequently offered) rather than employ additional manpower, firms can sub-contract suitable work, employ part-timers or utilise existing employees on overtime.

(e)   The inflexible use of labour because of demarcation and other rigid

Figure 11:1 Significance of Technological Change 1977—1987

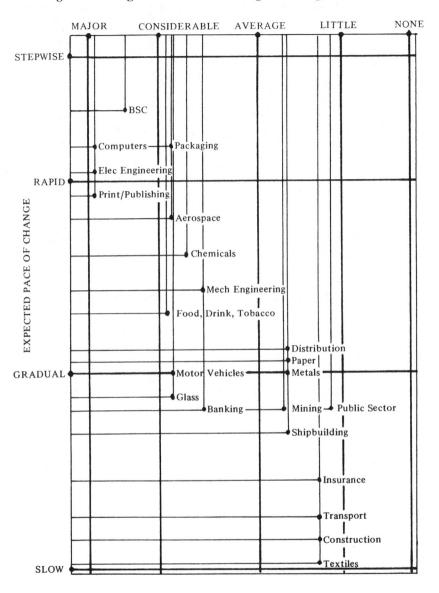

Source: MSC *Training for Skills* (1977)

manning policies — trade unions are blamed for operating closed shop and rigid demarcation policies to protect their own members' employment to the perceived detriment of others.

(f) Bad working conditions — it is suggested that certain jobs, which involve unpleasant conditions and long and unsocial hours, do not attract employees because of those working conditions and low levels of pay, e.g. hotels, the retail trade and other personal service jobs.

(g) Low productivity — this prevents the production of goods cheaply and efficiently so that they sell against foreign competition and generate more employment.

(h) Lack of manpower planning — organisations are often criticised for not attempting to plan their manpower needs more efficiently and for long enough into the future to enable them to signal skill needs to the labour market.

(i) Lack of labour mobility — (discussed above under **4. MOBILITY OF LABOUR**).

(j) The reaction of industry to cyclical and frictional changes — in past recessions industry has been prepared to reduce intakes of skills requiring long training, which has particularly created shortages of skills at various times. This has affected the ability of some young people to take apprenticeships because, by the time demand has picked up, they are too old to enter those occupations.

(k) The constraints of incomes policy — firms have occasionally been prevented from adjusting wage levels, in times of low supply of essential skills, to attract people into those occupations.

(l) The rate of technological change will have a differential impact from one industry to another. The likely significance of technological change was estimated in the MSC report *Training for Skills* (1977), as Figure 11:1 shows.

Chapter 12
The Government and the Labour Market

1. THE EMPLOYMENT SERVICE

The Government has long involved itself in the labour market to encourage the match of people with relevant skills to employer demand. The first public labour exchanges were established in 1910, with the stated aim of bringing employers and unemployed people together to reduce the costs of both recruitment and seeking employment. Initially the labour exchanges had close links with the administration of unemployment insurance to check whether claimants were entitled to benefits or not, i.e. if unemployed, were they also available for work? This role increased between the two World Wars and the labour exchanges became associated with the 'dole queue', often tucked away down back streets so that those in work would not be embarrassed by the sight of those waiting to collect their benefits and vainly hoping for work.

Because of this close relationship of the employment service with unemployment benefit administration, employers tended not to use the labour exchanges during the 1950s and 1960s, unless they were absolutely desperate for employees, and when they did it was primarily for those with very low levels of skills. In consequence, workers very seldom tended to use them to seek work.

To investigate the possibilities of improving the recruitment service against a background of labour shortages, major studies of the employment service were undertaken in 1968 and 1971, leading to the publication of a policy document in December, 1971 *People and Jobs*. The document suggested that, although most labour exchanges were designed especially for the unemployment side of their work, they had begun to develop the employment side and were receiving, at that time, notification of around 2 million vacancies and filling about 1½ million of them. It was recognised, however, that this represented only about 20 percent of all job changes.

As a result of these studies, five objectives were determined for the employment service:

(i)   To convince employers that it was to their benefit to inform the service of their vacancies.

(ii) To persuade workers who were already in employment, but who were actively seeking new jobs, that a visit to the employment office as one of the sources of potential vacancies, was worthwhile.

(iii)   To provide an effective placement service, not only for unskilled and semi-skilled workers, but also for other kinds of employees including skilled, white collar, executive, technical, scientific and professional vacancies.

(iv)   To improve the ability to advise workers about alternative jobs, training facilities available and help in moving to other areas to take up employment; and

(v)   To advise employers of labour market changes.

To accomplish these objectives meant having to lose the dole queue image of the labour exchanges. This required the separation of employment work from the administration of benefits. Efforts were made to upgrade employment exchanges so that information about vacancies could be presented more efficiently; improvements in training were made of the staff employed in the service; and closer liaison was encouraged between organisations and employment service staff.

People and Jobs thus led to a modernisation of the employment services and the establishment of a jobcentre network with more attractive premises and placed in the 'High Street' rather than the back streets; the first jobcentre was opened in Reading in May 1973.

On 1st January 1974, the Government established a new body to coordinate its labour market services of employment and of training help with two executive arms, the Employment Services Agency and the Training Services Agency. Following a further review of the services in 1977, further modifications were made, the main details of which follow. By 1978/79 the number of vacancies notified had risen to 2.68 million and the number of placings were around 1.8 million. Despite this success, a survey by Social and Community Planning Research in 1977 *A Survey of Employers' Recruitment Practices,* over the period of April—June 1977, indicated that only about one third of vacancies were being notified.

2.   THE MANPOWER SERVICES COMMISSION

The Manpower Services Commission was formally set up on 1st January 1974 as a result of the Employment and Training Act 1973. Through its executive arms, now named the Employment Division and the Training Division, the Commission now administers Britain's employment and training services. These bodies have been developed to secure the social and the economic advantages of a comprehensive manpower policy. There are two main thrusts of government policy in this area:

(a)   to facilitate the development of the country's manpower resources so that they can contribute effectively to the economic success of the nation; and

(b)   to ensure that each individual worker in society can take advantage of the new opportunities by availing themselves of the services to develop a satisfying working life.

In 1976 the Manpower Services Commission published *Towards a Comprehensive Manpower Policy* setting out these aims in the Commission's broad purpose:

'to enable the country's manpower resources to be developed and contribute fully to economic well-being; and to ensure that there are available to each worker the opportunities and services he or she needs in order to lead a satisfying working life.'

The MSC's *Review and Plan 1977* set out four aims of the comprehensive manpower policy which the Commission was developing through its operating divisions and links with other organisations, and a fifth aim which was specifically for the Commission to pursue. These aims were:

1. To contribute to efforts to raise employment and reduce unemployment.
2. To assist the development of manpower resources and contribute fully to economic well-being.
3. To help secure for each worker the opportunities he or she needs in order to lead a satisfying working life.
4. To improve the quality of decisions affecting manpower.
5. To improve the effectiveness and efficiency of the Commission.

The Commission itself is made up of ten Commissioners, three appointed after consultation by the TUC; three after consultation with the CBI; two after consultation with local authority associations; one after consultation with professional further education interests; and finally, an independent Chairman.

As well as advising the Secretary of State for Employment on broad manpower policies which take into account the information obtained regarding the state of the labour market, via the Manpower Intelligence and Planning Division, the Commission through its operational arms has the responsibility for services aimed at helping individuals to train for and obtain jobs, and thus realise their potential, and helping employers find suitably qualified employees. The Headquarters and regional organisation of the MSC as laid out in 1985 can be pictured as in Figure 12:1.

Within the lifespan of the MSC, the economic recession has considerably increased the unemployment level in the UK.

In framing its Corporate Plan for 1985-89, the Commission had laid down the following objectives:

1. To safeguard the provision of skilled manpower for industry's present and future needs, with increased emphasis on helping people and smaller businesses to respond to the pace of technological change.
2. To ensure that all unemployed 16 and 17 year olds have access to programmes for training and work experience, as part of efforts to

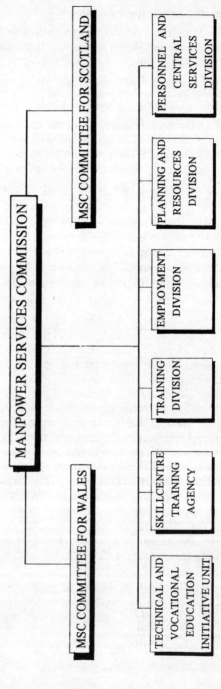

Figure 12:1 The Manpower Services Commission

MANPOWER SERVICES COMMISSION

MSC COMMITTEE FOR SCOTLAND

MSC COMMITTEE FOR WALES

TECHNICAL AND VOCATIONAL EDUCATION INITIATIVE UNIT

SKILLCENTRE TRAINING AGENCY

TRAINING DIVISION

EMPLOYMENT DIVISION

PLANNING AND RESOURCES DIVISION

PERSONNEL AND CENTRAL SERVICES DIVISION

improve access to training and vocational preparation for all young people.

3. To provide an efficient and cost-effective employment service to meet employers' and jobseekers' needs.

4. To do all that is practicable to place in permanent employment, in training and in temporary employment, those unemployed jobseekers who most need help in returning to work. (MSC *Corporate Plan May 1985*).

A. Regional Manpower Boards

Regional Manpower Services Directors and their Boards have specific responsibility for coordinating action at regional level on skill shortages, hard-to-fill vacancies, and other local manpower matters. The primary objective is to provide a broader base for labour market information and assessment of local needs for the MSCs operational planning in the regions, for the Secretary of State for Employment, local authorities, employers and jobseekers.

Each region has Regional Manpower Intelligence Units whose task is:

(a) to obtain, collate, analyse and interpret manpower information for the executive services of the MSC so that they can plan and operate effectively;

(b) to identify emerging manpower problems at regional, district and local level;

(c) to carry out special manpower studies in the regions as need arises;

(d) to provide managers of the Jobcentres in the field with a professional manpower intelligence back-up as required; and

(e) to interpret national trends as they might affect their regions and advise the MSC about developments in their region.

B. MSC Committees for Wales and Scotland

The Committees for Scotland and Wales have been established to advise the Commission on the specific manpower and training problems and, in particular on the implementation of the MSCs plans and programmes in those countries.

(i) MSC Committee in Scotland

The MSC Committee in Scotland was established in January 1977; from April 1978, the financial responsibility for this Committee was assumed by the Secretary of State for Scotland and given the following responsibilities:

(a) to give advice to the Commission on general or specific issues referred to the Committee by the Commission;

(b) to put forward on its own initiative matters it wishes to draw to the Commission's attention;

(c) to consider and approve, with or without modifications, proposals made by either the Divisions or the Office of the MSC in respect of Scotland, and to submit these to the Commission who, with or without modifications arising from its assessment of the national situation, would incorporate them in its Great Britain plans and programmes for submission to the Secretary of State for Employment and the Secretary of State for Scotland;

(d) to receive reports from the Divisions and the Office of the MSC on the implementation of their plans and programmes in Scotland, to consider them and advise the Commission;

(e) to be responsible under the Commission for the Area Manpower Boards in Scotland; and

(f) to be responsible for such other functions or activities as the Commission might from time to time invite the Committee to undertake.

The Committee is chaired by a Scottish nominee chosen by the MSC and the Secretary of State for Scotland and the other members of the Committee are three members nominated by the Scottish TUC, three nominated by the CBI, Scotland, two nominated by local authority representative bodies and one nominated by professional education representative bodies.

(ii) MSC Committee in Wales

Financial responsibility for the MSC Committee for Wales passed to the Secretary of State for Wales from 1st April 1978. The functions of the Committee mirror those of the Scottish Committee as follows:

(a) to give advice to the Commission on general and specific issues referred to the Committee by the Commission.

(b) to put forward on its own initiative matters it wishes to direct to the Commission's attention;

(c) to consider and approve, with or without modifications, proposals made by either the Divisions or the Office of the MSC (OMSC) in respect of Wales; to submit these to the Commission, who with or without any modifications arising from its assessment of the national situation, would incorporate them in its Great Britain plans and programmes for submission to the Secretary of State for Employment and the Secretary of State for Wales;

(d) to receive reports from the Divisions and the OMSC on the implementation of their plans and programmes in Wales, to consider them and advise the Commission;

(e) to be responsible under the Commission for the District Manpower Committees in Wales;

(f) to advise the Commission's Chief Officer in Wales, and the Commission's Director of Manpower Intelligence and Planning, of research required to enable the manpower needs of Wales to be satisfactorily identified and met; and

(g) to be responsible for such other functions or activities as the Commission might from time to time invite the Committee to undertake.

As in Scotland, the membership of the permanent Welsh Committee comprises three members nominated by the Wales TUC, three nominated by the CBI, Wales, two nominated by local authority representative bodies and one nominated by professional education representative bodies.

C. Area Manpower Boards

Area Manpower Boards were established in 1983 to succeed the 29 Special Programmes Area Boards and 88 District Manpower Committees.

There are 54 of them to help ensure an effective response by the MSC to local problems and needs. Each Board includes local representatives of employers, employees, local authorities, the education service and professional education interests, and voluntary organisations.

Their terms of reference include:

— Advising on the planning and delivering of MSC training and employment services in their area.

— Assisting MSC in promoting the use of these services, encouraging sponsors to come forward with schemes and advising potential sponsors.

— Encouraging training and development activities in their area. Promoting links between MSC and local bodies which could influence manpower decisions.

— Advising on resource allocation.

— Approving area training plans.

— Approving schemes in their area and assisting in monitoring and assessing them, especially as regards the YTS.

— To give local data to the MSC to help make recommendations to Government.

D. Corporate Services Division

The Commission attempts to improve its own efficiency and effectiveness and centrally the Commission's Corporate Services Division has a role here. The objectives of the Division are to ensure that the MSC has the resources of money, equipment and personnel it needs to carry out its agreed programmes of work and to assist other Divisions in seeing that these resources are used efficiently.

E. Manpower Intelligence and Planning Division

This division's aim is to assist all parts of the MSC to produce and implement appropriate and effective manpower policies and plans to develop the MSCs role and knowledge of manpower matters. This function is achieved through its policy and planning, economics and statistics branches and its central development group for regional manpower intelligence.

3. EMPLOYMENT DIVISION

The Employment Division was established as the Employment Services Agency in October 1974 and renamed in 1977. The aims of the ED are, on the one hand, to help people choose, train for and get the jobs they want and, on the other, to help employers to get the recruits they want as quickly as possible. Thus, one of the main purposes of the Division is to assemble and make available information about vacancies and people who are seeking work so as to help the labour market to work more efficiently and effectively.

These aims were outlined by the MSC in the 1979/80 Annual Report as:

(a) by completing the introduction of Jobcentres, to establish the basic job finding and job filling services on a satisfactory level throughout the country by the end of 1983/84;

(b) to improve the accessibility of information about the labour market and the full range of employment, training and other services of the MSC;

(c) to improve the provision of help and advice available for job seekers who need it to select, train for, obtain and retain suitable employment;

(d) to ensure employers are able to obtain information and advice on recruitment and other manpower matters;

(e) to improve cost effectiveness.

A. Jobcentres

By the end of March 1985 there were around 1,000 Jobcentres in operation:

(i) They operate vacancy display boards for people who want information on a self-service basis. Evidence collected by the ED suggests that more vacancies are attracted into Jobcentres than were attracted into the old-style employment offices and that they are filled more quickly. Thus for example, a survey in 1978 showed that unemployed people are helped into work on average 2.4 days sooner than in the traditional-style employment offices and that 50% of users of Jobcentres use the self-service facility.

(ii) Advisory interviews are given for people needing help in finding jobs or training opportunities. In addition to this service the ED is creating a system of Job Libraries in major towns and cities to give the public the ability to obtain information themselves about careers, occupations, training, qualifications required and further education availability.

B. Help for Disabled People

The handling of employment services for disabled people, through the Disablement Resettlement Officers, is an important part of the EDs task, especially as recession has an adverse effect on the employment prospects of the disabled. The ED also administers the quota scheme under which employers with over 20 employees have a statutory obligation to employ a minimum of 3% of their employees from the registered disabled. Special schemes are available for the disabled including *The Job Introduction Scheme* where employers take on a disabled person on a trial basis for up to 6 weeks. In addition the Disablement Resettlement Officers can recommend a disabled person to an employer under the *Individual Training Throughout with an Employer Scheme:* an individually biased training programme designed with the employer which can last from 4 weeks to more than a year and is monitored by the TD, who pay an allowance for up to 13 weeks, after which the employer contributes. The employer must be able to employ the person for 6 months after the training period is due to finish. In 1984 Jobcentres placed 720,000 disabled people in jobs and 27,000 benefited from other MSC schemes of training.

Fares to work scheme The MSC can assist those registered disabled who, because of their disability are unable to travel to work by public transport, by partial help with up to 75% of taxi fares.

C. Employment transfer

Grants and allowances are available through the ED to people who are prepared to find jobs outside of their present area of residence, to encourage mobility. Special allowances are available under the *Job Search Scheme* for financial assistance to attend interviews. Unemployed people, together with those under threat of redundancy, are given financial assistance if looking for a full time, non-seasonal job outside their own locality. There must, however, be no reasonable possibility of a suitable job locally and no suitable unemployed in the area being visited. In addition, the Employment Transfer Scheme provides help with removal expenses.

D. Professional and Executive Recruitment (PER)

PER provides a specialist employment service at professional, managerial, executive, scientific and technical levels. It operates on a commercial basis and charges employers for its recruitment and selection services. Vacancies are notified by a weekly magazine *Executive Post*.

E. Employment Rehabilitation

The ED provides courses at Employment Rehabilitation Centres to help those people who, after sickness, injury or long periods of unemployment, wish to enter or re-enter employment. These courses aim to improve the individual's work ability, restore confidence and, at the same time, give some guidance on the most appropriate work.

F. Sheltered employment

Under these programmes financial support is given to local authorities, voluntary bodies and Remploy, which enables them to provide work under sheltered conditions for disabled people whose handicaps are so severe that they are unable to obtain and retain employment in open industry. To help sheltered workshops to find more work, especially from Central and Local Government, and to provide a consultancy service expert in the use of such workshops, an organisation called Sheltered Employment Procurement and Consultancy Services (SEPACS) was set up in August 1979.

4. JUSTIFICATIONS FOR A PUBLIC EMPLOYMENT SERVICE

The Annual Report of the MSc for 1984/85 declared that 1.82 million people were placed in work through job centres which in total handled 2.36 million vacancies; a success rate of nearly 78% of vacancies notified which were estimated to be 33% of the vacancies in the economy.

As there are imperfections in the operation of the labour market, especially in terms of information flows, the MSC argues in *The Employment Service in the 1980s* (1979), that there are the following reasons for a public employment service:

(i)   Because it is costly to look for work and to recruit employees, a country wide employment service has economies of scale and can

240

handle large numbers of registrations and vacancies, reducing costs.

(ii) It is not reasonable for the individual seeking work to pay fees to obtain information about jobs or training opportunities or to get advice about his own potential or eligibility to enter a particular career.

(iii) Vacancies can have a wider circulation from region to region than through a private system.

(iv) Vacancies are likely to be filled more quickly than through other methods.

(v) It provides opportunities for members of the public to obtain data about other manpower services.

(vi) Through Jobcentres, a picture can be formed of national labour shortages which are likely to hinder the full development of the economy.

(vii) It can aid in checking the individual's entitlement to State benefits.

(viii) As the objective is not profit, more time can be spent with each individual, if required.

(ix) Private agency services are not evenly spread geographically or occupationally.

Criticisms of the Jobcentre network include:

(a) By separating the employment and the placement service, the unemployed have to attend two different places, to collect benefit and to seek work, and, additionally, it is difficult to monitor whether a person obtaining benefit is actively seeking work;

(b) The self-service facility does not enable the employment service to question and 'filter' applicants for particular vacancies as much as some employers, especially smaller ones, would wish. Additionally, the employer may be faced with a large number of applicants for each vacancy and this can be time-consuming. In a research funded in 1981 by the ED and conducted by J. Ford, E. T. Keil, A.D. Beardsworth and A. Bryman 'How employers see the public employment service' *Employment Gazette,* November 1982, it was reported that employers wanted the Jobcentres to screen applicants. However it was emphasised that screening was likely to favour the short term unemployed rather than the long term unemployed with the potential danger that the Jobcentres would face irreconcilable demands from the jobseeker and the employer.

With these problems in mind, the MSC argues that the employment service activities need to be constantly monitored to ensure their benefits, both in terms of economic cost and efficiency and that simple measures of success such as 'placement penetration' and market share of vacancy placement are not necessarily appropriate measures of success.

5. TRAINING DIVISION (TD)

This Division was set up as a statutory body responsible to the MSC in April 1974. The aims of the TD are:

1. To assist the development of a national training system to meet the manpower needs of the economy;
2. To offer training to individuals, consistent with their ability and interests, in skills for which there is, or likely to be, a demand;
3. To promote the efficiency and effectiveness of training generally;
4. To coordinate the work of the remaining Industrial Training Boards;
5. To encourage and assist in the development of training in occupations not covered by the Industrial Training Boards.

In this they work with the ED, which has an important role in recruiting trainees, especially for the Training Opportunities Scheme (TOPS) and, at the end of their training, helps to place them in suitable employment, thus aiming to meet industry's vacancies for skilled manpower. The ED, in tandem with the Careers Service, is responsible for the recruitment and placement of participants in the various youth training programmes.

(a) Job Training Programme & Wider Opportunities Training Programme

These replaced the Training Opportunities Scheme which was introduced in 1972 and offered a wide range of courses, primarily designed to help adults who, for whatever reason, needed training in order to seek new employment. The MSC through this programme aimed to meet both its social function in helping people to improve their employment prospects, and its economic function in helping to meet the needs of the labour market. The Government requires that priority is given to areas of crucial national importance, such as technician training, training in skills of electronics and micro-electronics, and courses for people starting new businesses.

1984/85 was the last full year of operation of the TOPS scheme. The 1984-1988 Corporate Plan of the MSC laid down the Commission's plans to develop two new programmes to replace TOPS — the Job Training Programme and the Wider Opportunities Training Programme.

(i) *The Job Training Programme* is designed to help employees, employers, the self-employed and the unemployed, and focuses on meeting the expressed needs of employers and employees and on encouraging and helping to create new businesses. Under this overall heading come a number of schemes:

— A National Priority Skills Scheme to help employers to train employees in priority areas of skill shortages which are identified by either the seven remaining ITBs or the non-statutory Training Organisations (ITOs) which are active. (There were 131 of these identified in 1985).

— A Job Training Scheme which directly replaces the training for unemployed people previously encouraged and developed by TOPS itself. The scheme provides a wide choice of training for unemployed people by adding to the skills they already have or by developing the new skills which more employers are demanding.

— A Training for Enterprise Scheme which aims to provide training for those starting their own business (including those who participate in the Enterprise Allowance Scheme), and to provide training for owner/managers of existing small businesses to stimulate growth through evening or weekend training modules in key subjects such as finance and marketing.

— An Access to Information Technology Scheme which attempts to promote increased awareness of information technology and its uses.

— Local Consultancy Grants

— Local Training Grants

— A Management Development Initiative designed to improve the quality of training and development for managers.

— The Management Extension Programme which matches experienced unemployed managers to small firms which have plans for growth but lack the resources necessary to carry them through.

(ii) *The Wider Opportunities Training Programme* is designed to help unemployed members of society to improve their work related skills, retain employability and cope with the changing content, and different patterns of work. There are two parts to the programme:

— To build on existing work preparation provision and training aimed to meet individual needs relevant to local labour market opportunities.

— To provide additional Training, linked with participation in the Community Programme, combining the experience of temporary work with relevant training opportunities.

(b) Direct Training Services to Industry and Commerce

The TD also offers help and advice in the form of direct training services. This training can either be done at Skills Centres or at the firm or plant concerned, e.g. Training Within Industry (TWI), or the Mobile Instructor Service. The Skills Centre Training Agency, established in 1983, now administers the Skills Centre training provision. It has the target of reaching a position in 1986 where it no longer has to depend on public subsidy to finance its activities. Employers can buy courses for their employees, individuals can buy courses, or the MSC can buy places for those in the Adult Training Strategy.

(c)   Industrial Training Boards.

(See section on Government initiatives in training).

6.   SPECIAL PROGRAMMES

Programmes are designed and monitored to soften the effects of unemployment amongst young people and adults.

On 29th June 1977, the Secretary of State for Employment announced that, because of the increasing level of unemployment especially amongst young people, the Government wanted the MSC to introduce two new programmes — the Youth Opportunities Programme (YOP [YOP was replaced in 1983 by the Youth Training Scheme — YTS]) and the Special Temporary Employment Programme (STEP). (STEP was replaced in April 1981 by the Community Enterprise Programme, now renamed the Community Programme.)

These programmes were intended to focus on the needs of the unemployed individual, to provide a constructive alternative to prolonged unemployment, and to have the aim of improving the ability of the individual to respond to employment opportunities.

A special Programmes Division was created in 1977 and its work was transferred to the Training Division in April 1983. The ED now exercises general oversight of the development and operation of the programmes through the Youth Training Board with responsibility for the day-to-day running of the programmes devolved to local level and, in particular, to 29 Area Boards comprising representatives of employers, trade unions, voluntary organisations, local authorities and education interests. These plan and oversee the provision of the programme in the area, monitor progress and assist in their marketing. These are supported in turn by 41 area offices which are responsible for developing, administering and monitoring opportunities and projects.

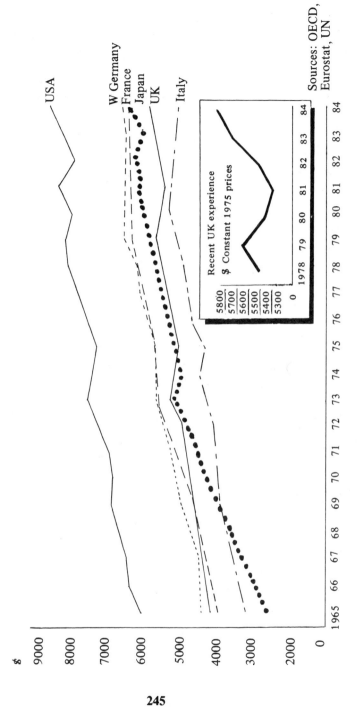

Figure 12:2 Standard of living: real GDP per head

USA

W Germany
France
Japan
UK

Italy

Recent UK experience
$ Constant 1975 prices

5800
5700
5600
5500
5400
5300
0

1978 79 80 81 82 83 84

Sources: OECD,
Eurostat, UN

$

9000
8000
7000
6000
5000
4000
3000
2000
0

1965 66 67 68 69 70 71 72 73 74 75 76 77 78 79 80 81 82 83 84

245

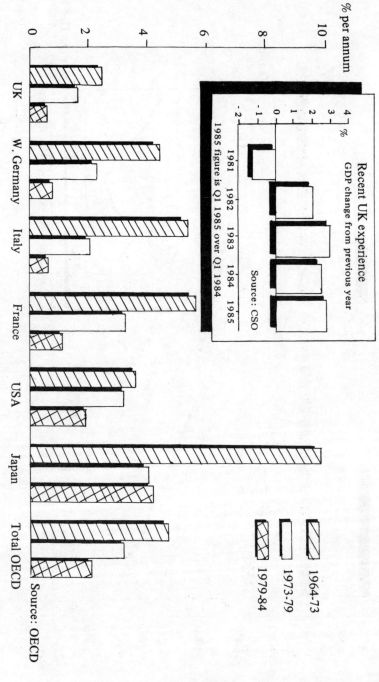

Figure 12:3 Growth: average annual increase in real GDP

Recent UK experience
GDP change from previous year

Source: CSO

1985 figure is Q1 1985 over Q1 1984

% per annum

UK W. Germany Italy France USA Japan Total OECD

1964-73
1973-79
1979-84

Source: OECD

246

Figure 12:4 Productivity by sector

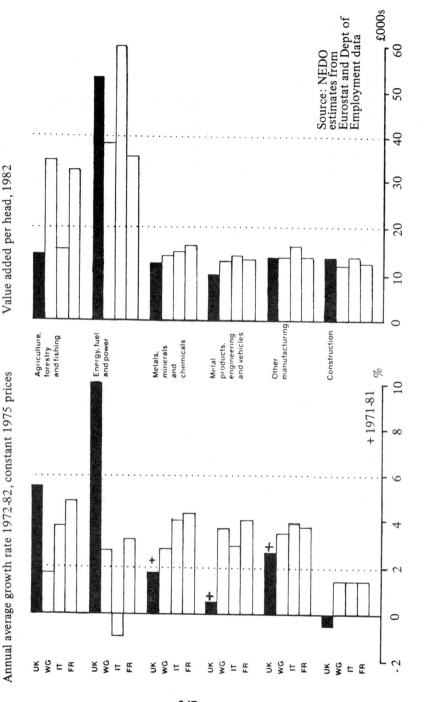

Annual average growth rate 1972-82, constant 1975 prices

Value added per head, 1982

Source: NEDO estimates from Eurostat and Dept of Employment data

247

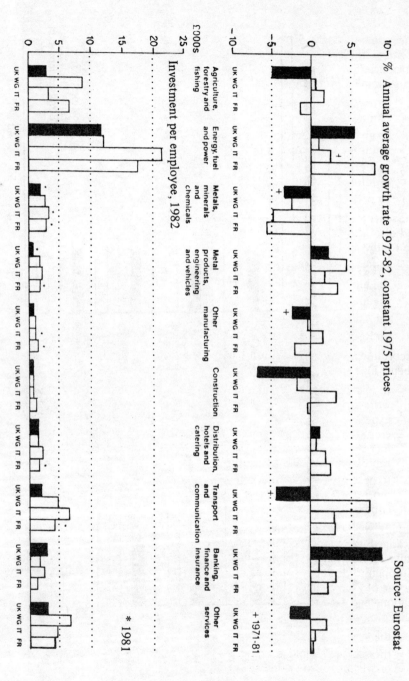

Figure 12:5 Investment by sector

Source: Eurostat

% Annual average growth rate 1972-82, constant 1975 prices

£000s

Investment per employee, 1982

+ 1971-81

* 1981

248

(a) Youth Training Scheme (YTS)

The Youth Training Scheme was announced in the White Paper *A New Training Initiative — a programme for action* MSC, 1981 and was introduced to replace the much criticised Youth Opportunities Programme in September 1982. It aims:

(i)   to equip young people to adapt successfully to the demands of employment;

(ii) to give them a full understanding and appreciation of the world of industry, business and technology in which they will be working;

(iii) to develop the basic and recognised skills which employers will require in the future;

(iv) to prepare young people for adult life.

The scheme therefore exists to give people skills in particular occupations and also general abilities which are transferable from job to job. Thus the following skills must be imparted:

— the necessary communication skills;

— the ability to work as part of a team;

— the ability to use numbers;

— the ability to work with their hands;

— an insight into computers and handling information.

According to the MSC Youth Task Group report in April 1982, the scheme also aims:

(i)   to provide for the participating employer a better equipped young workforce which has acquired some competence and practical experience in a range of related jobs and skills, thus enabling the employer to operate more productively and effectively in an increasingly competitive trading environment and a period of often rapid and far reaching technological and market changes;

(ii) to develop and maintain a more versatile, readily adaptable, highly motivated and productive workforce which will assist Britain to compete successfully in the 1980's and beyond.

Initially the scheme offered a one year training and work experience package but, from April 1986, 16 year old school leavers have the opportunity of two years' training and 17 year olds one year. The scheme is also open to disabled young people who leave full time education up to the age of 21. Schemes should be open for all, regardless of sex, race or religion, and recruitment may be direct or via the Careers Office. Five Principles must underpin each approved scheme:

(i)   the scheme should be voluntary;

(ii) the scheme should be coherent and consistent with other training provision for the same age group;

(iii)   the scheme should provide high quality training and be seen to do so;

(iv)   the scheme should be flexible for both trainee and provider;

(v)   the scheme should be simple in its operation.

Standards are monitored by a Training Standards Advisory Service. The schemes provide initial broad based training for the first year and progress towards more occupationally related training in the second year, which will give the individual the opportunity to obtain vocational qualifications. At least 20 weeks off-the-job training is required over the two years. A training agreement is drawn up between the trainee and those responsible for the training. This should set out the respective rights and responsibilities including details of the training programme. These agreements are to ensure that individuals know the skills they are expected to acquire, the competencies they need to attain, who is going to assess competence and what they are expected to acquire through off-the-job training.

Those offering the training receive a basic grant for each filled place each month plus the possibility of a premium grant to meet the special needs of trainees and localities (employers who give training to the disabled receive help to adapt their premises where necessary). In addition, there is a management fee for each contracted place each year.

Trainees receive a weekly trainee allowance, which rises in the second year, and receive 1½ days holiday per month plus public bank holidays. They must have the right to join the appropriate trade union.

The YTS scheme, in certain instances, has been criticised on a number of grounds:

—   the inability of many trainees to secure employment at the end of their training;

—   the likelihood that trainees are being substituted for full time permanent employees;

—   the quality of the training; in some cases trainees have been used as cheap labour;

—   trainees are not legally employees and are, therefore, not protected by the employment legislation;

—   trainees have not necessarily been placed on the courses most appropriate for their needs.

What programmes are offered within your own organisation? How do they run? What training is given? Who looks after the trainees? How successful do trainees and ex-trainees feel they are?

(b)   Community Programme

The programme provides temporary work for long term unemployed adults. It is open to people aged 18-24 who have been unemployed for six months out of the previous nine and those over 25 who have been unemployed for 12 months out of the previous 15. This was introduced in April, 1981 as the Community Enterprise Programme (to replace STEP) and its purpose is to 'help long term unemployed men and women improve their prospects in obtaining normal employment, by giving them worthwhile temporary employment, on schemes of benefit to the local community', e.g. adapting buildings for public use, setting up adventure playgrounds, clearing up derelict land etc. Projects must be ones which otherwise would not be done for two years; do not put existing jobs at risk; would not have been carried out on a voluntary basis; and have the support of trade unions and employers' organisations. Individuals cannot be employed under the programme for more than one year, except in special circumstances. Places are allocated on a regional basis. Sponsors (which can include any organisation or group of individuals, e.g. local authorities, private companies, trade unions, voluntary bodies, charities and community groups) receive payments to cover operating costs, management and supervision for each participant. People leaving the programme are said to have twice as good a chance (40% against 15-20%) of finding a job in the next 12 months as those who have not been on the programme.

(c) Young Workers Scheme (YWS)

Introduced in January, 1982, the scheme is designed to encourage employers to take on more young people under the age of 18, but at wage rates which reflect their inexperience and lack of training. The scheme is open to all employers, except the public services and domestic households, and jobs must be full time, i.e. over 35 hours per week and permanent, and the young person's average gross wages cannot be more than £50 per week. A grant is available towards wages for up to twelve months. Studies have shown that in many cases the subsidies were paid for jobs which would have existed anyway. It also operated, as it was intended to, against older workers' employment prospects. A Department of Employment investigation by Robert Bushell, 'Evaluation of the Young Workers Scheme' in *Employment Gazette* May 1986, suggests that since its introduction YWS has helped employers to give jobs and a start in the working community to nearly 440,000 young people.

(d) New Workers Scheme

In order to help young people under the age of 21 set out in the work environment and encourage employers to create more job openings of at least 35 hours per week for young people who earn £55 per week or less, if they are under 20, *or,* £65 per week maximum at age 20. It thus complements YTS for the slightly older age group.

(e)   Community Industry Scheme

In addition, the ED contributes towards the funding of the Community
Industry Scheme which was established in 1972 by the National Association of Youth Clubs, and provides temporary jobs for unemployed,
disadvantaged 17 — 19 year-old young people. The characteristics of the
young people referred to CIS are such that, even in times of full employment, they would have problems in finding and keeping jobs, i.e. those
with histories of frequent job changes, behavioural problems, truancy,
lack of motivation, poor literacy and numeracy, petty criminal offences,
poor home backgrounds and mental and physical handicap. Three main
types of opportunity are offered — site, workshop and placement
projects.

In May, 1985 the MSC reported that special unemployment measures
aimed to provide nearly 600,000 places per annum.

YTS	390,000 p.a.
Community programme	200,000 p.a.
Young Workers Scheme	61,000 p.a.

7.   ADDITIONAL GOVERNMENT SCHEMES

(a)   Job Release Scheme

This provides for full time employees nearing retirement age to be replaced by unemployed people who would otherwise not have been employed.
It applies to men aged 64 and women aged 59 and disabled men of 60 + .
The employees who are released are paid an allowance until normal
retirement age.

(i)   Part-time job release scheme — the scheme is open to all men aged
        62—64, women aged 59 and disabled men aged 61—64, and allows
        people to change to part-time work and receive a weekly allowance,
        provided an unemployed person is recruited by the employer as a
        result.

(ii)   Full-time job release scheme — this version offers older workers a
        weekly allowance from the date they leave work until the State
        Pension age, provided the employer agrees to replace the applicant
        by a person who is unemployed.

(b)   Enterprise Allowance Scheme (EAS)

EAS was launched in 1983 and is aimed at helping some 80,000 people
p.a. This scheme pays unemployed workers of over 18 years of age a
grant each week for 12 months while they set up their own businesses. It
also offers help by providing management advice from experienced

business people. Most of the businesses established are in the service sector.

(c) Job Splitting Scheme

This scheme, introduced in January 1983, is designed to encourage employers to split existing jobs into two part-time jobs and so open up more opportunities for the unemployed. The two part-time jobs must have total hours which are broadly comparable with those of the full-time job, with a minimum of 15 hours. The employer receives a grant, which is paid in instalments, for each job which is split or for each two new jobs which are created and filled by people leaving other Government schemes, especially YTS, or for combining overtime hours of existing staff to create jobs which can be split.

(d) Voluntary Projects Programme

This programme aims to provide opportunities for unemployed people to do voluntary work, but of a constructive work-related type which meets individual needs and improves the individual's employment prospects. The programme categories are of two main types.

— Community work activities which assist other members of the community and can include decorating and gardening for the elderly and disabled; furniture renovations; improvements to community buildings etc.
— Education and training projects which provide the unemployed with literacy, life and social, computer, or basic craft skills.

(e) Job Start Scheme

Launched in January 1986, jobless people are offered a £20 per week (for 6 months) top up to their wages if they take jobs paying less than £80 per week. The scheme started in nine pilot areas — Billingham (Cleveland), Dundee, Ealing, Huddersfield, Crawley and Horsham, Plymouth, Port Talbot, Neath, Preston and Stoke on Trent. The grant is taxable but is not counted towards employer and employee nationalinsurance contributions. It is paid directly to the individual.

(f) Loan Guarantee Scheme

Under the scheme guarantees are provided by the Government for loans in support of viable business propositions.

(g) Business Expansion Scheme

Independent investors are given tax relief on equity investments in unquoted small businesses.

(h) Schemes to help Particular Areas

In addition to help and guidance in the working of the labour market, the Government also operates a system of incentives for investment in regional aid programmes. The assisted areas comprise Northern Ireland, development areas and intermediate areas. To help employers and potential employers who wish to take advantage of any of these schemes, the Department of Trade and Industry offers the help of Industrial Expansion Schemes, giving practical advice on the availability of funds for some 64 different schemes of help.

(i) *REGIONAL DEVELOPMENT GRANTS:* these are automatically available in the Special Development Areas and Development Areas for capital expenditure on buildings, plant and machinery for manufacturing industry and allied scientific research. In special Development Areas the grant is 22%, in Development Areas 15%.

(ii) *ENTERPRISE ZONES:* these were established in 1981 for areas of high unemployment and offer special incentives in addition to any other regional assistance, e.g. capital allowances for commercial and industrial buildings; exemption from rates on industrial and commercial properties; exemption from ITB levies, where applicable.

(iii) *NATIONAL SELECTIVE ASSISTANCE:* major projects involving substantial new investment can qualify for a cash grant, wherever it occurs in the UK, providing it can be shown that the project is of benefit to the UK economy and is in the national interest.

(iv) *REGIONAL SELECTIVE ASSISTANCE:* covers more industries than Regional Development Grants and Intermediate Areas of development, and is provided in the form of a grant towards fixed and capital working expenditure, providing the projects create additional jobs or maintain or safeguard existing jobs by, for example, modernising existing production units. As the grants are discretionary, the amount of assistance provided is negotiated individually. They take the form of negotiable grants for each job created, a fixed grant for essential employees moving with their work and grants towards essential training schemes.

(v) *NEW ENTERPRISE ALLOWANCE:* this is available to unemployed people who start their own business, but is restricted to three areas — Coventry, the Medway Towns and North East Lancashire.

(vi) *GOVERNMENT FACTORIES:* these are built in areas of expan-

Figure 12:6 Regional aid map

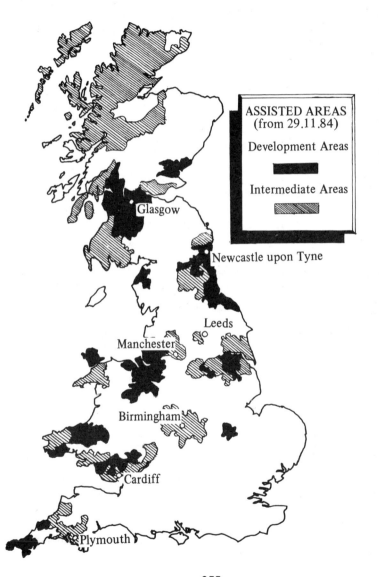

ASSISTED AREAS
(from 29.11.84)

Development Areas

Intermediate Areas

Glasgow

Newcastle upon Tyne

Leeds

Manchester

Birmingham

Cardiff

Plymouth

sion and are available for projects creating additional employment, either on a rental, lease or freehold basis.

(vii) *SUPPORT FOR INNOVATION* — offers support to research and development projects leading to new projects and processes.

8. EUROPEAN FINANCIAL HELP

(i) Some finance may also be made available from Europe; for example, the European Social Fund gives financial support to training schemes, retraining schemes, resettlement schemes, rehabilitation schemes and job creation programmes which offer 200 hours training of which at least 40 hours are devoted to new technology. Schemes to be eligible must assist:

— training programmes for technological change;
— people leaving agriculture;
— people leaving the textile industry;
— migrant workers within or from outside the EEC, e.g. Vietnamese boat people;
— unemployed young people under the age of 25;
— women over 25 who are unemployed or returning to work after bringing up a family;
— rehabilitation, training and retraining of disabled.

The Fund is mainly reserved for schemes helping workers in regions of high unemployment.

(ii) In addition, the European Coal and Steel Community provides loans to help create work for redundant coal and steel workers. These projects must be located in coal and steel producing areas.

9. PUBLIC SECTOR INVOLVEMENT IN TRAINING

Employers have always been concerned with the provision of training, both for existing employees to update or uplift their skills, and for new entrants to industry. This enables a direct link to be made between the training provided and the needs of the job itself, which ensures some form of guarantee that training will be both realistic and cost effective. The role of the public authorities, therefore, should be to intervene and provide training where it is felt necessary to support, supplement or encourage the efforts of employers. It is argued that the role of public finance in training should be to provide additional funds, where necessary, not to enable employers to rely on training at public expense, instead of providing their own. Public training should help individuals to cope with labour market demand changes, which cannot easily be handl- ed by industry itself, for example, in areas where there is a growth in demand for skills which outrun current supply; where there is structural

256

labour market movement; and where there are geographical shifts in demands for skills, which workers are unable to follow.

(a) Investment in Human Capital

Both education and training give work skills to the labour force and the potential labour force. They represent a form of investment for society itself and for employers; this has been termed — investment in human capital. G S Becker, in *Human Capital,* Columbia University Press, 1964, suggests that the acquisition of education and training gives the individual a higher earnings potential, and thus the individual will invest his time and money in education and training which gives him the highest future return. (If we consider that the opportunity cost of education and vocational training, where not paid for by an employer, is the wages which otherwise could be earned if the individual continued working — even the individual studying in the evening may be passing up the chance to work overtime.) In economic terms organisations also will invest in any training which provides potential returns of increased productivity from the individual worker, which are greater than the costs of training. Costs include the costs of equipment; facilities; materials used in training; the value of the employee's wages whilst undergoing training; and the cost of the trainers. There are also less measurable returns on training which, although not completely relevant to the individual's job, encourage him to remain with an employer, perhaps because the training meets the individual's need and provides intrinsic satisfaction.

(b) Specific versus General Training

Becker (see above) also argues that we can differentiate between specific and general training.

(i) *General training* is useful to many other organisations besides those providing it, as it increases the productivity and effectiveness of the individual. There is thus a danger that those providing the training may not reap the benefits of it if employees take advantage of job opportunities elsewhere. In economic terms, it can be argued that firms will only carry out general training if it is heavily subsidised, either by low wages while the training is taking place (this is not normally possible due to both union agreements and the non-attractiveness of taking jobs at low wages), or because the State provides grants towards the costs of such training. Examples of general training include many professional study programmes, clerical and typing training and skilled and semi-skilled machine operating in engineering and other sectors.

(ii) *Specific training.* If training is completely specific, individuals will not be able to improve their job prospects by moving elsewhere. Organisations often regard such training as valuable because they will reap all the benefits and employment stability is likely to be increased. On the other hand, turnover is more costly in jobs where specific training has been undertaken because no equally skilled and efficient employee can be obtained. Firms may pass some of the benefits of specific training onto the employee by offering higher wages: employees will have less incentive to leave and organisations less incentive to dismiss them. Training can be specific to one organisation or specific to an industry. Often where internal labour markets operate, which give preferences on promotion to existing employees, there will be specific training. For example, much of the training in the Civil Service could be considered specific. Can you think of any examples of specific training within your own organisation?

(c) Government Initiatives in Training

Since 1925, when the first Government Training Centre (GTC) was opened in the UK, the Government has intervened in the labour market to provide training directly, especially in skills of which there were shortages. However major governmental influences to encourage training are a relatively recent phenomenon. By the late 1950s it was becoming evident that training provision, based entirely on perceptions of individual employers of their own needs and their perceived ability and willingness to meet them, had led to serious skill shortages, which had prevented consistent economic growth. Long standing skill shortages, questioning of the quality of training and employers' complaints that those who were investing in training were losing employees to those not incurring such investment, led to increasing criticism of the philosophy that industrial training should be left entirely to the whims of industry. After the 'Carr Report', in 1958, *Training for Skill,* pressure for change led to a White Paper in 1962, the passing of the Industrial Training Act in 1964 and the establishment of the Industrial Training Board (ITB) system. The main objectives of the 1964 Act were:

(a)   To ensure an adequate supply of properly trained men and women at all levels in industry.

(b)   To secure an improvement in the quality and efficiency of training.

(c)   To ensure that the proper attention and importance to training is given by the management of firms.

(d)   To share the costs of training more evenly between firms.

Thus it was hoped that the Act and the Industrial Training Boards, which were established as a consequence of the Act, would result in a raising of the overall standards and volume of training. The first 5 boards were set up in 1964, and over the next 6 years 27 in all were established, covering industries employing about 15 million people. Neither the Government nor the ITB's could force an employer to train his employees. The detailed functions of the ITB's included the following:

(i) Establishing training policy within each industry, including such questions as admission to training, length of training, registration of trainees and provision for appropriate attendances at colleges of further education.

(ii) Establishing standards of training and syllabuses for different occupations in the industry, taking into account the associated technical and professional education required.

(iii) Providing advice and assistance about training to firms in the industry.

(iv) Devising tests to be taken by apprentices and other trainees during, and on completion of, their training.

(v) Establishing qualifications and tests for instructors.

(vi) Running training courses in their own establishments.

(vii) Assisting individuals in finding facilities for being trained for employment in the industry.

(viii) Carrying out or assisting other persons in carrying on research, into any matter relating to training, for employment in the industry.

(ix) Making payments to persons in connection with arrangements under which they or their employees make use of courses and other facilities provided or approved by the Board, including travelling and maintenance expenses and course fees, and making grants or loans to provide adequate facilities for training.

The Central Training Council of the Department of Employment recommended eight principles of training which should underpin an organisation's training philosophy:

(i) The aim should be to establish training systems in which initial training and further training opportunities are available, subject to employment demands and prospects, to all employees capable of benefiting from such opportunities, irrespective of age, sex, length of service.

(ii) Programmes of training should be based on an analysis of relevant jobs. The initial training of young people should be broadly based and subsequent training geared more closely to specific requirements.

(iii) The duration of training should be a function of what requires to be learned, flexibility being allowed to take account of the maturity, experience and learning ability of the individual trainee.

(iv) All young trainees should receive the further education necessary to complement and reinforce their industrial training.

(v) Apart from the initial and complementary further education for young people, there should be a recognisable correspondence between the training provided for young people and that provided for adults, particularly as regards the standards of competence achieved at the end of training.

(vi) To meet the requirements arising from changes in technology and other factors influencing the work situation, including, for example, the growth of new industries in areas of special development, opportunities should be provided for workers to receive such training and further education as may be necessary throughout their working life.

(vii) Apart from industry's foreseeable and immediate requirements, workers should be encouraged to take courses likely to improve their prospects for more highly skilled employment.

(viii) Systematic means of assessment should be increasingly used, both for the selection of people for training, and to establish their competence during the training itself. Subject to availability, skilled jobs should be open to any worker who has established his competence to do them.

To encourage training within their industry, the ITB's tended to operate a levy/grant scheme whereby firms over a certain size — this varied from Board to Board — paid a training levy at the beginning of the training year and received a grant at the end of the year towards their training costs, providing the training was of an approved standard. Board levy rates in the 1960s varied enormously; some charged a percentage rate of payroll, from 3.8% by the Air Transport and Travel ITB for British Air carriers to 0.04% in Electricity supply, and others charged a per capita rate, e.g. in Iron and Steel £4.50 per head to £45 per head in certain sectors of the Construction Industry. In assessing the success of the ITB system in 1972 in *Training for the Future,* the Department of Employment showed that, from 1964 — 1968, the number of persons undergoing training had increased by about 15%, with a marked increase in the training of managers, scientists and technologists, technicians and operatives; an increase over the period from 1964 — 1971 in the total numbers of people in GB released from work to attend courses in further education; a substantial increase in the number of training officers and instructors employed by firms; and a large increase in the number of cooperative group training schemes, from 60 in 1964 to 700 in 1972. Managers had certainly come to recognise the need for training and its provision had increased substantially.

There were, however, a number of criticisms of the system which fell into two distinct categories (a) the whole philosophy on which the 1964 Act was based and (b) the weaknesses of operation:

(a) Philosophy

(i) The Act neglected the distinction between general and specific training. Where firms were investing in specific training, there was no need for subsidy because the organisation providing it got a return from that investment. Whereas the ITB's had provided an increase in the amount of general training conducted, some of this would probably have been carried out anyway because of labour shortages.

(ii) No additional funds were created for training; the levy/grant scheme merely reallocated funds from one employer to another.

(iii) There was no central logic in the establishment of the ITB's who were working as hard in the declining industries as in the growth industries, a possible waste of resources.

(iv) The system encouraged training for the sake of training, i.e. to get the levy back, rather than a genuine assessment of the economic returns on training.

(v) The elaborate bureaucracy and costly structure of the ITB's which were funded by employers, was an unnecessary drain on resources.

(vi) The Training Board system was not equipped nor designed to deal with problems of labour redeployment. It could not contribute to a better distribution of labour because it was industry based.

(b)   Operational weaknesses

(i) Because of the requirements of record keeping and paperwork, small firms especially felt that Boards were too rigid in assessing training needs, which were often based on 'good practice' in large organisations.

(ii) Occupations which were common to the ITB's (e.g. clerical, managerial and computer training) were not efficiently covered as there was duplication of effort.

(iii) The effect of the Act on quality and quantity of training was not steady and continuous: a good example of this was the 50% reduction in the number of apprenticeships offered in 1972.

(iv) The use of training staff, including instructors and emphasis on off-the-job training methods, may have actually increased training costs unnecessarily.

(v) There were problems in measuring the quality of training done: should it be the standard based on the best firms or the average for the industry?

(vi) Some areas of importance to the economy were not covered, e.g. local government, banking and finance.

(vii) The system failed to adopt new industries quickly enough, e.g. North Sea oil extraction, production and refining.

The Government introduced the Employment and Training Act 1973 partly because of these criticisms, and also in an effort to bring together the role of the ITB's and other direct Government training schemes, e.g.

the Government Training Centres and the Training Opportunities Scheme, and also to introduce a more comprehensive service which linked employment and training initiatives. The Act established the Manpower Services Commission (MSC) the Training Services Agency (TSA), and the Employment Services Agency (ESA) to provide coordination and redevelopment of national employment and training policies. It sought to distinguish between the training needs of industry and changes in industrial structure through the coordination of the ITB's and other training measures by the TSA; the training needs of individuals who were forced to change skills, through the TSA; and to exempt those firms with adequate training facilities so that the ITB's could concentrate on those needing most help. Other changes made by the 1973 Act included:

(i) The abolition of the Central Training Council of the Department of Employment, its duties being taken over by the TSD.

(ii) The replacement of the ITB's 'mandatory duties' to provide or secure the provision of courses and other facilities for training, to make training recommendations and to impose a levy with enabling powers to do those things if they wished.

(iii) The limitation of levy to a maximum of 1% of the employer's payroll: ITB's were only able to raise a levy above 1% if there was consensus support by employers representing 50% of the firms liable to levy, and if those firms accounted for over 50% of the levy raised.

(iv) The transfer from industry to the Exchequer of responsibility for funding the ITB's administrative expenses, including staff training advisory services and capital expenditure.

(v) The MSC had a responsibility for promoting training in the sector of the economy not covered by the ITB's.

(vi) The TSA had a responsibility to look after and finance regional problems.

The MSC has based its activities on its power to influence in the non-ITB sector, backed by the financial help which it could provide. Its prime objectives have been:

— to improve the planning of training;
— to help to identify key training needs;
— to secure cooperation on cross sector problems;
— to stimulate the exchange of manpower and training information;
— to stimulate the creation of new voluntary training organisations in specific industries.

In the ITB sector the imposition of the TSA (latterly called the Training Division (TD)) with its introduction of direct training activities, led to difficulties in the late 1970s. ITB's found difficulty in coping with the dual responsibility to their industry and to the MSC, which at times they found incompatible. ITB's came to feel that they had insufficient influence in shaping national training policy. They became more dependent on Government funds and, from 1975, when public spending was being reduced, the following irritations arose:

— the inability to carry forward unspent money;
— inability to obtain final commitment of funds for more than one year;
— close scrutiny of ITB staff and conditions.

In *Outlook on Training — a Review of the Employment and Training Act 1973* MSC (July 1980), the performance of national training arrangements was analysed again. Evidence suggested that, despite national provision, skills shortages had arisen, which suggested that under-training was still a problem. Organisations tended to train to meet their own needs and the amount of training investment was reduced in times of downturn in business activity. Small firms still found it difficult to establish appropriate training arrangements. There was a failure to link industrially biased training arrangements with cross sector skill problems: most ITB's were unable to relate their operations to local labour markets, despite some success in the field of North Sea oil. The CBI had expressed doubts in their evidence as to whether national arrangements had actually increased the quality of training. It was also still evident that organisations valued their independence and did not always see the relevance of an external body responsible for training.

However, research had indicated that levy exemption arrangements had caused an improvement in training quality and the following results were quoted to justify this statement:

— training was perceived as an important function of management;
— there was a much increased use of trained instructors and qualified training staff, who portrayed greater professionalism in assessment of training needs and the management and execution of training. There were 1,532 qualified training officers in 1964 and 3,148 in 1978;
— the quality of training had improved in occupations covered by specific training recommendations;
— group training schemes had continued to spread.

Yet current training arrangements were still not fully conforming to the philosophies envisaged in the MSC report *Training for Skills: A programme for action* (1977), which commented on the setting and achievement of standards; on training programmes, which should be appropriate in content and realistic in length; and that there should be greater opportunities for trainees of different ages and experience to enter training and qualify for skilled work. The report saw that the main thrust of future public policy was likely to arise within the following areas, with the MSC acting as leader and industry training organisations and employers playing a part:

— Securing adequate training for unemployed and young people geared to the needs of individuals and the labour market;
— Training for cross sector occupations;
— Meeting training needs in particular localities;
— Reforming training systems to meet contemporary needs;
— Securing the provision of reliable and consistent manpower intelligence, especially at local level;
— Promoting training during times of recession;
— Retraining for the new skills required with new technology.

To do this it was not suggested that the existing ITB's system should be scrapped or altered radically, as any new bodies would take time to gain credibility and influence. The Committee accepted that a better approach could be developed for local and cross sector needs, but considered that the existing statutory framework could be adapted to cope with it. It made the following recommendations:

(i)   MSC, ITB's and others should be given clear responsibility and effective authority in their own spheres.
(ii) The funding of ITB's operating costs should be returned to industry. MSC should provide supplementary funds where necessary.
(iii) The 1% levy maximum should be abandoned.
(iv) Power to exempt employers from levy should become discretionary.
(v)   Special facilities and services should be established to help determine small firm's training needs.
(vi) In order to improve ITB's accountability to their own industries, it is important for adequate and relevant information to be supplied to the industry through the annual publication of strategic plans and budget proposals.
(vii) More emphasis should be put on the establishment of contacts at local level, e.g. local steering committees.
(viii) MSC should develop a better information system and standardise the collection of data by ITB's.
(ix) MSC should take an active lead in formulating training programmes for newly emerging and expanding occupations.
(x)   More emphasis should be given to *Training for Skills* guidelines.
(xi) Special funds should be made available for firms to provide training for young people.

Subsequently, the MSC published, in May 1981, *A New Training Initiative,* which spelt out the objectives for the 1980s as a framework for the national training system as follows:

(i)   to develop skill training, including apprenticeship, in such a way as to enable young people entering at different ages and with different educational attainments to acquire agreed skill standards appropriate to available jobs and, in addition, to provide them with a basis for progression through further learning;

(ii)   to move towards a position where all those under 18 years old have the opportunity, either of continuing full time education, or of entering training or a period of planned work experience, which combines work related training and further education;

(iii)   to make available widespread opportunities for adults whether employed, unemployed or returning to work, to acquire, increase and update their skills and knowledge throughout their working lives.

Arising out of the 1981 document, the Government published a White Paper *A new training initiative; a programme for action* in December, 1981, which set out detailed recommendations of the structure of the Youth Training Scheme. The elements such a scheme would have to provide were listed as follows:

— induction and asessment;

— training in basic skills, such as the use of tools and machinery and basic office operations;

— occupationally relevant occupational training both off and on-the-job;

— guidance and counselling;

— recording and reviewing of progress.

In addition the MSC considered that there should be an urgent review, sector by sector, of the training arrangements across the whole of industry in order to draw up the most appropriate arrangements to meet training needs in the 1980s. This was published in July 1981.

In the same month, a new Employment and Training Act was given royal assent. The main purposes of the 1981 Act were:

(a)   To allow the Secretary of State for Employment to set up, abolish or change the scope of an Industrial Training Board, after consultation with the MSC.

(b)   To enable a Board to finance its operating expenses from a levy on employers.

(c)   To widen the scope of exemptions of an employer of levy from an ITB.

(d)   To exempt establishments in Enterprise Zones from having to pay levy or provide information to an ITB.

(e)   To enable a Board to use for its operating expenses money obtained from past levies.

(f)   To enable the Secretary of State to direct Boards to publish information which they hold, subject to safeguards about confidentia-
lity.

In November, 1981 the number of ITB's was reduced from 23 to 7 and,
where the Boards were abolished, industries were expected to develop
alternative voluntary arrangements. Where Boards were retained, they
would be funded by the relevant industry.

The ITB's retained are Clothing and Allied Products, Construction,
Engineering, Hotel and Catering, Road Transport, Plastics Processing
and Offshore Petroleum. These 7 Boards (the Department of Employment estimates) have about 30% of all employed persons in their scope.

The Industrial Training Act 1982 consolidated all the legislation
relating to Industrial Training Boards. The current philosophy in the UK
is, therefore, that employers should provide for their own needs in the
same way as they provide for investment in capital equipment: the
Government has indicated a general preference for voluntary training
arrangements within the overall philosophy of national training objectives. Thus, the purpose of the Government's Adult Training campaign
in 1985 was to bring home to employers that investment in training
brings results, in terms of improved company performance and growth.
The extent to which the demise of the Boards has reduced training activity will vary from industry to industry, and the effects on national skills
provision can only be judged as time passes.

A number of schemes have been initiated to encourage training in
particular areas. These include:

(a)   **The Technical and Vocational**
      Education Initiative

(TVEI) provides a four year course of full-time technical, vocational and
general education including appropriate work experience. This scheme
applies to 14—18 year olds and aims to stimulate technical and vocational education across the range of ability to link the world of work and
the world of education. Computer literacy and information technology
tend to be prominent features. The Careers Service is concerned with
assessing the individual's needs and arranging programmes of work
experience.

(b)   **Priority Skills Programme**

Through this scheme the Government offers help to employers for training where there are nationally identified skill shortages, especially in
computer skills.

(c) Information Technology Centres

These provide unemployed young people under the age of 18 with training and work experience in new technology. They are jointly funded by the Department of Trade and Industry and the MSC.

(d) New Technology Access Centres

These offer training and development programmes, usually of a few days in length, which give familiarisation in basic operating skills, or longer courses to learn how to maintain and test complex equipment. Employers can go to the centres to try out equipment before they invest in it.

(e) Local Training Grant Scheme

Introduced in July, 1985 this scheme offers grant aid to employers to help them provide or purchase training for new or existing employees. Grants may be used to update or broaden skills required for hard-to-fill vacancies and training can be up to 40 days per employee. Grants are to help employers to do the required training urgently.

(f) Local Consultancy Grants Scheme

Introduced in July, 1985 this scheme makes Grants available to purchase specialist professional advice to analyse an organisation's training needs as a result of changes within the firm. Grants may also be used to assist with reviews of company performance that are intended to lead to the development of employee training. Up to two thirds of the consultant's fee (subject to a maximum) can be paid.

Whatever the effects of changes in statutory training influence, training and retraining is required to remove bottlenecks in the labour market and to remedy the problems of unemployment to raise national output and efficiency. There are also social, psychological and political benefits associated with investment in training. The costs of investment in retraining and initial training in periods of high unemployment are reduced because there is little loss in output, which would otherwise be incurred if training took place in times of economic boom. From 1975 onwards, the MSC has been forced, to encourage a programme of counter-cyclical training, especially for the young unemployed. The prime difficulty for the public authorities is to obtain sufficient data on industry's future needs to provide relevant training; in addition, there are difficulties in maintaining the motiviation of those who have undergone training if job opportunities are not immediately available. It is essential that for the greatest value to be obtained from current public training investment, employers develop and implement effective manpower policies and plans to foresee as far as possible their future needs for skills and numbers of employees. Experience of past economic upswings has shown that bottlenecks occur in labour supply and skills to reduce the impact of these requires cooperation between industry, trade unions and the relevant Government agencies. David Felton in *The Times* on 31/12/85 suggests that British industry's training performance compares badly with its competitors with British companies committing only 0.15% of turnover to training compared with 1-2% in other countries and this attitude is being addressed by the MSC.

Chapter 13
Unemployment

This has been one of the key influences on governments over the last ten years and is likely to be so for the remainder of this century. In order to be able to examine the implications of high levels of unemployment, we need to understand the different concepts of the term.

The labour market, as we have inferred, is in continuous motion as people move from one job to another. In 1979 it was suggested, based on the number of P45's issued, that there were between 8 and 9 million job changes every year. Because unemployment and vacancies coexist, we cannot view unemployment as a residual state in the labour market which results when all vacancies have been filled. For, as the MSC has illustrated in most of their annual reports, there are always a number of hard-to-fill vacancies in some sectors and regions. There are also variations in supply and demand in different labour markets. Unemployment is therefore a state through which most individuals pass within their lifetime. But, what is evident, is that some categories of employees have more frequent and longer spells of unemployment. It has been suggested that overall rates of labour turnover do not vary much over the economic cycle; what varies are the reasons for that turnover. Thus, when the economy takes a downswing, the lay-off or redundancy rate increases, i.e. involuntary unemployment, whereas, when the economy is booming resignations increase, i.e. the voluntary leaving rate increases.

1. VOLUNTARY *VS* INVOLUNTARY UNEMPLOYMENT

It has therefore been suggested by economists that policy makers need to distinguish between voluntary and involuntary unemployment, in trying to solve unemployment problems.

Voluntary unemployment: people leave because they do not think the prevailing wage rates or job opportunities within the organisation are adequate for their perceived level of skill and experience.

Involuntary unemployment: people cannot find work at a suitable rate of pay.

Some people are unemployed even where full employment exists, and the definition of full employment varies and has been considered over the years to exist when between only 1% and 5% of workers are unemployed. More realistically, it is a situation where, although demand exists for goods and services, supply cannot be increased because of labour shortages: there can be said to be a *natural rate of unemployment,* which is influenced by the industrial mix of the economy; the custom and practice arrangements regarding employment in the labour market, e.g., trade union/management agreements on the basic skills required for employment; the speed of technological and industrial change; and the preferences of the labour force as to their degree of participation. Thus, while the labour force adjusts to changes in the labour market and obtains the raw skills necessary for changed work practices and the search for new jobs, there will be an inevitable level of unemployment which will be difficult to avoid and to control.

2. TYPES OF UNEMPLOYMENT

In order to consider the likely success of Government measures it can be useful to define other types of unemployment, based on reasons which can be broadly classified into:

(a) Unemployment that occurs because of a low level of demand for labour — seasonal unemployment, cyclical unemployment and growth gap unemployment.

(b) Unemployment which occurs because of changes in skill requirements and the necessary adjustments which take place in the labour market — hard-core unemployment, frictional unemployment and structural unemployment.

A. Demand affected unemployment

(i) *Seasonal unemployment:* occurs in those sectors of society where the work is of necessity of a seasonal nature; regular bouts of unemployment are likely, the pattern varying from industry to industry. The construction industry used to suffer seasonal unemployment but new techniques and improved raw materials have reduced the bad weather lay-offs which used to occur. A current example is the tourist industry where hotels and travel firms often take on staff only for the the summer season. Governments tend to adjust the unemployment figures to reduce the impact of seasonal unemployment.

(ii) *Cyclical unemployment:* few economies or industrial sectors achieve a smooth trade cycle and thus there are always peaks and troughs through growth and deflation. Vacancies may exist, but in the 'wrong' jobs.

(iii) *Growth gap unemployment:* growth gap unemployment or stagnation unemployment occurs when a country's economy has suffered from depression for a considerable period of time and there is little prospect of increasing economic activity. Thus, long term high rates of unemployment persist.

    Sustained demand — deficient unemployment tends in the end to produce structural unemployment as production capacity and skills become obsolete.

270

B. Labour Market maladjustment unemployment

(i) *Hard-core unemployment:* this exists because any society has a number of workers who, because of their physical and mental conditions, age or work attitudes, are unlikely to be employed. These groups are possibly about 1% of the working population, according to the Department of Employment.

(ii) *Frictional unemployment:* or 'search unemployment' occurs because it takes time to match people and jobs' skill requirements; people have to either adjust their skills for the work which is available or adjust the wages at which they will offer themselves for employment. Each unemployed worker can technically be said to have a reservation wage which he feels represents the value of his skills; over time, if he cannot find work at what he considers an adequate wage, he may adjust his expectations and, therefore, his reservation wage has to be reduced to take account of the prevailing wage and salary structure as he perceives it. Because of poor information about available job opportunities, the job search process is hampered while individuals assess the extent of the market demand for labour. Economies are dynamic, therefore job mobility will be required as new firms and industries develop. There will inevitably be some level of frictional unemployment while the supply of skills adjusts to demand in the short term. Usually frictional unemployment implies that the number of vacancies exceeds the number of job seekers and that the unemployment period is of short duration.

(iii) *Structural unemployment:* this can be thought of as a long term form of frictional unemployment. The unemployed have not the necessary skills for the available job vacancies and, in order to obtain work, they will either have to change their skills or change their location of residence. Throughout the period of industrialisation, industries have grown up and declined in importance in the economy. The skills requirements of society have developed, grown and declined in parallel. Few industries or types of work are guaranteed indefinite survival and, as an industry declines, the demand for labour falls quicker than the supply can readjust. Unemployment is created because the economy's industrial structure is itself changing. Often declining industries are grouped geographically, e.g. shipyards and, therefore, whole regions have a disproportionate level of unemployment because of these structural changes.

With structural unemployment it usually means that the worker has not left his job voluntarily but has been forced to do so. The shift in Britain from manufacturing employment has been an important feature in the unemployment distribution

271

Table 13:1 Employees in Employment (Millions)

	June 1974	June 1979	June 1984
Manufacturing	7.7	7.1	5.5
Construction	1.2	1.2	1.0
Distribution	3.1	3.3	3.3
Financial Services	1.5	1.6	1.9
Public Administration	1.9	1.9	1.8
Education and Health	2.5	2.8	2.8
Other	4.4	4.7	4.5
Total	22.3	22.6	20.9

Source: *Department of Employment Gazette,* August & December 1984

Between 1974 and 1979 there was already a fall in employment in the manufacturing industry, but this was compensated for by both public and private services. However, between 1979 and 1984, the decline in manufacturing employment was very significant, a fall of about 25% in five years; this was not compensated for by a rise in employment elsewhere in the economy. The position reversed somewhat between June 1984 and June 1985 as follows:

Table 13:2 Jobs: Gains and losses (June 1984 — June 1985)

Sector	Numerical Change (000s)	% Change
SERVICES		
Banking finance and insurance	+79	+4.3
Retail distribution	+57	+2.7
Hotels and catering	+41	+4.1
Other services (public & personal)	+24	+1.8
Wholesale distribution	+23	+2.0
Medical and other health services	+22	+1.7
Transport	-19	-2.2
MANUFACTURING		
Paper, paper products, printing & publishing	+5	+1.0
Mechanical engineering	+3	+0.4
Office machine, electrical engineering and instruments	+2	+0.2
Metal goods (misc.)	+2	+0.5
Motor vehicles and parts	-9	-3.1
Timber, wooden furniture	-10	-2.2
Textiles, leather, footwear & clothing	-11	-2.1
Other transport equipment	-13	-4.4
Construction	-34	-3.5
Coal, oil, etc.	-17	-5.9
Electricity, gas & water	-6	-1.8
Agriculture	-2	-0.6

Source: *The Times* 4.1.86

3. MEASUREMENT OF UNEMPLOYMENT LEVELS

There has long been criticism of official unemployment statistics: they are collected for two primary reasons. Firstly, as an indication of the demand pressures for labour,so that governments can help to lubricate the demand and supply in the labour market (in the UK through the auspices of the Manpower Services Commission). Secondly, as a means of assessing cases of social and economic hardship and the amounts which have to be allocated for unemployment and social security benefit from Government funds.

In the UK, the Department of Employment calculates the unemployment statistics by counting the number of people who are registered each month as claiming benefit at unemployment offices. One of the intrinsic problems with statistics of registered unemployment is that people register according to their previous occupation. Thus, rather than measuring the true labour supply position for that occupation the statistics may actually reflect the number of people who have left that occupation. The figures may also not fully represent the extent of involuntary unemployment because they do not include in the employment count those who are not entitled to benefit for one reason or another. For example, some of those who will soon be entitled to retirement benefit may only register to obtain unemployment benefit to tide them over. In October, 1983 there were 199,000 unemployed people who were 60 years old (and no longer required to register) but who would have been registered as unemployed had the definition of unemployment been those actively seeking work. Another problem with the official statistics is that, in including those actively seeking work, they do not count those 'unemployed' who are undergoing Government training and subsidy programmes of one sort or another, who technically would enter work if it were available. The *Employment Gazette* labour market data commentary in March/April 1986 claims that at the end of January 1986 668,000 people were being assisted by the employment and training measures and that 495,000 people were in jobs, training or early retirement as a result of the schemes, instead of an equivalent number claiming unemployment benefits. In March 1986 the numbers involved in some Government employment measures were as follows:

Table 13:3 Numbers involved in Government employment measures March 1986 (GB)

Enterprise Allowance Scheme	55,000
Community Industry	8,000
Community Programme	200,000
Job Release Scheme	43,000
Job Splitting Scheme	270
Young Workers Scheme	51,000
Youth Training Scheme	265,219

Source: *Department of Employment Gazette*

In March 1981, it was estimated that the registered unemployed for that month would have been 345,000 greater than the published figure of 2,380,000 because of these measures.

Estimates, from the General Household Survey, suggest that one-fifth of the unemployed are not entitled to benefit; these have been termed the *hidden unemployed*. They are defined as those who would like to work, but who have become so discouraged about finding jobs in the prevailing economic situation, that they have ceased active searching. This figure from the General Household Survey, although shocking enough, may be a gross underestimate for, if we take the monthly average unemployment rate for 1971, it stood at 806,800 people (the highest figure that year was for November when there were 926,100 unemployed), whereas the 1971 Census of Population showed that 1,366,000 people said that they were 'out of employment', an increase of nearly 41%! Groups which fall into the hidden unemployed category include married women, who would take suitable part-time work; those on an organisational pension, who are not eligible for unemployment benefit for it has run out, but who would take work if it was available; and those active people who are over the State pension retirement age who would work to supplement their pensions.

The statistics also ignore what has been termed *labour hoarding*. Organisations tend to retain surplus labour at the beginning of a depression to avoid incurring termination costs, for example, redundancy pay and redundancy enhancement and the potential future costs of recruitment, selection and training. They will thus tend to cut overtime first and then under-utilise existing employees. When organisations have a hierarchy of tasks they will, when faced with a continued decline in demand for their products, tend to retain the most skilled employees, especially those that they have invested in training, and will start the termination process with the least skilled who are easier to replace. The reasons for labour hoarding can be listed as follows:

(a) Different sorts of employee have different sorts of contractual agreements with employers as, for example, in the Employment Protection (Consolidation)Act minimum notice periods.

(b) In some processes a certain man/machine ratio is required. Unless production is rationalised and different methods introduced, it may not be possible to vary the ratios and organisations will initially introduce short-time working or get work done more slowly.

(c) Hiring and training costs make employers unwilling to lay off skilled employees who will tend to be retained as a precautionary measure.

(d) Workers tend to prefer stable employment and so organisations may be slow in reducing employment levels, to avoid an adverse reaction from trade unions.

At the onset of a recession, labour is not simultaneously cut back with output but labour utilisation will fall. With an upturn in the economy, increased output can be achieved without the need to obtain more workers because the labour utilisation rate can increase; there will thus be a lag in reducing unemployment levels. In the UK, manufacturing output declined slowly over the 1970s and initially labour hoarding took place but, as the depression deepened without any real signs of a recovery, organisations began the process of shedding labour. This has been especially noticeable in textiles, mechanical engineering, car manufacture and metal manufacture. In 1980/81 manufacturing output fell by about 10% and, generally, there was an increase in the numbers of redundancies which has continued into 1982; the redundancies notified to the Department of Employment in 1980, for example, were three times the average of 1975—1979. The CBI in their *Economic Situation Report* of 1984 estimated that there was a bank of 300,000 'hidden' unemployed in the existing labour force, in addition to the unregistered unemployed of approximately 490,000.

4. DIFFERENTIAL IMPACT OF UNEMPLOYMENT

What is evident is that the impact of unemployment will be felt with increasing severity on particular sectors of the labour market. In terms of the types of unemployment defined above, the current UK unemployment situation is, on the one hand, *growth gap unemployment,* caused by the general economic recession, but is also more fundamentally *structural unemployment,* which has hit hardest those with the skills once required by the declining industries.

Both these factors working together have led to an increase in the duration of unemployment. According to the 1985 White Paper, *Employment: the challenge for the Nation* (March 1985), more than 1.3 million in the UK had been out of work for at least one year, 760,000 for more than two years and 450,000 for more than three years.

Table 13:4 Number of unemployed by age and duration April 1985 (000's)

Source: *MSC Annual Report 1984/85*

	No. of unemployed in April 1985 by age				Percentage change April 1984—85			
Duration	**Under 25**	**25—44**	**45 +**	**All Ages**	**Under 25**	**25—44**	**45 +**	**All Ages**
0—6months	530	461	220	1212	+ 4	+ 6	-4	+ 3
6-12 months	296	235	135	666	+ 3	+ 8	-7	+ 2
1—2 years	181	200	142	523	-8	+ 1	-2	-3
2—3 years	86	113	92	292	+ 7	-2	+ 1	+ 2
Over 3 years	73	200	184	458	+ 37	+ 41	+ 33	+ 37
Total unemployed	1167	1210	774	3150	+ 3	+ 9	+ 3	+ 5

(i) Skill distribution

In spite of low investment in the UK compared with many other industrialised nations, there has been a consistent trend in the British manufacturing industry over the last decade towards new technologies and more capital-intensive methods of production. This has been brought about because of advances in computer systems technology and micro technology. This trend is likely to continue and the occupations which are in decline, and which will continue to decline, are those involving the least skill, whereas those on the increase involve more skill and more training. In a study published by the MSC in February 1980 *A study of the long term unemployed,* evidence was gathered which showed that almost 75% of the long term unemployed interviewed in the survey had previously been manual workers, the majority of whom had done semi-skilled or unskilled jobs. The prospects for those people are slim for, within the employed labour force, there have been major changes in occupational structure. For example, between 1971 and 1978 the number of non-manual jobs grew by 1¼ million, whereas there was a loss of 900,000 manual jobs with the largest job losses among the least skilled occupations and those craftsmen from the declining industries with non-transferable skills. Blue collar jobs are fewer and white collar jobs will outnumber them before the end of the 1980s. The new technologies will require a more highly skilled, better educated workforce, in which a larger number of professional and technical staff will be supported by workers performing a range of tasks in a process industry rather than repetitive assembly or manufacturing jobs. Those who, either through State intervention or through opportunities being created for existing workers within firms (or through firms being willing to take on new employees to train), cannot obtain the new skills are likely to remain unemployed and certainly, as regards business and commercial organisations offering training, the long term and inexperienced unemployed will be the ones least likely to be given opportunities.

(ii) Sex distribution

Unemployment is more prevalent amongst the male than amongst the female working population. Within the broad industrial sectors, male and female employment moved in different ways over the 1970s. In manufacturing the decline in employment affected males and females equally so that the shares of male and female employment were much the same at the end of the decade as they have been at the beginning. In the service sector, however, male employment only increased by 5%, whereas female employment went up 25%. In 1979 there were more women than men employed in the service sector. Yet, overall, female unemployment has risen steadily since the mid 1970s and this is likely to increase as reductions are made in the labour force in the public sector (almost 1¾ million women are employed in Local Government) and as technology infiltrates the white collar service sector; through word processors and information storage and retrieval systems in the office, and new stock control and inventory information systems in the retail and distribution centres. Dr Emma Bird produced a report for the Equal Opportunities Commission in 1980 *Information technology in the office: the impact on women's jobs,* which suggested that, by 1990, 17% of all typing and secretarial jobs will have been displaced by word processors. She also claimed, based on her investigations of the pattern in ten companies, that job opportunities will be reduced even more for unskilled and semi-skilled clerks.

Table 13:5 Unemployment rates by sex 1981-1986 (%)

Year	Male	Female
1981	12.9	6.8
1982	15.0	7.9
1983	15.8	8.9
1984	15.7	9.4
1985	16.1	10.0
April 1986	16.4	10.1

Source: *Department of Employment Gazette*

(iii) Regional distribution

There are different patterns of unemployment between regions, those hardest hit being the ones which have a high dependence on manufacturing industry (e.g. the North West and West Midlands); those with a reliance on metal processing (e.g. South Wales and the East Midlands); and those which are affected by the falls in shipbuilding output and the decline in demand for heavy construction for the oil industry. Nevertheless, the traditionally protected South East has also suffered over the last 5 years. Regional differences in unemployment are illustrated in Figure 13:2.

(iv) Age distribution

Young people usually face shorter unemployment periods than most of the other groups in the labour market. In recent years, however, young people have been finding it increasingly difficult to enter the labour market and periods of youth unemployment have become longer.

Unemployment is also highest amongst those aged under 34 (especially those under 18) and those who are aged 60 plus. The greatest concern presently is for the young unemployed who, without any significant work experience, or because they have been forced to take short term jobs, find it very difficult to find employment, even if an upturn occurs within

277

Table 13:6 Unemployment rates by region, April 1984, 1985 & 1986

PER CENT

REGION	April 1984	April 1985	April 1986
South East	9.1	9.9	10.1
East Anglia	9.7	10.8	11.2
South West	10.9	12.0	12.2
West Midlands	14.6	15.5	15.5
East Midlands	11.6	12.8	12.9
York & Humber	13.6	15.0	15.8
North West	15.3	16.2	16.3
North	17.3	18.8	19.1
Wales	15.4	16.9	17.3
Scotland	14.2	15.7	15.8
Great Britain	12.3	13.3	13.6

Source: *Department of Employment Gazette*

the economy. The psychological effects of unemployment are damaging enough but, for the young person who feels rejected by society and who has no source of income, the effects are likely to be even worse. The unlikelihood of obtaining employment, if the individual has few academic qualifications, is also likely to be reflected back into the school system and lead to lack of motivation, disinterest and potential discipline problems.

The changes in the Labour Market, with sectors becoming more efficient and needing a smaller number of employees to produce a given number of goods or services, is particularly affecting the young unemployed. New technologies are rationalising and eliminating jobs which once provided the first chance for young people entering working life.

Table 13:7 Number of unemployed by age — April 1986

Age	Number (000s)	% of Unemployed
under 18	186.6	5.6
18 & 19	314.6	9.5
20—24	682.6	20.5
25—34	805.2	24.2
35—44	510.2	15.3
45—54	447.7	13.5
55—59	301.0	9.1
60+	77.2	2.3
Total	3325.1	100.0

Source: *Department of Employment Gazette*

Table 13:8 Unemployment rates by age — April 1986

Age	%
Under 18	19.0
18 & 19	23.4
20—24	18.9
25—34	14.8
35—44	9.6
45—54	10.0
55—59	15.6
60+	5.9
All ages	13.7

Source: Department of Employment

(v) Other groups

Disabled employees — During recessions the number of disabled people who become unemployed always tends to rise less quickly than general unemployment, partially because some organisations wish to maintain their quota and partially because many organisations operate a policy whereby the disabled are retained until the last possible moment. For example, the proportion of disabled people who became unemployed from 1974—1977 only rose by 20% (to 14%) as against a general rise of 120% (to 5—6%).

Ethnic minority workers as a group have also tended to suffer disproportionately; from 1974—77 unemployment of ethnic minority groups increased by 350% and from 1979—81 by a further 220%. The problem is made worse by their age distribution as there is a high proportion of young people, and also by the fact that ethnic minorities are concentrated in certain regions which have been worst hit by unemployment — West Midlands, Yorkshire and Humberside.

5. UK UNEMPLOYMENT RATES COMPARED WITH OTHER COUNTRIES

At present (1986) Britain's unemployment rate is near the top of the international league, as figure 13:3 shows.

Most industrialised countries have high unemployment levels in the 1980s, compared with the last 10—20 years, and are increasingly uncertain about growth. Over the last 25 years most industrial economies have experienced a steady shift in the balance of economic ability from manufacturing and agriculture into service industries. In each of the nine major industrial countries listed below there has been a decline in the proportion of GDP which is contributed by manufacturing output with the decline accelerating especially after 1970 (see Figure 13:4).

Table 13:9 Unemployment rates in selected countries
APRIL, 1986

Country	% Rate of Unemployment
Belgium	16.2
Spain	22.2
Britain	13.2
Ireland	17.8
Holland	15.0
France	10.3
Italy	11.1
Canada	9.6
USA	7.1
West Germany	9.0
Australia	8.0
Greece	6.4
Japan	2.7
Sweden	2.8

Source: Department of Employment

Table 13:10 Share of manufacturing in GDP*
%

	1960	1970	1971	1972	1973	1974	1975	1976	1977	1978	1979	1980	1981	1982	1983
Canada	23.3	20.4	19.9	20.2	20.2	20.2	19.2	18.6	18.0	18.4	19.1	18.8	18.3	15.6	15.9
US	28.6	25.7	24.9	24.9	24.9	24.1	23.4	24.2	24.5	24.4	23.8	22.5	22.2	20.9	21.1
Japan	33.9	35.9	35.2	34.5	35.1	33.6	29.9	30.6	30.0	30.0	30.1	30.4	30.4	30.5	30.5
France	29.1	28.7	28.5	28.2	28.3	27.9	27.4	27.4	27.5	27.2	27.0	26.3	25.2	25.2	25.3
W.Germany	40.3	38.4	37.0	36.0	36.3	36.1	34.5	34.8	34.6	34.2	34.1	33.0	32.1	31.7	31.8
Italy	28.5	28.9	28.5	27.1	30.0	31.3	29.7	31.7	31.0	30.4	30.6	30.5	28.9	28.5	27.1
Netherlands**	33.6	28.2	27.2	27.1	26.8	25.5	23.7	23.9	20.9	19.5	19.0	17.9	16.9	17.1	17.0
Norway	21.3	21.8	21.1	21.5	21.5	21.9	21.7	20.1	18.9	18.0	18.2	15.6	14.7	14.3	13.7
UK	32.1	28.1	27.4	28.3	28.5	27.2	26.3	25.4	26.6	26.6	24.9	23.1	21.4	21.3	21.0

* Value added in manufacturing as percentage of current price GDP
**Figures for the Netherlands are estimates taken from national sources to reflect the exclusion of oil and gas extraction from the definition of manufacturing

Source: *OECD*

The share of manufacturing in total employment has also fallen in the same period and remains highest in West Germany with the UK now being comparable to France, Italy and Japan but with a higher share employed in manufacturing than the USA. See Table 13:5:

Table 13:11 Employment in manufacturing
% of total civilian employment

	1960	1970	1971	1972	1973	1974	1975	1976	1977	1978	1979	1980	1981	1982	1983
Canada	23.7	22.3	21.8	21.8	22.0	21.7	20.2	20.3	19.6	19.6	19.9	19.7	19.3	18.1	17.5
US	27.1	26.4	24.7	24.3	24.8	24.2	22.8	22.8	22.7	22.7	22.7	22.1	21.7	20.4	19.8
Japan	21.5	27.0	27.0	27.0	27.4	27.2	25.8	25.5	25.1	24.5	24.3	24.7	24.8	24.5	24.5
France	27.5	27.8	28.0	28.1	28.3	28.4	27.9	27.4	27.1	26.6	26.1	25.8	25.1	24.7	24.3
W.Germany	37.0	39.4	37.4	36.8	36.7	36.4	35.6	35.1	35.1	34.8	34.5	34.3	33.6	33.1	32.5
Italy	23.0	27.8	27.8	27.8	28.0	28.3	28.2	28.0	27.5	27.1	26.7	26.7	26.1	25.7	24.7
Netherlands	30.6	26.4	26.1	25.6	25.4	25.6	25.0	23.8	23.2	23.0	22.3	21.5	20.9	20.5	20.3
Norway	25.3	26.7	25.3	23.8	23.5	23.6	24.1	23.2	22.4	21.3	20.5	20.3	20.2	19.7	18.2
UK	36.0	34.5	33.9	32.8	32.2	32.3	30.9	30.2	30.3	30.0	29.3	28.1	26.2	25.3	24.5

Note: figures for Italy 1960-1976 and 1983 and for the Netherlands 1971-1974 and 1983 are estimates based on different classifications of employment.

Source: *OECD*

As we can see from the following table the UK has shown one of the lowest growths in GDP over the last 10 years or so:

Table 13:12 Percentage change in GDP/GNP and industrial production in selected countries 1973/1984

	GDP/GNP	Industrial Production
UK	2.2	12.3
USA	26.1	30.7
Canada	18.9	30.8
Japan	38.3	52.6
France	13.0	26.2
Germany	7.9	20.8
Italy	15.7	23.5

Source: *National Institute Economic Review*

We also have overall a lower productivity (although growth has been faster than competitors since 1979) and rate of investment than many other countries and a standard of living which has not kept pace with our industrial competitors in Europe and America.

6. ECONOMIC COSTS OF UNEMPLOYMENT

Money has been invested in the acquisition of skills, knowledge and experience of workers and not utilising those workers is wasteful and, therefore, is a cost to society. The cost of unemployment for society as a whole could be said to be partly made up from the value of production lost due to unemployment. In calculating such a cost we would have to consider a number of questions:

— Should lost production be calculated for the whole unemployed labour force? Perhaps not because at any level of economic activity there is always frictional unemployment and hard-core unemployment.

— Would the unemployed achieve higher or lower production results than those currently unemployed? It is sometimes believed that the unemployed would have a lower productivity rate than those actually working because the unemployed have below average qualifications and efficiency levels. Yet it could also be argued that this underestimates the contribution which the unemployed could make to Gross National Product.

— How can we calculate sectoral change effects and changes in work patterns? Production results will vary between individuals, dependent upon their sector of work, due to differences in the degree of capital intensity. The costs would also be different if we changed work patterns from full-time to part-time or from five to four days a week. Other difficulties in calculating the true cost of unemploy-

281

ment include:

—   The unemployment rate quoted by Government is not a total record of the unemployed. Evidence suggests that when the unemployment rate falls, the increase in employment is more than proportional to the reduction in the unemployment rate. This is due to the fact that in such circumstances, not only do the unemployed find jobs, but also other workers who were not registered as unemployed.

—   Also, when the unemployment rate drops, the average number of hours worked increases because, as part of the process, some part-time jobs are turned into full-time jobs and labour hoarding results.

—   In addition, as output increases, productivity tends to improve because improvements in economic activity lead to investment in new technology and an encouragement to use manpower more efficiently.

—   Where a community or region suffers from high unemployment, the loss of purchasing power has a consequential effect on producers of other products, who may run down production targets before they too lay employees off. The turnover of the providers of other services — hairdressers, football clubs, cinemas etc. — will also fall, which is a loss to those groups.

Unemployment will also lead to increased Government spending as financial resources are transferred to unemployment and supplementary benefits. Government budgets are also affected by losses in income tax revenue, VAT and Social Security Contributions. Actual unemployment expenditure is also affected by the structure of the unemployment.

—   If a large proportion of the unemployed are new entrants on the labour market, the unemployment benefit cost is low because of the qualification rules.

—   If a large proportion are long term unemployed many may not be entitled to supplementary benefits after unemployment benefit runs out after 12 months.

Other costs, however, include income tax rebates and subsidies like free school uniforms and school meals or uniform grants, rent and rate rebates.

These are not the only costs to the community or the Government for the State will be forced to spend money on measures to try and stimulate employment; these will include training grants for individuals, the cost of operating training programmes in both the Government sector and the private sector and, perhaps, subsidies to create jobs, e.g. regional aid, and wage subsidies.

282

7. THE OVERALL INFLUENCE OF UNEMPLOYMENT

The problems of structural changes will not be easy to handle; redundancies in some of the traditional industries are heavily concentrated in particular regions, e.g. the reduction in steel manufacture and its effects on towns like Consett and Corby. Although it can be suggested that some of the decline in industries like motor car manufacture, steel production and in other manufacturing sectors is due to a degree of growth gap unemployment caused by the recession, other factors in the world economy could mean that, even with an upturn, there will not necessarily be an increased demand for those products. One significant effect is that the developing countries, who traditionally used to import many finished products, are creating their own home-based industries, often with the help of large multinational companies, to produce steel, motor cars and electrical appliances for themselves. This may, in the long term also result in an over capacity in the world supply of those goods and only the most efficient will survive. Unless we match their technology, productivity and prices, an economic upswing will not help employment very much in the UK.

A number of problems have been identified which are likely to influence the UK's ability to increase levels of employment:

(a)   Increases in product or service demand in the short term, because of labour under-utilisation, will mean only a small initial flow of additional job opportunities in those industries influenced at first for a time, therefore, remaining spare capacity will have to be absorbed.

(b)   With developments in technology in many industries, less labour is likely to be required in the future to produce the levels of goods demanded. Evidence of this is already clear in new motor car production technologies using robotics.

(c)   Public sector employment is unlikely to grow in the same way as in the past because of public concern about the levels of public expenditure.

(d)   Firms having suffered a fairly long term recession are likely to favour a more intensive use of their existing labour force as an alternative to recruitment or may initially only hire labour on a fixed term contract.

Of course, whether technological developments are likely to cause more serious unemployment is debatable. Historically, investment in technology created more employment through the creation of additional wealth and increases in gross domestic product; unemployment problems have, to a large extent, proved transitional, although employment is not necessarily created in the same industries and sectors. Technology can have long term benefits for the economy and for individual welfare. Technological developments can lead to investment and increased employment in those industries providing the technology and, if the technology lowers costs, and thus prices, it can have a beneficial effect on real incomes and demand can be stimulated overall with consequent further employment effects.

It is likely that the impact of information processing technology will be greater than before, especially due to its potential impact on the service jobs which previously have been areas of growth in employment. According to an institute of manpower studies report in mid 1985 by David Parsons, *Clerical Labour Markets: changes and trends in the UK,* between 1971 and 1981 clerical, secretarial and related work grew at 2.4% and, between 1980 and 1982, 250,000 clerical jobs were lost in the production sector. Examples of the actual effect of word processors on particular organisations are quoted by an article 'Jobs in Jeopardy and the Trade Union Response' in *Personnel Management* by Tim Webb (July, 1979).

'In Bradford Metropolitan Council (a 50% reduction in the number of typists in the word processor area) the British Standards Institute (33% reduction) and the Provident Financial Group (37% reduction in full-time typists and 79% reduction in part timers).

A choice will inevitably have to be made in the UK between accepting and investing in the new technolgies and of refusing or opting out of them to retain levels of employment. If we do not adopt them, and our competitors do, then there could be a resultant loss of exports, an increased threat from imports and, eventually, a more serious threat to levels of employment.

8. MEASURES TO REDUCE UNEMPLOYMENT

A number of measures have been suggested to attempt to deal with the problems of unemployment. The extent to which they are likely to be successful and the impact they are likely to have on organisations will vary. The measures also need to be evaluated against the causes of unemployment.

To some extent it can be argued that unemployment is a matter of definition; it presumes that employment means that people will work from the age of 16—65 (or 60); that they will work continuously; and that they will work a 35.0 or 39 hour week. The first set of measures deals with removing these parameters.

(i) Reduction in working hours

Logically, reducing the length of the working week would increase the amount of employment, but a reduction in working hours would not create more work if there was a corresponding increase in overtime. Certainly a reduction in working hours is favoured by the TUC as a way of reducing unemployment and, at the TUC annual conference in 1979, they passed a resolution which read:

'Congress expresses its deep concern at the continued persistence of high unemployment...Congress notes that there was a general resistance on the part of employees to the 35 hour week clause in many unions' claims during the last pay round...Congress recognising likely technological developments, calls upon the General Council and its affiliated unions to give top priority in bargaining to reductions in the working week without loss of pay, with a reduction in overtime.'

Figures show that, although the working week in most industries and firms is technically between 36 and 40 hours per week, the average hours worked in manufacturing and certain other industries were as follows:

Table 13:13 Average weekly hours worked 1977-1985 full time manual, males

Year	Hours
1974	46.5
1975	45.5
1976	45.3
1977	45.7
1978	46.0
1979	46.2
1980	45.4
1981	44.2
1982	44.3
1983	43.8
1984	44.3
1985	44.5

Source: Various

Reductions in hours of work need to be combined with overtime reductions or levels of employment are little affected.

Evidence, from the 3 day week in 1972, also suggests that a reduction in working hours may in itself lead to higher productivity from the existing workforce, with no consequential demand for additional workers. This is confirmed in a report by M White and A G Habadean 'Shorter working hours in practice' Policy Studies Institute, 1984, which was a study of firms who reduced working hours in 1981—82 in the engineering and printing industries who reported higher productivity and yet no increases in unit costs.

The problems for employers of such a measure would be the effects on costs and competitiveness if those working fewer hours receive the same levels of pay as before, and there is no increase in productivity. The effect of employing additional labour to obtain the same output would be to raise unit costs, which could damage competitiveness and lead to higher unemployment. It was estimated in the *Department of Employment Gazette* (April 1978) in an article, Measures to alleviate unemployment in the medium term : work sharing, that a working week of 35 hours would create between 100,000 and 500,000 jobs, together with an increase of 6—8% in labour costs, with no loss of pay with the reduction. Figure 13:5 illustrates:

Table 13:14 Percentage increase in labour costs resulting from reducing normal working hours without loss of pay

		35 Hours	38 Hours
1.	Large employment	+ 7.0	+ 2.5
2.	Intermediate employment (low productivity)	+ 8.5	+ 3.0
3.	Intermediate employment (high productivity)	+ 6.1	+ 2.2
4.	Small employment	+ 6.4	+ 2.2

(Source: Department of Employment Gazette)

Although the TUC believes that costs will rise, it also believes that a reduced working week will lead to increased productivity. Figures for France and Germany compared with Britain seem to bear the TUC out, as in Figure 13:6.

Table 13:15 Working time and productivity in major industrial countries

	UK	France	W.Germany
Annual hours 1975	1932	1831	1671
Annual percentage reduction 1976 — 1979	-0.5	-1.7	-1.1
Annual increase in productivity 1976 — 1979	+ 1.0	+ 2.8	+ 3.0

(Source: Department of Employment Gazette)

(ii) Reductions in overtime

This could increase employment for, even with high levels of unemployment, overtime is being worked in many industries; it is thought to be, in the long term, a cheaper method of finding additional production than employing extra people. It has the benefit that it can be cut quickly, whereas the organisation will incur higher costs in terminating employees.

If we take the total overtime hours worked in week ending March 8th 1986 and presume that the average working week in manufacturing is 38 hours and that all overtime could be converted into jobs, then we could create, at a stroke, 3.06 million jobs.

In some industries compulsory reductions in overtime could create employment where equipment is available for additional employees to operate, but, in some cases, if overtime were reduced, individuals might suffer because overtime can be a vital element in earning levels. Reduc-

Table 13:16 Average overtime hours worked per week
1980-1986 (Manufacturing industries)

Year	Operatives (000s)	% of all Operatives	Hours of Overtime Worked	
			Average per Operative working overtime	Actual hours of Overtime (millions)
1980	1422	29.5	8.3	11.76
1981	1137	26.6	8.2	9.37
1982	1198	29.8	8.3	9.98
1983	1209	31.5	8.5	10.30
1984	1311	34.3	8.9	11.59
1985	1332	34.9	9.0	11.94
March 1986	1314	34.8	8.9	11.64

Source: *Department of Employment Gazette*

tions in overtime do not necessarily create work where man/machine systems already have the required number of employees and there is no way of adding staff without incurring higher investment costs.

(iii) Worksharing

It has been suggested that a combination of a shorter working week, longer holidays, early retirement and less overtime could provide employment opportunities for the out of work. Worksharing has its aim of redistributing the total work available more evenly among the population. One of the difficulties in Britain is that working time is not influenced by statute, except in the Wages Council Industries, nor are holiday entitlements, except the public holidays. Whereas countries, such as Belgium and West Germany, have legal limits to the amount of overtime worked, the UK only has such limits under the Factories Act and the regulations regarding driver's hours under the Transport Act. Otherwise all these matters are subject to agreement in the UK by the process of collective bargaining and in recent years there have been some significant negotiations which have reduced the working week and increased holidays.

Trade unions generally seem to be in favour of shorter hours of work and many employees, when questioned, have argued that they would prefer to work shorter hours for the same pay than attempt to significantly increase their pay for current hours.

Jobsharing is a form of employment whereby two or more worksharing individuals voluntarily share the responsibility for one full-time position with the salary and fringe benefits being split between them according to the time they work. One of the pioneers in the field of job sharing in Britain was GEC Telecommunications in their Coventry and Atcliffe plant. Many organisations in the public and private sector now have schemes. (A form of job sharing has been encouraged by the MSC Job Splitting Scheme — see Chapter 12). Advantages of job sharing schemes include:

287

— the opening up of opportunities for part-time workers in areas where only full-timers were previously employed. (But are these opportunities going to help the registered unemployed or the hidden unemployed?)
— reduced labour turnover, increased efficiency and greater flexibility of employees.
— greater continuity of work coverage as it is unlikely that the job sharers will both be absent or leave together.
— can be a good way of helping the future retiree to wind down.
— reduction in costs to the Exchequer.

Disadvantages include

— part-time jobs are created, not full-time ones.
— may limit promotion opportunities.
— where less than 16 hours per week is worked, there is no protection from the EP (C)A 1978.
— more time and expense of training for employers.
— extra cost of payroll administration protective clothing, facilities, like lockers, which cannot be shared.

These are general job sharing advantages and disadvantages and the Government's Job Splitting Scheme has a number of particular ones.

Main opposition to worksharing has come from employers' organisations because they argue W.S. will increase costs, and therefore reduce competitiveness, and hence mean lower profits (e.g. *CBI News* No.20 October 1983).

N. M. Meltz, F. Reid and G. S. Swartz in *Sharing the Work,* an analysis of the issues in worksharing and jobsharing University of Toronto Press, 1981, suggest that there is evidence that worksharing does not necessarily lead to increased labour costs

— when there is a leisure/income agreement and restrictions in overtime.
— worksharing can remove some of the administrative costs of holiday coverage, replacement problems when somebody leaves etc.
— by retaining workers during a recession and training new ones during periods of low demand, it helps to reduce the recruitment, selection and training costs once trade recovers.
— it may prevent the rusting of skills and problems of motivation amongst those who would be otherwise unemployed.
— shorter hours may reduce absenteeism.
— reorganising working time could allow more capital utilisation and greater flexibility, leading to higher productivity.

(iv) Raise the School Leaving Age

It is becoming apparent that to exclude young people from the labour market by keeping them within the educational system is not equally appropriate for all young people, e.g. the poorly motivated, and furthermore that not all families have the economic capacity to maintain their children in a financial sense.

This would incur increased economic costs for the Exchequer, for it is likely to require investment in more school buildings in some areas and the employment of extra teaching staff. Thought would also have to be given to what is done in that additional school time to improve the likelihood of young people obtaining work.

Certainly some moves have been made thus in November 1982 the Prime Minister invited the MSC to launch a major new educational initiative — the Technical and Vocational Education Initiative (TVEI). The target group of TVEI is the whole ability range of the 14—18 age group. In 1983/84 there were 14 pilot Local Education Authorities (LEA's) and in 1986 74 LEA's were operating schemes. The general aim of the scheme is to give young people the knowledge and skills necessary to prepare them for the world of work. Thus the scheme attempts to promote a balance between educational and vocational needs, to develop each individual's personal effectiveness and link the work of schools with the world of business, commerce and the public services.

Whilst there are a variety of schemes with variation in content from area to area the common characteristics of schemes include a strong emphasis upon project based learning; the development of real and simulated experience of work problems, the development of problems; the development of problem solving, study skills, computer awareness, communication ability, numeracy, business management and technological initiatives.

Table 13:17 TVEI students per year 1983/1984 & projected to 1992/1993

Year	New entrants to schemes	Total numbers on schemes
1983/84	4,000	—
1984/85	16,000	20,000
1985/86	19,000	39,000
1986/87	26,250	65,250
1987/88	22,250	83,500
1988/89	10,250	77,750
1989/90	7,250	66,000
1990/91	—	39,750
1991/92	—	17,500
1992/93	—	7,250

Source: MSC Figures & Estimates

The TVEI scheme has a counterpart in the Certificate of Pre-

289

Vocational Education (CPVE) which is a one year programme, launched in 1984 and aimed at the 17 + group. Its general aim is to assist the transition from school to work by developing in the students basic skills, experience, knowledge and the relevant personal and social competence which will be required outside of the education world. The CPVE provides a framework of knowledge and has three components:

1. To develop, core competence in the areas of personal development, communication, numeracy, information technology and industrial studies.

2. Vocational studies are organised in five main categories; business and administration services, technical services, production, distribution and personal services.

3. Additional studies which are based on individual choice.

The emphasis is on activity based learning, the development of individually relevant work experience and personal counselling support.

There is a danger however that extra education could raise individuals job aspirations to levels which may not be capable of being met by industry and commerce. Certainly, to keep people at school merely to keep them off the streets has limited value. To transfer back into the education system some of the existing training and work experience schemes could be an attractive proposition, but then we are incurring the costs even for those who can get work and not specifically for those who need it. It would also have repercussions for current apprenticeship and higher education processes.

Table 13:18 School leaving age
(1985)

Belgium	14
Denmark	15
France	16
Germany	15/16
Greece	14
Ireland	15
Italy	14
Luxembourg	15
Netherlands	16
Sweden	16

(v) Lower Wages

The argument has been used by employers and politicians that young people especially, but also others (for example, in the Wages Council Industries) cannot be employed because the costs are too high. It was estimated by the Department of Employment in 1983 that a 1% fall in the wages rates of young males would lead to a 1.2% rise in their employment. Whilst it must be agreed that the cost of the employee is an important factor when deciding who and how many to employ, wages are only one element of cost. It is the demand for the product and service which is of crucial importance.

A number of studies, both in the UK and abroad, have shown that even where the young have relatively lower wage rates there is little impact on the levels of employment. For example a study by the Labour Research Department *Bargaining Report 30* in December 1983 analysed the relative rates of pay of young people under 18 and, although these have declined, there has been no increase in employment in the UK.

Table 13:19 Under 18s gross weekly pay as % of adult average

Year	All Male	All Female
1974	38%	58%
1979	40%	58%
1980	39%	59%
1981	39%	55%
1982	38%	54%
1983	36%	51%

Source: Labour Research Department — December 1983

Even where studies have shown lower wages leading to small increases in youth employment, it is extremely difficult to ascertain whether this apparent improvement in the situation is at the cost of someone else's job or to the benefit of total employment in society.

(vi) Lower the retirement age

This also would have the effect of raising Exchequer costs; to retire people early increases social security spending and creates the need to develop leisure facilities. In July 1980, a written reply was given to the House of Commons on the costs of reductions in male pension ages by Reg Prentice, the then Minister for the Disabled. The reply was as follows:

'On the assumption that the pattern of retirement amongst men in the five years following the new pension ages would be the same as the present pattern amongst men aged 65 or 70, and that two thirds (the figure of two-thirds is assumed because not all retirements would create vacancies, and because some vacancies would not be filled, since there would be insufficient unemployed with the necessary qualifications in the right localities) of the jobs created by men in employment retiring earlier were filled by persons on the unemployment register, the net cost to Central Government funds for a full year, at November 1980 rates, would be in the order of:

Reduction of age to:	64	63	62	61	60
Cost £ million	300	600	900	1,300	1,800

However, in a situation of full employment, when there would be significant job replacement by persons on the unemployment register, these costs could rise considerably. To give some indication of this, if the effect of job replacement on the above calculations were disregarded, the costs, on the same basis as those above, would be of the order of:

Reduction of age to:	64	63	62	61	60
Cost £ million	600	1,200	1,900	2,600	3,600

These figures take account of the net cost to the National Insurance Fund, the loss of National Insurance surcharge, National Health Service, Redundancy Fund and Maternity Pay Fund income, a broad estimate of the loss of income tax revenue and a saving in supplementary benefits. There would, in addition, be important implications for occupational pension schemes.'

According to the DHSS's best estimate in 1982, a male pension age of 60 would cut registered unemployment by 420,000, of which 200,000 would be currently unemployed 60 — 64 year olds. There is some doubt whether the other 220,000 jobs released would actually be filled by others on the unemployment register because it can be argued that many of these close to retirement are retained by organisations because of a perceived moral obligation to 'long serving' employees.

(vii) Employment Subsidies

Employment subsidies to reduce unemployment are based on the idea that employment is extremely costly in economic, psychological and social terms and that Government expenditure to support jobs is preferable to paying social security benefits. In addition to major investment in organisations like British Leyland and British Aerospace, recent subsidies have included the Temporary Employment subsidy; Recruitment Subsidy for school leavers; Temporary Short Time Working Compensation Scheme; the Youth Employment Subsidy; and various grants to encourage the employment of additional labour and to encourage employers to offer training programmes — including the Youth Opportunities Programme, Young Workers Scheme, and the Youth Training Scheme. The arguments for subsidies as a weapon against unemployment are:

(i)   Cash subsidies are a simple method of reducing the costs of hiring labour, (i.e. wage rate minus the subsidy); therefore, employment is stimulated because hiring costs are reduced.

(ii) They are cheap in terms of public finance — there are savings in social security payments, and income tax and national insurance revenue will increase as the level of employment rises.

(iii) They have a dampening effect on inflation:
   — employment subsidies have a direct cost-reducing effect on unit labour costs of subsidised firms and, as prices tend to be linked to costs, employment subsidies work directly to keep prices down;
   — employment subsidies means a lower Public Sector Borrowing Requirements (PSBR) as compared with the costs of unemployment benefits.

292

Whether there is a long term dampening effect on prices is debatable, as is the idea of reducing the PSBR. There is a danger that employment subsidies will be 'wasted' on employers who will have to reduce their labour force in the long run, for example, British Steel received the Temporary Employment Subsidy. Subsidies which reduce the relative costs of one firm over another may discourage consumer expenditure on the products of non-subsidised firms, whose output and employment may be reduced: they could have an effect in delaying structural change in the rundown of older industries and distorting long term labour changes and investment decisions.

Although recruitment and training subsidies appear to have the advantage of accelerating the progress of firms who are expanding, rather than a Temporary Employment Subsidy which can help declining firms, it tends to favour those who are leading the recovery and this can induce a labour supply problem for those who recover later. Another major problem for a government is to know when to terminate the subsidies.

Even subsidies and training grants cannot create work where work does not exist, so their benefits may be illusory. There may be a substitution displacement effect with employers retaining labour at public expense or, if subsidies are used to create jobs, changes in the pattern of labour demand to take advantage of public funds and displace normal recruitment policies.

(viii) Lower Unemployment Benefit

The idea has been put forward that people today are less interested in having a job because of the possible disincentive benefit of unemployment pay, which is said to increase the amount of voluntary unemployment. Yet the majority of serious investigations have tended to support the view that unemployment benefit at its present levels does not in most cases increase 'voluntary' unemployment (e.g. A. B. Atkinson *et al.* Unemployment Benefit Duration and Incentives in Britain: How robust is the evidence. *Journal of Public Economics* 1984 Vol 23 No. 1/2).

The problem in setting unemployment benefit levels is the difficulty of ensuring adequate income for those unlucky enough to be unemployed whilst, at the same time, avoiding a disincentive to work.

There are two main state schemes that provide income support for the unemployed:

(a) National Insurance unemployment benefit is a contributory scheme for which an individual becomes eligible if in the previous tax year he has paid sufficient N.I. payments. It can be paid for a maximum of 52 weeks in a spell of unemployment and is a flat rate payment.

(b) Supplementary benefit depends, not on past contributions, but is payable if a claimant who, when means tested, needs it. The degree of need is assessed, taking into account family circumstances and whether the claimant is the head of the household.

Once the need has been established, and provided the claimant's circumstances do not change, eligibility for supplementary benefit runs indefinitely from July 1982. Both National Insurance unemployment benefit and supplementary benefit have been made subject to tax.

The argument against an incentive to remain unemployed, created by N.I. Benefit, is made stronger when we realise that not all the unemployed at any one moment are receiving N.I. unemployment benefit. In 1984/5 when there were on average two million unemployed, only 30% were in receipt of unemployment benefit (according to the DHSS estimates used in the Green Paper on the Social Security Review June 1985). In addition, the DHSS Social Security Statistics (1984) show that in November 1979, 18% of the registered unemployed males were receiving neither N.I. benefit nor supplementary benefits. The reasons for non receipt of N.I. unemployment benefit include:

— awaiting the DHSS to determine eligibility for benefit.

— insufficient contributions — for example many married women who wish to enter the labour market after a break are not entitled to benefit and, in addition, those married women who have continued to pay the reduced N.I. stamp are not entitled.

— disqualification from benefit — disqualification for up to six weeks may occur where a person quits his job voluntarily without just cause (i.e. the N.I. Commissioners would expect that the employee had made every effort to secure alternative employment before handing in his notice), or where an individual is sacked for misconduct (in general however a dismissal is assumed to be involuntary unless misconduct is proved).

— denial of eligibility for benefit where the claimant has entered employment with wages paid in lieu of notice.

Certainly OECD evidence from eight countries on young people's attitudes to work rejects the argument that young people do not wish to work because unemployment benefit is high. Thus CER, *Education and Work, the Views of the Young* Paris, 1983 concluded:

'We should perhaps be permitted to repeat one of the more important findings of the present enquiry, namely that evidence drawn directly from young people in eight OECD countries does not confirm the widespread belief that their attitude to work is largely one of rejection.'

(ix) Regional policies

Regional imbalances in the level of economic activity and the availability of work, and thus the level of unemployment, has been a feature of post-war Britain. Even in times of so-called full employment, there has been a higher than average level of unemployment in the development areas of Scotland, Wales, North and North West England, Northern Ireland and the South West, whereas the Midlands and South East have tended to have a continuous shortage of labour until the last 5 years.

One of the main causes of this differential level of unemployment, in areas outside of the Midlands and South East, has been that these areas have housed the declining industries, for example, coal mining (i.e. those pits which are considered no longer economical to mine), shipbuilding, textiles, and, latterly, steelmaking; the unemployment is thus primarily structural. It has also proved difficult to encourage new firms to move into these areas, mainly because of their distance from major markets in Europe and elsewhere and the costs of transportation or the unreliability or unsuitability of the transport available.

Methods used to tackle regional problems have included grants for investment, tax allowances against building and capital costs, cheap factories to rent and employment subsidies to reduce the cost of employing labour. Some local authorities have also refused to grant permission to firms to set up in specific areas, unless they were likely to create a significant amount of work. This has been tried by local authorities around the London area to prevent maufacturing units being replaced by warehouses. Individuals have been given financial assistance to move from high unemployment areas to those where jobs are more readily available.

Regional policies do not seem to have been very successful, especially in recent years, but this must be judged against the prevailing level of economic activity, and business uncertainty generally has been a reason for organisations' unwillingness to establish themselves in new areas or to expand.

(x) Increased use of temporary work

Whilst temporary work has been a traditional feature of a number of industries (especially those where work levels follow a seasonal pattern e.g. retailing, tourism and agriculture) a view has developed that employers across a wide spectrum are making an increased use of temporary and fixed term contracts as part of a move towards more flexible manning strategies in work organisation.

Evidence from the 1984 Labour Force Survey suggests that in April 1984 there were around 1½ million people in GB who are either in seasonal or casual temporary jobs or in fixed term contracts — around 6½% of the total labour force.

The highest proportion of temporaries are found in the Service Sector with high concentrations in the educational professions, literary, artistic and sports jobs, sales, waiters, waitresses and shop stewards. Outside the service sector the contruction industry especially includes temporaries.

The principal reasons for use of temporary workers include:
— to cover for absence

Table 13:20 Industrial distribution of temporary workers (GB) 1984

(Source: 1984 Labour Force Survey)

Industry division	Proportion of employment which is temporary (%)	Proportion of total Temporary employment (%)
Agriculture, forestry & fishing	8.0	3.1
Energy and water supply	3.1	1.5
Other mineral & oil extraction & Manufacture of metal	3.1	1.7
Metal goods, engineering & vehicles	2.7	4.6
Other manufacturing	4.2	6.5
Construction	7.8	9.2
Distribution, hotels & catering	7.9	24.7
Transport & communication	2.7	2.6
Banking, finance, insurance etc.	5.0	6.6
Other services	9.1	38.2
Other sectors	12.2	0.3
All industries	6.4	10.0

Table 13:21 Occupational distribution of temporary working as a proportion of total employment 1984

Occupations	% of Temporary Employees	Total employment (000s)
Managerial & administrative	3.3	3219
Higher level service	7.6	3415
Higher level industrial	4.8	1145
Lower level service & supervisory	8.1	6823
Craft & foreman group	4.5	3509
Lower level industrial & others	7.2	4802

— to cope with seasonal work load peaks

— to cope with fluctuating work load when employers are unsure of the potential longevity of increased demand

— to cover shortages while recruiting regular staff

— to ease problems of reorganisation or for short term projects

— to avoid a commitment to permanent employment in the face of uncertainty of future labour needs

— to increase the degree to which flexibility of manning is possible

— whilst providing training

Between 1983 and 1984 the number of temporary jobs in the economy increased by 150,000 according to the Labour Force Surveys and have continued to increase since. It is however questionable whether temporary workers are being pulled off the unemployment register or whether they are a different category of worker who do not want a permanent job.

Unemployment is likely to remain at around 3 millions for at least the next four years, according to the MSC's *Corporate Plan for 1982 — 86,* as the labour market remains relatively dormant. The numbers of long term unemployed are likely to rise. There will be a continued shift from manufacturing into service industry and from manual to non-manual jobs.

Chapter 14
British Industrial Relations System

No understanding of the problems of personnel management in context can be complete without some examination of the workings of the British Industrial Relations System. Whether the problems are unemployment, the level of wages, training and development of staff, the mobility of labour or the behaviour of individuals and groups within an organisation, the effects of the trade union movement are likely to be felt. However, this chapter can only give a very superficial introduction.

1. NUMBERS OF UNIONS

According to the Certification Officer's Report for 1985, there are 413 unions in the UK as defined by the Trade Union & Labour Relations Act 1974, ranging from small organisations (the Halifax & District Power Loom Overlookers Association) to the giants (the Transport & General Workers Union and the Amalgamated Engineering Union). Twenty-one unions have over 100,000 members (see table), a combined membership of 8,769,279 out of a total of 10,773,953.

Table 14:1 Unions with over 100,000 members as at 31.12.84

(Source: Certification Officer's report, 1985)

Union	No. of Members
Transport & General Workers Union	1490555
Amalgamated Union of Engineering Workers (now AEU)	1000883
Technical Administrative and Supervisory Section	220000
General Municipal Boilerworkers and Allied Trades Union	846565
National and Local Government Officers Ass.	766390
National Union of Public Employees	673445
Association of Scientific, Technical and Managerial Staffs	390000
Electrical Electronic Telecommunication and Plumbing Union	394283
Union of Shop Distributive & Allied Workers	392307
National Union of Mineworkers (includes retired members & widows)	318084*
Union of Construction Allied Trades and Technicians	249961
National Union of Teachers	259366
Royal College of Nursing of the UK	245000
Confederation of Health Service Employees	214321
Society of Graphical and Allied Trades 1982	210118
Union of Communications Workers	195374
Civil and Public Services Association	190347

Banking, Insurance & Finance Union	154579
National Association of Schoolmasters and the Union of Women Teachers	164295
National Union of Railwaymen	136435
National Graphical Association (1982)	131584
National Communications Union (Engineering & Clerical Groups)	125387

*1983 figure

2. UNION STRUCTURE

Each union has its own problems of control and representation: some believe in centralised control, whereas others prefer to decentralise. Some unions have a left-wing bias in their administration, others are much more conservative in their approach to particular issues. Approximately 91 unions are affiliated to the Trades Union Congress, representing over 90% of trade union members.

It is customary to divide British trade unions into three categories — craft, industrial and general — but these divisions must be treated with caution because, on the whole, the unions do not conform to any one of these structures; they do not develop in a vacuum and the social and economic environment is a continuously varying influence on their growth and development (see Henry Pelling — *A History of Trade Unionism* (1968)). Some categories can be identified as:

(a) *Craft Unions* — customarily recruit their membership from some distinct skilled trade or occupation, normally entered through apprenticeship. The object, historically, was to protect the jobs within that craft for members of the trade union exclusively. In a dynamic economy the main focus of the craft is likely to be changed due to technological innovation and, to survive, the craft unions have had to change their boundaries. Examples of craft-based unions include the AEU, EEPTU and ASLEF. (Appendix 1 at the end of this chapter, gives some commonly used trade union acronyms.)

(b) *Industrial Unions* — seek to recruit all the workers within a given industry, regardless of their occupations. Industrial unionism is not very pronounced in Britain because craft sectional and occupational unionism, which developed in the 19th century, established itself across industrial boundaries or as tightly organised segments within industries before industrial union organisation really developed. The National Union of Mineworkers represents the nearest approach to an industrial union; however, another example quoted is ISTC, the steel industry union, although it does not organise all steelworkers.

(c) *General unions* — by definition, general unions recruit across all occupational and industrial boundaries and recognise no restrictions on their potential membership. The largest union in the country, the TGWU, is a good example. Nowadays the categories of occupational and white collar unions are often added to the list.

(d) *Occupational unions* — organise workers in a particular occupation or related groups of occupations, without the rigidities of the old craft union system. Some, like the Association of Professional Executive Clerical and Computer Staffs, cover many industries; others recruit only in one industry, e.g. Fire Brigades Union.

(e) *White collar unions* — concentrate on non manual occupations, e.g. ASTMS, NUT, BIFU. These distinctions, as we can see, are not perfect and other classifications exist in modern writings, e.g. horizontal and vertical unions, open and closed unions; but all classifications tend to be imperfect.

3. DENSITY OF UNION MEMBERSHIP

There are around 10.8 million trade union members (about 54% of the UK working population), although trade union membership has actually declined since 1979, between 1969 and 1979 membership increased by 28.8% due primarily to white collar union growth, whilst the number of unions declined by 24.4%. This overall density of trade union membership figures is somewhat misleading for there are differences between blue-collar union density and for white collar union density.

TABLE 14:2 — MANUAL & WHITE COLLAR
UNION MEMBERSHIP & DENSITY IN GB
Selected Years 1911—1979

Source: Price R and Bain G S, Union Growth in Britain: Retrospect and Prospect,
BJIR March, 1983

YEAR	MANUAL			WHITE COLLAR		
	Union Memb. (000s)	Potential Union Members (000s)	Union Density (%)	U.M.	P.U.M.	U.D. %
1911	2730.9	13141	20.8	398.3	3297	12.1
1920	7124.1	13271	53.7	1129.2	3847	29.4
1931	3544.0	14157	25.0	1025.4	4639	22.1
1948	7055.7	14027	50.3	2062.1	6243	33.0
1968	6636.9	13322	49.8	3056.0	9381	32.6
1970	7095.0	12852	55.2	3533.0	9688	36.5
1973	6968.9	12468	55.9	3966.3	10266	38.6
1974	7082.3	12362	57.3	4130.8	10458	39.5
1975	7112.1	12327	57.7	4488.8	10715	41.9
1976	7321.6	12322	59.4	4632.3	11004	42.1
1977	7445.3	12265	60.7	4837.9	11251	43.0
1978	7549.7	12168	62.0	5029.1	11467	43.9
1979	7577.5	12035	63.0	5124.7	11652	44.0

There are also wide variations in density between industries and also between firms.

Table 14:3 Trade union membership and density by sector in Great Britain 1979

(Source: Price R and Bain G S, Union growth in Britain: Retrospect and Prospect, *BJIR* March, 1983)

Sector	Union Memb. (000s)	Potential Union Memb. (000s)	Union (%)
Public Sector	5189.9	6297.2	82.4
Manufacturing	5157.4	7385.8	69.8
Manual	4234.6	5273.5	80.3
White Collar	922.8	2112.3	43.7
Construction	519.7	1415.2	36.7
Agriculture, Forestry & Fishing	85.8	378.3	22.7
Private Services	1214.5	7283.6	16.7

N.B. Road transport and sea transport are not included in any of the sectors.

(i)   Comprises National Government; Local Government and Education; Health Services; Post and Telecommunications; Air Transport; Port and Inland Water Transport; Railways; Gas, Electricity and Water and Coal Mining. The nationalised iron and steel industry is included in manufacturing.

(ii) Comprises Insurance; Banking, Finance, Entertainment; Distribution and Miscellaneous Services.

Breaking this down further industries with less than 40% density include:

Agriculture and forestry	22.7%
Fishing	20.5%
Construction	36.7%
Distribution	14.9%
Hotels and catering	5.2%
Professional Services	3.7%
Timber and furniture	34.7%
Leather, Leather goods and fur	28.3%

Whereas, for example, the following industries have over 80% of employees in trade unions:

Coal Mining	97.1%
Footwear	81.2%
Tobacco	95.8%
Cotton & Man Made Fibres	98.2%
Printing & Publishing	93.8%
Gas, Electricity & Water	93.0%
Railways	97.8%

Road Transport	95.1%
Sea Transport	99.6%
Port & Inland Water Transport	94.7%
Air Transport	93.6%
Post & Telecommunications	99%
Education & Local Government	77.5%
National Government	91.3%

(Source: Price R and Bain G S, Union growth in Britain: Retrospect and Prospect, *BJIR* March, 1983)

The density of membership between males and females also varies with male density at around 64% and female density at around 40%.

4. OBJECTIVES OF TRADE UNIONS

One of the major issues in society over the last 20 years has been Government concern and action to ensure that trade unions do not reduce the ability of the UK economy to grow and develop. To consider this debate realistically, it is important to realise that trade unions develop and are in existence, to serve their members and to improve or maintain their terms and conditions of employment. Whilst some trade unions can be justifiably criticised for their internal trade union democratic processes, it is to the members that trade unions are directly responsible and they should be judged on their success in reaching their members' objectives and not on the degree of cooperation which they maintain with Government or employers.

We can perceive the following objectives of trade unions:

(a) To prevent legal interference in the collective bargaining process

Britain's industrial relations framework is based primarily on the concept of voluntary collective bargaining and there are no stronger champions of this philosophy than the trade unions. For a significant period in post-war Britain there has been some form of restraint on bargaining, but this has not weakened their resolve that bargaining should be conducted freely between employers and trade unions. Whilst the unions and the TUC are prepared to tolerate Government intervention to create a more favourable industrial climate through new labour laws to protect workers, they have an inherent dislike of policies to restrict incomes even in the short term.

Trade unions do have a number of legal rights established by some of the Acts of Parliament summarised in Chapter 8 (i.e. Health and Safety at Work etc. Act, the Employment Protection Act; the Employment Acts; the Transfer of Undertakings (Protection of Employment) Regulations; the Employment Protection (Consolidation) Act and also the Social Security Pension Act 1975). These rights are:

- the right to appoint safety representatives and to establish safety committees;
- the right to be consulted on pensions if employers wish to have a pension scheme which is contracted out of the State Pension Scheme;
- the right to consultation on proposed redundancies;
- the right to information and consultation on business transfers;
- the right to disclosure of relevant information for collective bargaining purposes;
- the rights of trade unions and employers to apply to the Secretary of State for Employment for exclusion in respect of dismissal and redundancy proceeding agreements;
- the right to hold secret ballots on employers' premises when there are more than 20 employees;
- the right to reimbursement of certain costs of postal ballots from public funds through the Certification Officer;
- the right of officials to time off for trade union collective bargaining and organisation duties.

(b) To improve wages of members

All unions exist to try to improve the material wealth of their members, both in real and in money terms. The pressure on them to do so is greatest under inflation, which reduces the purchasing power of real wages. Often success has an added bonus of increased membership.

(c) To improve other terms and conditions of employment

Britain's unions can be fairly criticised for not widening the scope of collective bargaining, especially over the 1950s and 1960s. A concentration of cash in the wage packet has led to neglect of better fringe benefits. During the 1970s, however, under the constraint of incomes policies, other fringe benefits became the target of trade unions. This has continued in the 1980s. Policies for a shorter working week, early retirement, longer holidays, better pensions and sick pay schemes are being increasingly adopted; the first three being a direct result of high levels of unemployment.

(d) To be involved in the determination of national economic and industrial objectives

It is natural that trade unions should wish to be involved in the determination of national and economic objectives and in decision making on industrial strategy because, in the long term, it is going to have an effect on their members. Trade unions are now involved in a whole range of official institutions and have become so since 1962 when they were invited to sit on the National Economic Development Council (NEDC), the 'little NEDDIES', and industrial sector working parties. They also participate, along with management representatives, in such organisations as the Health & Safety Commission, the Manpower Services Commission and the ITB's. The trade union movement is also prominent in the work of ACAS and the Industrial Tribunals. Unions have generally agreed to participate in organisations set up by both the major political parties so that the viewpoint of their members can be represented in Governmental policy decisions.

(e) Health and safety at work

In the opinion of the Robens Committee in 1972, which examined health and safety at work:

> 'the most important single reason for accidents at work is apathy'.

The appointment of safety representatives (since 1978) from the workforce, who consult with employers on organisational health and safety questions, has underpinned the role and responsibility of unions in this area.

(f) Protection of members' job opportunities

Britain's unions are often criticised for their refusal to abandon restrictive practices, which is said to hinder technological change and a rise in levels of productivity. Overmanning is seen as a feature of the 'British disease' and union custom and practice, far more than lack of investment in plant and machinery, often gets blamed for our lack of competitiveness. Yet unions must be seen by their members to be protecting job interests as far as possible and certainly demarcation disputes are of reducing importance in annual figures of industrial conflict.

(g) To improve public and social services

Trade unions have to represent their members' needs and interests in the broader sense. Though their prime function is industrial representation, they have to take into account that workers are also consumers and parents; tenants and actual, or potential, homeowners; sometimes sick or unemployed; and, eventually, old-age pensioners. So trade unions have not only to fight against deprivation and inequality at work, they also have to act as a pressure group to ensure social justice in the widest sense. Inequality is, in any case, indivisible, whether it be in the place of work or in the community. Many sociological studies have shown how inequality in the workplace is at least in part shared by other inequalities — in family conditions, housing, education etc. A trade union movement which confined its concern to the workplace would not be furthering its members' interests. The era of the Social Contract especially showed union concern with this wider role.

(h) To have a voice in Government

In their early years, trade unions preferred to use their industrial power, and it was not until 1900 that they formed a political party to represent their views. As the unions contribute to Labour Party funds, they have a very powerful influence over Labour as a political party and in staffing its national, regional and local machinery:

Table 14:4 Labour Party funds

Year	Total (£m)	Trade Unions %	Constituencies %	Miscellaneous %
1980	2.55	80	15	5
1981	3.22	78	17	5
1982	3.59	78	16	6
1983	3.77	79	15	6
1984	3.99	74	18	8

Source: Labour Party NEC Annual Report 1985

Under the Trade Union Act of 1913 as amended [by the Trade Union Act 1984] trade unions are allowed to make donations for political purposes, providing they are made out of a separate political fund and there are regular review ballots every ten years at least. At the end of 1983 there were 58 trade unions with political funds and, apart from the Civil Service unions, the only major union not affiliated to the Labour Party was NALGO. Trade union members do not have to contribute into their union's political fund and must be allowed to 'contract out' of that proportion of their trade union fees.

The annual report of the Certification Officer for 1984 shows that in 1984, within the 53 trade unions who had political funds, something like 75% of members paid the political levy. This figure hides wide variations between unions, for example, in the TGWU, 96% pay the political levy, whereas in the NUM (Northumberland area) only 33% pay it (see Table 14:5 on page 306).

The TUC has issued a statement of guidance to trade union affiliates which sets out clearly the action which trade unions should take to ensure their members are fully informed about their rights as regards the political levy.

(i) Industrial democracy

Many, but not all unions, wish to increase their members' involvement in the decision making process in their work organisations. All political parties and many firms have stated their commitment to the principle of worker participation. In 1976 the Labour Government published the

Table 14:5 Trade unions paying political levy (%)
and political fund expenditure

Union	1983 Political fund Expenditure (£)	% Paying political levy	Union	1983 Political fund Expenditure (£)	% Paying political levy
ATWU	16,693	94	NUB	2,344	48
AUEW			NUM		
Engineering	781,524	65	(National)	477,465	60
AUEW(TASS)	205,326	58	NUPE	1,260,727	98
ASLEF	61,383	93	NUR	303,280	96
ACTT	6,773	7	NUS	38,353	76
APAC	3,805	63	NUTGW	91,720	89
APEX	140,953	70	NUTFLAT	27,622	88
ASTMS	115,000	30	POEU	205,847	74
BFAFU	26,323	96	SOGAT'82	183,332	44
CATU	20,017	98	TWU	18,985	56
COHSE	274,036	92	TGWU		
EETPU	206,375	78	(National)	1,354,478	96
FBU	39,082	63			
FTAT	21,506	61	(Regional)	241,824	
GMBATU	1,436,176	82	TSSA	86,740	83
ISTC	61,627	52	UCW	251,136	94
MU	5,147	62	UCATT	136,595	65
NACODS			USDAW	442,909	92
(National)	14,486	97			
NGA	74,260	42	TOTAL	8,639,336	
NSMM	15,485	83			

- 47 trade unions with a membership of 8 million have political funds.
- 81% of their members, or 6.5 million, pay the political levy.
- In 1983, the income from the political funds was £8,197,750. Six large unions accounted for nearly 70 per cent of this.
- 82½ per cent of the political fund is given to the Labour Party; 14 per cent is spent on administering the fund; 3½ per cent is spent on other items.
- 79 per cent of the Labour Party's national income comes from the unions; 16 per cent is given by constituency parties and 6 per cent from miscellaneous sources.

Source: *The Times* 13/3/85

results of the *Committee of Inquiry on Industrial Democracy,* chaired by Lord Bullock, and published a subsequent White Paper in early 1978. So far, nothing has transpired from these discussions, partly because of the differences of opinion as to what system of worker participation we should introduce, and partly because in recent years trade unions have been more concerned with other issues. Under Section 1 of the Employment Act 1982 there is a requirement that all publically quoted firms with over 250 employees must make a statement in their Annual Reports as to what they are doing in the area of employee involvement.

5. ORGANISATION OF UNIONS

For most members the union only matters at the place of work when something is going wrong and the person to whom they look for support is the local shop steward. Yet, like all other organisations, unions have a hierarchical structure.

(a) Branches

Each member of the union is a member of a branch which has the task of organising meetings where problems can be raised and strategems discussed; organising elections for various officers; and acting as a medium of communication between the member and the senior officers of the union. Members may be allocated to a branch, either because of their place of residence, or because of their place of work. Branches will usually have a Chairman, a Secretary and a Treasurer who are lay officers of the union elected by the branch members; these will administer the branch operations. The attendance of members at branch meetings varies considerably from union to union, but it has been calculated that average attendance is no more than about 5% of the membership.

(b) District Committees

District committees act as a focal point for major decisions which affect a particular locality and coordinate activity within that locality; they also help to spread information on local conditions amongst the members. Membership of District committees can be determined in several ways, but the most common system is that each branch sends representatives to sit on the District Committee.

(c) Area or Regional Committees/Trade Group Committees

In some unions, above the district committees there are a network of Area or Regional Committees to act as a further coordination or communication body. In addition, some large general unions recognise the need for coordination between members of the same trade on matters of mutual interest and also have a series of Trade Group committees as well as regional committees (e.g. TGWU).

(d) National Executive Committee or Council

The senior council within the union may consist of a mixture of full time and lay trade union officials or may be dominated by one group or the other. There is normally a full time General Secretary who is the senior executive; he may be elected by union members and is often appointed for life. He controls the administrative machinery of the union; acts as the chief negotiator and chief spokesman; and ensures that the union follows the policy laid down by the NEC. Other members of the Executive will be elected, either from constituencies based on regions or trade groups, or by votes cast at delegate Conference. The Executive sets out the policy of the union, based on the wishes of the membership.

(e)   Delegate Conferences

The membership elect representatives to go to regular annual or biennial conferences to discuss the activities of the union over the previous period and to agree or initiate new union policies on wages and working conditions; social economic and political matters; and other matters which are considered urgent. These conferences enable the NEC to keep in touch with the 'grass roots' feeling of the union members and are useful for the informal and formal dissemination of information. Some unions e.g. GMBATU have industrial conferences for the same purposes.

6.   TRADE UNION CONGRESS (TUC)

At the centre of the trade union system in the UK is the TUC. It was initially founded in Manchester in 1868 and acts as the chief representative for the affiliated unions — 91 of them (1986) — with Government, government bodies and internationally.

Circular calling the first TUC 1868

The document which led to the formation of the TUC in 1868 read as follows:

PROPOSED CONGRESS OF TRADES COUNCILS

AND OTHER

Federations of Trades Societies

Manchester, February 21st, 1868.

Fellow Unionists,
   The Manchester and Salford Trades Council having recently taken into their serious consideration the present aspect of Trades Unions, and the profound ignorance which prevails in the public mind with reference to their operations and principles, together with the probability of an attempt being made by the Legislature, during the present session of Parliament, to introduce a measure detrimental to the interests of such Societies, beg most respectfully to suggest the propriety of holding in Manchester, as the main centre of industry in the provinces, a Congress of the Representatives of Trades Councils and other similar Federations of Trades Societies. By confining the Congress to such bodies it is conceived that a deal of expense will be saved, as Trades will thus be represented collectively: whilst there will be a better opportunity afforded of selecting the most intelligent and efficient exponents of our principles.
   It is proposed that the Congress shall assume the character of the annual meetings of the British Association for the Advancement of Science and the Social Science Association, in the transactions of which Societies the artizan class are almost entirely excluded: and that papers, previously carefully prepared, shall be laid before the Congress on the various subjects which at the present time affect Trades Societies, each paper to be followed by discussion upon the points advanced, with a view of the merits and demerits of each question being thoroughly ventilated through the medium of the public press. It is further suggested that the subjects treated upon shall include the following:-

1. Trades Unions an absolute necessity.
2. Trades Unions and Political Economy.
3. The Effect of Trades Unions on Foreign Competition.
4. Regulation of the Hours of Labour.
5. Limitation of Apprentices.
6. Technical Education.
7. Arbitration and Courts of Conciliation.
8. Co-operation.
9. The present Inequality of the Law in regard to Conspiracy, Intimidation, Picketing, Coercion, etc.
10. Factory Acts Extension Bill, 1867: the necessity of Compulsory Inspection, and its application to all places where Women and Children are employed.
11. The present Royal Commission on Trades Unions: how far worthy of the confidence of the Trades Union interest.
12. The necessity of an Annual Congress of Trade Representatives from the various centres of industry.

All Trades Councils and other Federations of Trades are respectfully solicited to intimate their adhesion to this project on or before the 6th of April next, together with a notification of the subject of the paper that each body will undertake to prepare; after which date all information as to place of meeting, etc., will be supplied.

It is also proposed that the Congress be held on the 4th of May next, and that all liabilities in connection therewith shall not extend beyond its sittings.

Communications to be addressed to Mr. W. H. Wood. Typographical Institute, 29, Water Street, Manchester.

By order of the Manchester and Salford Trades Council,

S. C. NICHOLSON, President.
W. H. WOOD, Secretary.

(a) The Annual Congress

Congress is composed of delegates from trade unions who must be members of the unions they represent. Moreover, under Congress rules and standing orders, delegates must either be working at the trade at the time of their appointment or be full time paid officials of the union they represent.

Congress always meets on the first Monday in September and four following days. Unions are entitled to send delegates on the basis of one for every 5,000 members (or part thereof), but only the smaller unions tend to take up their full quota. They vote according to their affiliated membership and, if there is a doubt about the view of the Congress on an issue after a show of hands, the matter is decided by a card vote. At a card vote each union casts a vote equivalent to its total membership; if the large unions vote together, they can dominate the smaller ones. The order of business of Congress is arranged by the General Purposes Committee of five delegates elected at the previous Congress — they are not members of the General Council.

Congress forms policy in two main ways:

(i)   by considering, paragraph by paragraph, the detailed Report of the

General Council about their work in the past year; and

(ii)   by endorsing or rejecting motions submitted by affiliated unions, each union being entitled to submit two motions.

The report of the General Council and a list of the motions and amendments submitted by unions is circulated two weeks before Congress.

(b)   The General Council

In 1985 there were 51 members of the TUC General Council. Since 1983 the General Council has been chosen by a mixed system of automatic representation and secret ballot.

Section A

(i)   Automatic representation: all affiliated unions with over 100,000 members are now entitled to a seat on the General Council and a sliding scale of seats operates depending on size of union. Thus unions with
100,000 — 499,999 members have 1 seat automatically
500,000 — 749,999 members have 2 seats automatically
750,000 — 999,999 members have 3 seats automatically
1 million — 1,499,999 members have 4 seats automatically
1.5 million + members have 5 seats automatically.

Thus 22 unions controlled 33 seats on the General Council in 1985.

(ii)   Secret Ballot — there are two elements to this:

Section B

(a)   11 seats are voted for by the unions with a membership of less than 100,000 members, with each union having the right to make a nomination.

Section C

(b)   Consists of 6 women members who are voted for by all the affiliated unions. This tends to lead to the larger unions whose vote can dominate, e.g. NALGO, NUPE, AUEW, TGWU, ASTMS AND GMBATU (1984), getting extra power on the Council.

The remaining seat is that of the TUC General Secretary.

The General Council acts as the executive body of Congress and its ultimate responsibility is to carry out the decisions of Congress. However, on most matters which come before the General Council, it would not be possible to delay a decision pending a reference to Congress and the Council acts on matters as they arise, reporting back to the next Congress via the Report.

The General Council meets once a month and is mainly concerned with examining the detailed work carried out by its committees. The Standing Committees are composed entirely of General Council members; these committees are Economic, Education, Employment Policy and

Organisation, Equal Rights, Finance and General Purposes, International, Social Insurance and Industrial Welfare.

There are a number of committees for major industries on which General Council members sit with representatives from affiliated unions — Construction, Fuel, and Power, Health Service, Hotel and Catering, Local Government, Printing, Steel, Textiles, Clothing and Footwear, Transport.

Finally, there are a number of joint committees on which representatives from other bodies of national importance (e.g. CBI, Health and Safety Executive, Commission for Racial Equality) sit with General Council and/or union representatives; Arts, Entertainment and Sports Advisory Committee, BMA—TUC Committee, CBI—TUC Committee, Media Working Group, National Council of Labour, NEDC, Nationalised Industries Committee, Public Services Committee, Race Relations Advisory Committee, Trades Councils' Joint Consultative Committee, Standing Advisory Committee of the TUC Centenary Institute of Occupational Health, TUC Labour Party Liaison Committee, Womens' Advisory Committee.

Table 14:6 Top 25 TUC unions by membership 1984/85 and 1985/86

Union	1985—86 Member ship	General Council seats	1984—85 member ship	General Council seats
Transport and General Workers Union	1,490,555	4	1,547,443	5
Amalgamated Union of Engineering Workers	1,000,883	4	943,538	3
General Municipal Boiler-makers and Allied Trades Union	846,565	3	875,187	3
National and Local Government Officers' Association	766,390	3	780,037	3
National Union of Public Employees	673,445	2	689,046	2
Union of Shop, Distributive and Allied Trades	392,307	1	403,446	1
Association of Scientific, Technical and Managerial Staffs	390,000	1	390,000	1
Electrical, Electronic, Telecommunications and Plumbing Union	355,000	1	363,000	1
Union of Construction, Allied Trades and Technicians	249,961	1	260,000	1
Amalgamated Union of Engineering Workers (Tass)	220,000	1	215,052	1

National Union of Teachers	214,361	1	210,499	1
Confederation of Health Service Employees	214,321	1	222,869	1
Society of Graphical and Allied Trades '82	210,462	1	213,605	1
National Union of Mineworkers	200,000	1	208,051	1
Union of Communication Workers	195,374	1	194,426	1
National Communications Union	166,483	1	129,950	1
Banking Insurance and Finance Union	154,579	1	156,476	1
Civil and Public Services Association	149,782	1	190,832	1
National Union of Railwaymen	136,315	1	143,218	1
National Association of Schoolmasters/Union of Women Teachers	126,435	1	119,668	1
National Graphical Association (1982)	126,267	1	129,231	1
Association of Professional, Executive and Computer Staff	94,846	?	100,177	1
Institution of Professional Civil Servants	90,242	?	93,090	1
Society of Civil and Public Servants	85,957	?	93,481	0
Iron and Steel Trades Confederation	79,082	?	91,006	1

Source: *Financial Times,* 27.6.85

Independent Review Committee

The Independent Review Committee exists to consider appeals from individuals who have been dismissed, and given notice of dismissal from, or of having been refused admission to, a union in a situation where trade union membership is a condition of employment. Established under the auspices of the TUC, and its secretariat drawn from the TUC, its members were appointed in consultation with the Secretary of State for Employment and the Chairman of ACAS. The Committee is completely independent in reaching its decisions.

The following procedure is part of the Committee's Terms of Reference:

(a) The Committee must be satisfied, before considering an appeal, that an individual who has been dismissed has exhausted all internal union procedures;

(b) The Committee will discuss the case with the union and the individual concerned and will try to resolve the matter by agreement;

(c)   If agreement cannot be reached, the Committee will make a recommendation about whether or not the individual should be admitted to the union, or in the case of a member who has been expelled, whether or not he should be taken back into the union and, if so, upon what conditions. There is then a clear responsibility on the part of the union concerned to act upon such a recommendation.

(c)   Regional and Local Structure of the Trade Union Movement

The TUC Regional Councils (of which there are eight regions in England) and the Scotland and Wales TUC form the machinery through which TUC policy is administered. These Councils are also responsible for the formulation and development of trade union policy in their areas on all matters solely affecting a particular region. They are composed of representatives of those TUC affiliated unions with members in the region. The general duties of the TUC Regional Councils are:

(i)   To make representations to bodies throughout the region including Government departments, Local Authorities and other bodies on economic, political, industrial, social and environmental questions pertaining to the region.

(ii)   To appoint representatives to bodies within the region designated by the TUC General Council.

(iii)   To support such representatives and to receive and consider reports from them about the activities of the bodies of which they are members.

(iv)   To perform a public relations function for the trade union movement within the region.

(v)   To keep the TUC informed of developments within the region.

(vi)   To give effect to policies adopted by the TUC and to keep trade unionists in the region informed of these policies.

(vii)   To promote an exchange of information between unions in the region.

(viii) To assist unions in the recruitment of members in the region.

(ix)   To encourage unions to take part in the work of Trades Councils in the region.

(x)   To give effect to any directions by the General Council.

(d)   Trades Councils

In most areas trade union branches join on a voluntary basis to form a local Trades Council, the main functions of which are to provide, to affiliated branches, services on a wide range of industrial, social and community issues. They, in addition, make representation to local authorities and nominate representatives to a number of statutory committees and tribunals. They communicate TUC policies and feed back local reaction and opinion. There are about 440 recognised Trades Councils in England and Wales.

7. CONFEDERATION OF BRITISH INDUSTRIES

The CBI is the major organisation of British employers. Founded in 1965 and incorporated by Royal Charter it combines the roles previously played by three former organisations:

1. The Federation of British Industries (FBI) which represented the larger private manufacturing organisations and trade associations.

2. The British Employers Confederation (BEC) which was primarily concerned with labour questions and had only employers organisations in membership.

3. The National Association of British Manufacturers (NABM) representing manufacturing firms and trade associations in commercial matters, and although there was no restriction in size, in practice the individual members tended to be small businesses.

In addition the CBI includes the main nationalised industries.
   The objectives of the CBI as stated in 1974 are:

(i)   to voice the collective views of its members;

(ii) to promote and protect its members collective interests;

(iii) to help its members play their full part 'in the creation, in a free market setting, of the wealth on which national prosperity and social progress depend.'

In fulfilling these objectives the CBI seeks to represent the interests of its members at national and international levels and to assist them individually with any problems concerning the running of business organisations. It is an independent body financed by its members in industry and commerce.

Membership

Membership includes individual firms, almost all the nationalised industries trade associations and employers associations. Some 12m people are employed by companies associated with the CBI either directly or indirectly through their trade association.

Structure and organisation

The governing body is the COUNCIL which meets monthly — approves the proposals that become official policy. Council has over 400 members including representatives from employer, trade and commercial organisations, the public sector, the Regional Councils and member companies.

Council is chaired by the PRESIDENT who is usually drawn from a major industrial company and is appointed for a two year period. In 1975 the machinery of the CBI was strengthened by the setting up of a PRESIDENT'S COMMITTEE consisting of about 25 leading representatives form the main sections of its membership — large companies, small firms, associations, nationalised industries and its main committees. The President's Committee meets monthly and advises the President on major policy issues and keeps the CBI's public position and overall strategy under review. (It could be compared loosely with the TUC General Council.)

The Council is served by some 20 STANDING COMMITTEES and a wide range of WORKING PARTIES and STUDY GROUPS. Collectively the Standing Committees serviced by the DIRECTORATE are responsible for the detailed work on policy making.

CBI Directorates

The CBI has a permanent staff of about 450 whose executive head is the Director-General who is appointed by the President with the approval of Council. The Directorates include Economic; Education, Training and Technology; Overseas; Social Affairs; Administration; Information; Company Affairs; and Regional and Smaller Firms.

Administration Directorate: One of two Standing Committees, Finance and General purposes which control major aspects of overall external and internal policy.

Company Affairs Directorate: has some 10 — 15 Standing Committees dealing with such aspects as Companies, Company law, Contracts, Industrial property, Energy policy, Environmental and Technical legislation, Transport, etc. In addition there are some 20 working parties and other subordinate groups.

Economic Directorate: has around eight Standing Committees including Economic policy, Financial policy, Economic situation, State intervention in private industry etc., with 16 working parties and other sub groups.

Education, Training and Technology Directorate: has four Standing Committees: Education and Training, Overseas and Scholarships Board, Production, Research and Technology, and 10 subordinate groups.

Overseas Directorate: Two main Standing Committees, overseas and Europe, and 10 subordinate groups.

Regional and small firms Directorate: Two Standing Committees, Smaller Firms Council and Marketing and Consumer Committee, in addition one subordinate group.

Social Affairs Directorate: has six major Standing Committees; Industrial Relations and Manpower, Employment policy, International labour, Labour and Social Affairs, Safety, Health and Welfare, Social Security and finally Wages and Conditions with 7 subordinate groups.

CBI Standing Committees

A representative organisation must work through a committee structure and therefore committees must be composed of members drawn from the industries or sectors of society which the organisation was set up to represent. At least 10% of the membership of a CBI Standing Committee must represent small firms interests. The functions of the CBI internal staff are to act as a secretariat, to provide central back up of services — research, information, publicity, etc. — and to carry out those policy decisions delegated to them by the committees to whom they are responsible. Each Chairman of committee is appointed by the President and committee members are appointed by the Director General.

Regional Councils

The CBI is also divided into 13 regions with the three largest areas by company membership being London and the South East, the West Midlands and Yorkshire and Humberside. Each region has a regional council which assesses membership opinions on proposed CBI policy and facilitates personal contact among local members and contact is maintained with local authorities, Government departments and constituency MP's.

The CBI nominates employer representatives to a range of public organisations including the NEDC, ACAS and Industrial Tribunals. It has extensive European and international affiliations and maintains an office in Brussels.

National Conference

In 1977 the CBI staged its first National Conference open to all its members. It is designed to provide a public platform for delegates from all sectors of British business, to project thinking on major issues and recommend action to the council.

Discussion

There are differences between the CBI and other employer and trade associations. In the majority of associations members of the functional committees are properly accredited representatives of their company. Members of the CBI committees, however, do not theoretically represent their own organisation. They are invited by the CBI to serve on the committee in question because of their perceived expertise in the subject. Naturally their opinions will be coloured by their own organisation's policy which they probably help to formulate and certainly assist to implement.

Nevertheless because the CBI aims to be the spokesman for the whole of industry, a truly representative system would not be practical, for the committees would have to be so large that they would not be able to achieve anything within a reasonable period of time.

Committees therefore are acutely conscious that they represent much wider interests than those of the immediate parent organisation which send the individual members. This is inevitable because the output of the committees deliberations go to the council where there is a reaction from a wide sector of industry. If the output from the committee is too narrow and insular it is likely to be referred back for moderation and amendment.

CBI's Weaknesses

1. Although it has a wide membership it has been unsuccessful in attempts to extend membership beyond the manufacturing sector so its membership coverage is not across British industry.

2. Even within the manufacturing sector the CBI is stronger in some spheres than in others. It is strongest among larger firms and despite the establishment of the Smaller Firms Council, the continued existence of a separate entity, the Smaller Business Association indicates that the CBI is an organisation whose policies are dominated by large firms.

3. Doubts have also been expressed about whether the CBI does really represent the views of its member firms. There is always potential tension in the CBI between those members who would prefer to see the organisation follow a strategy of cooperating with government in the implementation of its policies in the hope of securing concessions, and those who would like the CBI to engage in more frequent and more outspoken criticism of government policy even if this impairs the organisation's ability to negotiate concessions from government.

8. EMPLOYERS ASSOCIATIONS

(a) Employers Associations are defined in the Trade Union and Labour Relations Act 1974 in Section 28(2) as:

'........an organisation, whether permanent or temporary which either,

(a)   consists wholly or mainly of employers or individual proprietors of one or more descriptions or is an organisation whose principal purposes include the regulation of relations between employers of that description or those descriptions and workers or trade unions, or

(b)   Consists wholly or mainly of:

        (i)   constituent or affiliated organisations which fulfil the conditions specified in paragraph (a) above (or themselves consist wholly or mainly of constituent or affiliated organisations which fulfil these conditions), or

        (ii)   representatives of such constituent or affiliated organisations and in either case is an organisation whose principal purposes include the regulation of relations between employers and workers or between employers and trade unions or include the regulations of relations between its constituent or affiliated organisations.'

They are thus those bodies which deal partly, primarily or even exclusively with labour and industrial relations masters. The list of employers organisations which complied with the above definition registered with the Certification Officer in 1984 included 158 organisations.

(b)   The largest employers associations on that list in terms of income included:

1.   Engineering Employers Federation and its local associations
2.   British Shipping Federation
3.   National Federation of Building Trades Employers
4.   British Printing Industries Federation
5.   Electrical Contractors Association
6.   Federation of Civil Engineering Contractors
7.   British Paper and Board Industry Federations Ltd.
8.   National Federation of Retail Newsagents
9.   Newspaper Society
10. Heating and Ventilating Contractors Association
11. Federation of Master Builders
12. Newspaper Publishers Association

Other large employers associations which were not listed at 31.12.84 included:

1.   National Farmers Union
2.   Freight Transport Association Ltd.
3.   Chemical Industries Association Ltd.
4.   Road Haulage Association Ltd.
5.   Publishers Association

(c)   The following table shows the year to year changes in the total employers associations listed between 1st February 1976 when the Certification Office was set up and 31.12.80:

Table 14:7		
Total employers'	1st February 1976	206
	31.12.76	205
associations 1.2.76 to	31.12.77	196
	31.12.78	194
31.12.80	31.12.79	190
	31.12.80	181
	31.12.81	172
	31.12.82	166
	31.12.83	157
	31.12.84	158

In addition the number of unlisted organisations known to the Certification Office at 31.12.84 was 192 compared with 290 in 1979.

There in fact no advantages from being listed for employers associations whereas for trade unions listing is essential as a preliminary to applying for a certificate of independence under Section 8 of the EPA 1975 and also entitles them to tax relief for expenditure on provident benefits.

(d) Historically employers associations were proactive bodies in British industrial relations and one of the greatest obstacles to the development of trade unionism was the hostility and collective action of employers. For example, in the 1850s and 1860s the 'document' became an important weapon of the employers in the engineering and construction industries especially, although its success was limited in the long term. Employers organisations were however often weak and temporarily established bodies but the 1869 Royal Commission encouraged the development of employers associations when it stated:-

'The employers cannot fail to see the advantage which the trade unions, in the conduct of strikes, have in attacking the employers.....the strike is with this view directed against a single employer, or against the employers in a single district, the workmen on strike being supported by those in the employment of other masters, the intention being, on the success of the first strike to take others in succession. To defeat this policy the employers resort to such expedients as they deem best for their own protection. The ordinary course is to form an association of their own in which they agree, in the event of a strike against any member of the association, to close the workshops of all, and in some cases by a subscription among themselves, to give pecuniary assistance to the employer against whom the strike is directed.'

Three main aims were identified for the early employers association:

(1) By collective action individual firms could be protected from being 'picked off'

319

(2)   To preserve the power to manage in conditions of change and growth

(3)   To establish national procedural agreements to deal with disputes between unions and employers (often in advance of strong trade unionism)

The Donovan Report Para. 77, emphasised the innovatory role of employers associations prior to 1914 but added:

> 'By contrast from 1914......nearly every important innovation in industrial relations which was not the work of the unions came from Government and individual companies.'

This prompted the Commission to ask why many firms still wished to belong to employers associations and it found the explanation in the continued existence of industry-wide bargaining despite its reduction in influence on the pay packet in many industries, the advice they offered on commercial matters (in those instances where they combined labour relations and trade association functions) and the general services and advisory functions they performed in such areas on representing members' views to Government, advising on the impact of legislative changes, the provision of training facilities and access to disputes procedures.

(e) Advantages perceived for association membership:

1.   Negotiation of wages and other terms and conditions of service for all members of the association — especially in those industries which include large numbers of small firms e.g. electrical contracting and construction.

2.   Advice on general industrial relations matters.

3.   Local meetings to discuss issues of mutual interest.

4.   Representation to Government, Government departments and other national bodies.

5.   Representation to the EEC and other international bodies.

6.   The availability of training services.

7.   Access to information on wage rates and working conditions.

8.   Advice on legal problems.

9.   Representation on legal matters.

10. Exchange of information.

11. Advice on specific industry health and safety matters.

12. Economic and trade advice.

13. Centralised procedures for the avoidance of disputes.

14. Access to trained personnel e.g. Membership of the General Council of British Shipping.

9. WAGES COUNCILS

Wages Councils, which are now governed by the Wages Council Act of 1979, were originally established as Trade Boards in 1909 by Winston Churchill to protect those working in the sweated trades. Churchill argued in the House of Commons on the 28th April 1909:

> 'Where you have no organisation, no parity of bargaining, the good employer is undercut by the bad, the bad employer us undercut by the worst...where these conditions prevail you have not a condition of progress but a condition of progressive degeneration...the degeneration will continue...for a period which compared with our brief lives is indefinite.'

The two objectives of the Wages Councils are to:

— protect unorganised workers
— promote collective bargaining

Wages Councils are tripartite bodies which have equal representations of the trade unions and of the employers represented in the industry and three independent members appointed by Government, who hold the balance of power. They are empowered to issue orders which fix the minimum wage rates and certain other conditions like holidays and holiday pay, hours of work, overtime rates and shift rates. These orders are mandatory on the employers and the policing force to ensure that organisations are complying with the Wages Inspectorate.

The 26 Wages Councils existing in 1985 fix the minimum conditions for some 2¾ million people (11% of the working population). 90% of the employees covered are in clothing, retailing and catering, all industries which are dominated by small firms where trade union organisation is currently weak and where trade union membership is expensive and difficult to organise.

In June, 1985 the Government renounced its ratification of the ILO Convention No 26 on Minimum Wage Fixing Machinery which underpins the Wages Council System; it decided to remove those under the age of 21 from coverage by the Councils; and also reduce the Powers of the Councils to require employers to meet terms and conditions other than pay and overtime rates for their adult workers. In 1986 a Wages Bill is currently before Parliament to make these changes.

10. STATUTORY JOINT INDUSTRIAL COUNCILS

The Wages Councils Act 1979 subsumes the provisions of the Employment Protection Act 1975, which provided the facility for Wages Councils to be converted after investigation by ACAS into a Statutory Joint Industrial Council (SJIC). An SJIC is similar to a Wages Council except there are no independent members, but disputes are settled by compulsory arbitration on the request of either the trade union representatives or the employers on the SJIC. Orders can still be enforced by the

Wages Inspectorate. The SJIC was an attempt to create a half-way house between statutory wage fixing and free collective bargaining. Whilst there was a recommendation to create an SJIC in the Toymaking Industry, so far none have been created.

Appendix
Commonly Used Trade Union Abbreviations

ACTS	Association of Clerical, Technical and Supervisory Staffs (white collar TGWU)
ACTT	Association of Cinematograph, Television and Allied Technicians
APEX	Association of Professional, Executive, Clerical and Computer Staff
ASLEF	Associated Society of Locomotive Engineers and Firemen
ASTMS	Association of Scientific, Technical and Managerial Staffs
AEU	Amalgamated Engineering Union
AUT	Association of University Teachers
BALPA	British Airline Pilots Association
BETA	Broadcasting & Entertainment Trades Alliance
BFAWU	Bakers, Food and Allied Workers Union
BIFU	Banking, Insurance and Finance Union
BMA	British Medical Association
CATU	Ceramic and Allied Trades Union
COHSE	Confederation of Health Service Employees
CPSA	Civil and Public Services Association
CSU	Civil Service Union
EESA	Electrical and Engineering Staffs Association (white collar EETPU)
EETPU	Electrical, Electronic, Telecommunications and Plumbing Union
EMA	Engineers and Managers Association
FAA	Film Artistes' Association
FBU	Fire Brigades Union
FDA	Association of First Division Civil Servants
FTAT	Furniture, Timber and Allied Trades Union
GMBATU	General Municipal Boilermakers and Allied Trades Union
HCSA	Hospital Consultants' and Specialists' Association
HVA	Health Visitors Association
IPCS	Institute of Professional Civil Servants
IRSF	Inland Revenue Staff Federation
ISTC	Iron and Steel Trades Confederation
MATSA	Managerial, Administrative, Technical and Supervisory Association (white collar GMBATU)
MU	Musicians Union

NALGO	National and Local Government Officers Association
NAS/UWT	National Association of Schoolmasters and Union of Women Teachers
NATFHE	National Association of Teachers in Further and Higher Education
NCU	National Communications Union
NUBOMCWKT	National Association of Blastfurnacemen, Ore Miners, Coke Workers and Kindred Trades
NUFLAT	National Association of Footwear, Leather and Allied Trades
NUHKW	National Union of Hosiery and Knitwear Workers
NUIW	National Union of Insurance Workers
NUJ	National Union of Journalists
NUM	National Union of Mineworkers
NUPE	National Union of Public Employees
NUR	National Union of Railwaymen
NUS	National Union of Seamen or National Union of Students
NUT	National Union of Teachers
NUTGW	National Union of Tailors and Garment Workers
POA	Prison Officers Association
RCN	Royal College of Nursing
SATA	Supervisory, Administrative and Technical Association (white collar USDAW)
SCPS	Society of Civil and Public Servants
SOGAT(82)	Society of Graphic and Allied Trades (82)
TASS	Technical and Supervisory Section (of AUEW)
TGWU	Transport and General Workers Union
TSSA	Transport Salaried Staffs Association
TWU	Tobacco Workers Union
UCATT	Union of Construction, Allied Trades and Technicians
UDM	Union of Democratic Mineworkers
USDAW	Union of Shop, Distributive and Allied Workers
WGGB	Writers Guild of Great Britain

References and Further Reading

CHAPTER 1

C Handy. *The Future of Work* Basil Blackwell, 1984.
C Howarth. *The Way People Work* Oxford University Press, 1984.
C Patterson & D Stevenson. Why the factory of the future is the challenge of today. *Personnel Management*, March 1986.
C Patterson & D Stevenson. *Towards the flexible craftsman* Technical Change Centre, 1985.
S Wood (ed). *The Degradation of Work* Hutchinson, 1982.

CHAPTER 2

P Armstrong & C Dawson. *People, work and organisations* 3rd edn, Elm Publications, 1985.
J Child. *Organisation : A guide to problems and practice* Harper and Row, 1977.
C G Handy. The Shape of Organisations to come *Personnel Management,* June 1979.
C G Handy. *Understanding Organisations* 2nd edn, Penguin, 1981.
C G Handy. The Organisation Revolution *Personnel Management,* July 1984.
P Johnson. *British Industry : an economic introduction* Blackwell, 1985.
J Raybould. Ten Years of Decentralisation *Personnel Management,* June 1985.
E H Schein. *Organisational Psychology* 3rd edn, Prentice-Hall, 1980.
G Thomason. *A Textbook of Personnel Management* 4th edn, IPM, 1981.

CHAPTER 3

M J Baker. *Marketing* Macmillan.
G Oliver. *Marketing Today* Prentice-Hall, 1980.

CHAPTER 4

K Lockyer. *Production Management* Pitman, 1983.
J D Radford & D B Richardson. *The Management of Production* Macmillan.
Joan Woodward. *Management and Technology* HMSO, 1958.

CHAPTER 7

W Brown. *Exploration in Management* Penguin, 1965.
S Coke. Putting Professionalism in its Place *Personnel Management,* February 1983.
H Mintzberg. *The Nature of Managerial Work* Harper and Row, 1973.
A Savage. Selecting Managers for a Permanent State of Flux *Personnel Management,* October 1981.
L Sayles. *Managerial Behaviour* McGraw Hill, 1964.
R Stewart. *Managers and their Jobs* Pan Books, 1967.
R Stewart. *Contrasts in Management* McGraw Hill, 1976.

R Stewart. *Choices for Managers* McGraw Hill, 1982.

R Stewart. It's not what you do...it's the way that you do it: implications of the choices in managerial jobs *Personnel Management,* April 1983.

D Torrington & J Weightman. *The Business of Management* Prentice-Hall, 1984.

CHAPTER 6

E Batstone. What have personnel managers done for industrial relations? *Personnel Management,* June 1980.

J Collerson. Labour Personnel or Staff Management : 50 years of the SMA *Personnel Management,* January 1984.

N Cowan. Personnel Management in the 80s *Personnel Management,* January 1981.

B Daniel. Who handles personnel issues in British Industry? *Personnel Management,* December 1983.

A Fowler. Proving the personnel department earns its salt *Personnel Management,* May 1983.

D Guest & R Horwood. Characteristics of the Successful personnel manager *Personnel Management,* May 1981.

P Honey. On the trail of the personnel professional *Personnel Management,* April 1976.

J W Hunt. The shifting focus of the personnel function *Personnel Management,* February 1984.

J Kenney & M Reid. *Training Interventions* IPM, 1986.

K Legge. *Power innovation and problem solving within personnel management* McGraw Hill, 1978.

P Long. *Personnel professionals : a comparative study of male and female careers* IPM, 1984.

M McCarthy. Personnel management in the health service *Personnel Management,* September 1983.

National Association of Health Service Personnel Officers. *Review of the NHS Personnel function,* 1984.

M M Niven. *Personnel Management 1913—1963* IPM, 1967.

P Prior. Toll the Knell for leadership : the personnel man cometh *Personnel Management,* October 1981.

J Purcell. Is anybody listening to the corporate personnel department? *Personnel Management,* September 1985.

Lord Sieff. How I see the personnel function *Personnel Management,* December 1984.

K Sisson & H Scullion. Putting the corporate personnel department in its place *Personnel Management,* February 1985.

J Stewart. Whatever happened to welfare work? *Personnel Management,* June 1983.

G Thomason. *A Textbook of Personnel Management* IPM, 1981.

K Thurley. Personnel Management in the UK — a case for urgent treatment *Personnel Management,* August 1981.

D Torrington & J Chapman. *Personnel Management* Prentice-Hall, 1979.

D Torrington & L Mackay. Will consultants take over the Personnel function *Personnel Management,* February 1986.

S Tyson. Is this the very model of a modern personnel manager? *Personnel Management,* May 1985.

CHAPTER 7

ACAS. *Industrial Relations Handbook* 1981.
B Robbins. The EEC's new social dimension *Personnel Management,* November 1985.

CHAPTER 8

S A Anderman. *Law of Unfair Dismissal* Butterworth & Co, 1985.
P Davies & M Freedland. *Kahn-Freund's Labour and the Law* Stevens, 1983.
G Janner. Implied Terms : the unwritten law of the employment council *Personnel Management,* September 1985.
D Lewis. *Essentials of Employment Law* IPM London, 1983.
K Wedderburn. *The Worker and the Law* Penguin, 1971.

Useful Journals include:
Industrial Cases Reports
Industrial Relations Law Reports
Industrial Law Journal

CHAPTER 9

N Cowan. Privatisation in the NHS : minor surgery or amputation *Personnel Management,* October 1984.

CHAPTER 10

A Ball. *The British Political Parties* Macmillan Press Ltd., 1981.
D Butler & D Kavanagh. *The British General Election of 1983* Macmillan, 1984.
D E Butler & A Sloman *British Political Facts 1900—1979,* Macmillan, 1980
G Gydford. *Local Politica in Britain* Croom-Helm, 1984.
S G Richards. *Introduction to British Government* Macmillan, 1984.

CHAPTER 11

J D S Appleton. *Labour Economics* McDonald & Evans, 1979.

CHAPTER 12

Coopers & Lybrand Associates. *A challenge to complacency : changing attitudes to training* MSC & NEDC, November 1985.
Department of Employment. *Training for the future,* 1972.
B Mansfield. Getting to the core of the job *Personnel Management,* August 1985.
R Milton. Double double toil and trouble : YTS in the melting pot *Personnel Management,* Macmillan, April 1986.
MSC. *Annual Reports*
MSC. *Outlook on Training — a Review of the Employment and Training Act 1973,* July 1980.
MSC. *Technical and Vocational Education Initiative,* 1983.
MSC. *Youth Training Scheme Review,* 1984.

R Upton. What next for youth training? *Personnel Management,* April 1985.
HMSO. *Education and Training for Young People,* White Paper, 1985.

CHAPTER 13

J Atkinson. Manpower strategies for flexible organisations *Personnel Management,* August 1984.
R Bushell. Valuation of the Young Workers Scheme *Employment Gazette,* May 1986.
S Cannock. Workforce flexibility : juggling time to task *Personnel Management,* October 1985.
C Cook. The company role in creating jobs *Personnel Management,* February 1986.
Department of Employment. *Employment : The Challenge for the Nation* HMSO, 1985.
L M Lynch & R Richardson. Unemployment of Young Workers in Britain *British Journal of Industrial Relations,* 1982.
N Meager. *Temporary work in Great Britain : its growth and changing rationales* Institute of Manpower Studies, 1985.
NEDC. *Education and Industry* NEDC, 1983.
A Rajan. New technology and jobs : the counter-argument *Personnel Management,* July 1985.
M Saks & R Dore. How the Youth Training Scheme helps employers *Employment Gazette,* June 1986.
M Syrett. How to make job sharing work *Personnel Management,* October 1982.
M Syrett. *Employing job sharers, part-timers and temporary staff* IPM 1983.
P Warr. What's new in unemployment *Personnel Management,* August 1984.
T Webb. Jobs in jeopardy : the trade union response *Personnel Management,* July 1979.
M White. *Long term unemployment and labour markets* Policy Studies Institute, 1983.

CHAPTER 14

G Anderson & J England. Trade Union Structure — is it moving with the times? *Personnel Management,* February 1978.
D Farnham & J Pimlott. *Understanding Industrial Relations* Cassell, 1983.
J Gennard. What's new in industrial relations? *Personnel Management,* March 1985.
J Raybould. Ten Years of decentralisation *Personnel Management,* June 1985.
HMSO. *Royal Commission on Trade Unions and Employers Associations* 1968. cmnd 3623.
T Swabe & P Price. The forgotton unions *Personnel Management,* April 1984.
J Weed. Is Donovan dead? *Personnel Management,* August 1985.

INDEX

331

People in Organisations, third edition
Pat Armstrong & Chris Dawson
isbn 0 946139 50 4   £6.90   Sewn paperback   1985

An introduction to the management of people at work, specially written for the BTEC Business Studies course at HNC/D level and suitable for Stage 1 DMS, IPM, IWM, CMS and other first level supervisory and management courses. Adopted by numerous colleges as a set text and by the Institute of Bankers for their diploma course reading list.

Tutor's Pack, revised edition
isbn 0 946139 75 X   £9.00
(free to tutors — see Terms & Conditions)
Looseleaf A4 binder   September,1986

10 classroom-tested exercises based on a simulated company with model answers/notes and carrying copying rights for student materials to purchasers.

People in organisations: basic business level
Pat Armstrong
isbn 0 946139 80 6   £4.95   Paperback   September, 1986

A new simply-written, basic level textbook on the management of people at work.

The book is intended for BTEC National level students in business and management and on other courses which include a core component about people at work.

People in organisations: basic level Tutor's Pack
isbn 0 946139 85 7 £29.00
(free to tutors — see Terms & Conditions)
A4 Looseleaf   October, 1986

12 classroom-tested exercises for trainees/students on basic level business courses with OHP masters/model answers/notes and other materials. Each pack carries copying rights for student materials and is looseleaf A4 format.

Textbooks in Management & Business Studies

Case Studies

Private Sector

Case studies in management: private sector, introductory level
£5.90 isbn 0 946139 31 8 (2/85)
Tutor's Pack £33.00 isbn 0 946139 36 9 (2/85)
John Lewington *et al*

9 tested short case studies for students of business and management
at beginner level; topical & based on real situations;
most need no special functional knowledge.

Public Sector

Public industry policy analysis: text & cases
£6.90 isbn 0 946139 16 4 (11/84)
Tutor's Pack £33.00 isbn 0 946139 21 0 (2/85)
Terry Garrison

British Leyland, National Coal Board, British Steel, British Rail,
London Transport & De Lorean - 6 well documented cases with
a large section on policy analysis for students of
management.